HUMANOID ENCOUNTERS

THE OTHERS AMONGST US

1995-1999

ALBERT S. ROSALES

Triangulum Publishing.

Copyright © 2015 Albert S. Rosales

ISBN-13: 978-1519446275

ISBN-10: 1519446276

Book designed by Ash Staunton

Central image from cover art used with permission by Vashta Art.

Figure 1. One of my early sightings in Santa Clara, Cuba, 1965?

Humanoid: *adjective* hu·man·oid \'hyü-mə-ˌnȯid, 'yü-\

Having human form or characteristics.

"Why?" You ask. Why do I go on, compiling events from worldwide locations and sources, why do I continue the struggle? Will this catalogue of uncanny events, someday be as important as I think it is? I hope so.

Humans are arrogant and this arrogant behavior has doomed this once beautiful planet. We have been warned on numerous occasions, about our war-like nature, our disregard for other species, destroying the environment, ignoring the writing on the wall, etc. There are indeed 'others' amongst us, perhaps they share this planet and are trying to prevent its destruction, perhaps they are remaining descendants coming from the future to warn us, or yes, wayfarers from distant stars concerned about our destructive and arrogant behavior, and even more likely visitors from other dimensions that co-exist with ours.

These visitations, encounters, abductions, whatever the case might be, have been occurring for perhaps thousands of years, I will never be able to collect each one of them, and many have gone and will go to their graves with their secrets and encounters that forever changed their lives.

This has never been an easy task, my obsession, if you will, has cost me dearly, relationships, financial hardships, etc, but I keep coming back

7

and trudging on. I always thought that writing a book about a compilation of humanoid encounters would be impossible, too much information and too little time. But with the encouragement of several fellow researchers, I will attempt to show events that have been mostly ignored or ridiculed, events that I believe are the key to the survival of humans on this planet.

In 1995, the first accounts of the so-called Chupacabra were reported in the island of Puerto Rico. The phenomenon spread to other areas in the region, including Central America, Mexico, Brazil and South Florida. Some of the cases in South Florida I was personally involved with.

1996 brought us many interesting events including the incidents near Varginha, Brazil. 1997 was a potpourri of varied cases including strange flying humanoids. There appears to have been a definite slowdown in 1998 but activity picked up in 1999 with South America, mainly Argentina and Chile being the focus.

All through the decade of the 90's, Hollywood seems to have been promoting the so-called "Greys," but as you will see, they were not the only ones intruding in our reality. Following, again, we present a listing of the most interesting cases covering this decade, the "Others" were still around, with a vengeance!

Of course it would be impossible to include all the cases, but included are the 'highlights' of the period, or the most interesting cases reported.

It would be impossible to mention each and every researcher and person that has helped me amass this incredible amount of information. I have been reluctant in writing a book with all the latest compilations. Many of them have used my research which is free for all to see on-line, they know who they are.

Without the encouragement and assistance of fellow researcher and experiencer Ash Staunton, I would still be debating this issue, I thank him.

I also received encouragement from many others, to name a few, Alexander Rosales, Jaime Brian, Wade Ridsdale, Hank Worbetz, Gerardo Macias, Sue Demeter St. Clair, Gladys Gonzalez, Daniel Garcia Ramos, way too many to name here, but they also know who they are.

I wish all the best in the future that is to come, sooner than later.

Albert S. Rosales

TYPES OF CE (Close Encounter) CLASSIFICATIONS:

- **Type A**: When an entity or humanoid is seen inside or on top of an object or unidentified aircraft.
- **Type B**: When an entity or humanoid is seen entering or exiting a UFO.
- **Type C**: When an entity or humanoid is seen in the immediate vicinity of a UFO.
- **Type D**: When an entity or humanoid is seen in the same area where UFOs or unknown objects have been reported.
- **Type E**: When an entity or humanoid is seen alone, without related UFO activity (Example: bedroom visitation).
- **Type F**: When there is a psychic contact between entities or humanoids, but a humanoid is not necessarily seen.
- **Type G**: When there is direct contact or interaction between a witness or witnesses and a humanoid or entity; either involuntary, as a result of a forced abduction, or as a voluntary contact.
- **Type H**: When there is a report of an alleged crash or forced landing of a UFO with recovery of its occupants, or when an anomalous entity is captured or killed either by a witness or military personnel.
- **Type X**: When the situation is so uncanny that it doesn't fit any of the previous classifications. A new classification, there are several such cases in the files already. I would call these cases "extremely high strangeness events."

1995

Location: Paracas Peninsula, Peru.
Date: 1995.
Time: Evening.

Well known Peruvian writer, photographer and artist, Juan Rivera Tosi, was alone in a remote area trying to obtain some inspiration for his next project when suddenly three tall, blond-haired, "nordic" appearing men appeared out of nowhere. All three wore similar metallic blue tight-fitting garments.

The three men approached Tosi and began to communicate with him both verbally and telepathically. They spoke mainly about 'philosophical' and earthly matters.

After about twenty minutes, the men turned around and vanished instantly, something that Tosi thought was impossible since the area was very wide open and it was arid flat desert terrain.

HC addendum.
Source: Carlos G. Tutor & Olga Canals in, Año Cero Nr. 03-260, quoting Alex Sender 'AstroUFO.'   Type: E

Location: Between Kinyara & Kitanosie, Uganda.
Date: 1995.
Time: Night.

The anonymous witness whilst walking home on a road through the sugar cane fields, abruptly stopped by the side of the road by an unfinished air strip and turned to his left and there stood a huge red colored winged creature with glowing blond curly hair and what seemed to be a halo effect surrounding his head. The sugarcane at the time had been left uncut for many years and stood about 16 ft. tall.

The "angel" was about 12 ft. tall and the most beautiful creature that he had ever seen, the being appeared to have an additional set of ribs that were below his normal ribs unlike a human being, at waist level his legs were fur like and it stood upon hooves instead of feet. They stood about 60 ft. apart and just looked at each other for about five minutes. The being exuded a very bright light from its body and his head, which gave a halo effect. The witness thrust his hand towards the being as a gesture of contact and at this point heard a message of a religious nature and of future warning for humanity, all in his mind.

After the message the "Red Angel" turned and his wings unfurled and trailed behind his body as he returned back into the sugar cane. The witness continued to walk towards home. About 150 yards further up the road the "Red Angel" appeared again standing amongst the cane. The witness turned and faced him again, this time standing about 30 ft. away, the being's face, although white was glistening black as if in shadow. Soon the bizarre humanoid disappeared into the sugarcane field again.

HC addendum.
Source: Direct from witness.   Type: E

Location: Raynham, Massachusetts.
Date: 1995.
Time: Night.

Bill Russo a retired ironworker who lived on a knoll just a few hundred yards away from the Hockomock Swamp had gone out on his nightly walk with his Rottweiler-German Shepherd mix, Samantha.

Samantha pulled Bill along into an area that he calls "The High Trees," and when they had gone about half a mile, they came to a break where a road cut through the swamp. At this point, Samantha began acting up, pulling hard on her leach and looking up at Bill. She trembled and her hair stood on end, and looked at her master for protection. Bill asked her, *"What's wrong Samantha? I don't see anything. It's okay baby. We'll go home now. Come on."* He tugged on her leash, but she wouldn't move an inch. She was afraid of something, and according to Bill, Samantha was not a dog that frightened easily. She just cried and quivered. It was cleared that something in the darkness was terrifying the poor dog.

It wasn't long before Bill began to hear the thing that was frightening his beloved dog. It was faint at first, but it was unmistakable. An eerie voice was calling through the night air, saying, *"Eee wah chu. Eee wah chu. Keer Keer. Eee wah chu."* The high-pitched unnatural voice repeated itself, getting louder and closer at the same time. At first Bill couldn't see anything, even though there was a streetlight about twenty feet ahead of him. The lamp cast a bluish circle of light on the pavement in front of him. And then, in Bill's own account, "into the circle walked a hairy creature about three to four feet tall which probably weighed a hundred pounds." What happened next has been haunting Bill for almost twenty years.

"Eee wah chu. Eee wah chu. Keer Keer. Eee wah chu." The creature said repeatedly. It stood straight on two legs and stared at Bill "with eyes that were too large for its head, like the eyes of an owl." Bill and his dog were paralyzed as they watched the creature, but the creature just stood there and didn't appear to be threatening. Samantha trembled, and then she looked at Bill as if to ask "What is it?" Bill looked at his dog and said, *"it's okay, Sam."*

In a somewhat unconvincing manner. The creature kept speaking and began to motion to him with its arms, asking him to come closer. The creature wasn't wearing any clothing to speak of and "was covered in course, unkempt hair that was about five or six inches long." The thing appeared to have a pot belly, and Bill "took it to be in the young stages of old age." Bill had no idea what in the world he was dealing with. Bill and Samantha stood there looking at the creature for what seemed to be hours, but in reality the encounter itself probably lasted only a few minutes. Although it appeared to be friendly and nothing overly

15

threatening could be detected in is mannerisms, Bill had heard stories from other people about bizarre things that they had seen in the swamps, stories that he could neither confirm nor deny. Bill was scared, the tiny creature was much smaller than he was, and yet he was still very frightened. Worse yet, it was the middle of the night, and the thing was talking to him!

Bill eventually worked up enough courage and asked the creature a few questions, but the only answer that he received was *"Eee wah chu"* over and over again. It was at this point that Bill and Samantha made a very big circle around the creature and went home as fast as they could. They didn't look back. That night Bill relived the entire experience over and over again in the confines of his living room. He wondered if he should've tried to talk to the creature more, or if he should have at least walked up to it. As near as he could figure, it was trying to speak English and was saying, *"We want you. We want you. Come here. Come here."* Bill took this to mean that there was more than one of these creatures.

HC addendum.
Source: Kyle Germann.   Type: E

*   *   *   *   *   *   *

Location: Sedona Arizona.
Date: 1995.
Time: Late night.

A middle-aged couple, William and Rose Shelhart was driving outside of Sedona when they spotted a bright light in the sky following them. It soon became apparent that the light was playing a game of cat and mouse with them as it chased them down the road and eventually landed in a field next to them. That was the last thing they consciously remembered.

Their next memory was arriving at a hotel in Sedona, several hours too late. Realizing they had missing time, they later sought out a hypnotist and recalled an incredible onboard UFO experience. They recalled being taken on board the craft and examined by nearly human looking uniformed extraterrestrials.

While William's recall was negligible, Rose was able to recall most of what happened, including an actual conversation that she had with the aliens. According to Rose, they were invited onboard and treated with kindness and respect. *"They were just saying that they were here to help us. They told me that William was in another room receiving additional messages."* Rose asked where they came from. The aliens gave a typically enigmatic and evasive answer, replying, *"We are from a place you don't know about yet."* When asked about their purpose for coming here, their response was decidedly positive. *"They said they are helping certain people here because they will help humanity."*

Rose was unable to obtain any further useful information. She and her husband continue to have sightings and encounters, and William reports that he was healed of carpel tunnel syndrome as a result of his interaction with the aliens.

HC addendum.
Source: Preston Dennett.   Type: G

* * * * * * *

Location: Feeding Hills, near Springfield, Massachusetts.
Date: 1995.
Time: 10:00 p.m.

The witness (involved in other experiences) was camping alone in the forest and had gone for a stroll from his campsite when suddenly he couldn't move. At that time he was approached by 5 small entities with large eyes and of "grayish-greenish" color.

The creatures spoke to him telepathically and he was under the impression that they wanted him to go to their planet which he described as somewhat barren (they also showed him images of their planet.) He did not see a craft at any time.

He said that he resisted them and refused to go to their planet. He then started praying and at once felt released from the paralysis. He said that he then moved towards the creatures and they at once disappeared. He then blacked out for several minutes.

He awoke and returned to his campsite. He then set up a "laser alarm" which would sound an alarm if any motion was detected in a given perimeter of his campsite.

Apparently the creatures did not return.

HC addendum.
Source: UFOs Northwest.   Type: E

Location: Pitahaya, Puerto Rico.
Date: January, 1995.
Time: Afternoon.

The witness, a retired military officer, was exploring the thick wooded areas of the local rain forest when he came upon a strange creature that seemed to be inspecting at very close range, the leaves of a nearby plant. The creature was described as three foot tall, with a large egg-shaped head, large oval shaped eyes, positioned vertically on his face, and very thin arms. The humanoid's skin was beige-brown in color. It appeared to be naked, and its body was totally covered with brown and black spots that seemed to interlace with each other.

The creature was looking strangely at the plant, moving his hands slowly up and down "as if feeling something from the plant." It suddenly became aware of the witness presence, and quickly turned his head, looking directly at the witness. The witness began walking slowly towards the creature, which remained standing motionless. The witness was briefly distracted and turned his head, whereupon when he looked back the creature had vanished.

HC addendum.
Source: Jorge Martin in Evidencia OVNI #6.   Type: E
Translation by Albert S Rosales.

* * * * * * *

Location: Feira de Santana, Bahia, Brazil.
Date: January 12, 1995.
Time: Evening.

A Mr. Beto Lima saw a small metallic saucer crash in a lake. A port opened and two creatures emerged. One was about one meter tall with a large baldhead and big eyes, and the other was a bit larger and hairy, except for the hands and face. Beto used a long stick to pull them to shore, and then took them to his house.

A report from an anonymous soldier of the 35th infantry battalion said that he was part of a team that went to the farmhouse and carried the creatures out. The hairy one protested. One solider made the sign of the cross and said, *"These are animals from another world."* Then Naval Intelligence officers arrived in a car and took control of the event. The saucer, being very light was put on a truck. Then a helicopter arrived and took the two humanoids. Another soldier confirmed the incident.

According to the military source, on this date, Jan 12th, there was a sudden blackout in the vicinity of Feira de Santana almost to the border of the state of Sergipe. Shortly after, a message was received at the

18

headquarters of the 35th infantry Battalion at around 5:30 a.m. canceling all soldier's leaves. Several squads were then transported to a location near a farm close to the above town.

Upon arrival the men thought at first that it had been a false alarm, since everything was quiet. There was no smoke to indicate a large fire in the pasture of any remains of any airplane. Curious, they searched the grounds of the farm and noticed the nervousness of its owner, Beto Lima and interrogated him, he then led several of the soldiers to his home. The commander entered the home followed by a contingent of armed soldiers. After searching the entire house, soldiers came out carrying what appeared to be a hairy sloth like creature and a small creature resembling a newborn child, but different, it seemed frail with large eyes. Both bodies were quickly placed in the back of a truck, as well as a few pieces of shiny metal. The smaller creature was moaning and appeared to be still alive.

As soldiers guarded the two small alien bodies another group was sent to the nearby lagoon where they saw something resembling a small car, partially sunk near the shore. They pulled it out and it was easy because it was very light weight. Soon a truck with several civilians and naval officers arrived, and then the beings and the object were loaded onto another truck which was the jurisdiction of the new arrivals.

According to the farmer, Beto Lima, he had been hunting near the lagoon when he found the strange object floating inside a pond in his farm. *"It was the size of a Volkswagen and was floating near the shore."* With the aid of a stick, he managed to pull it ashore. Suddenly a strange sticky liquid began to ooze from the object and two beings appeared at a portal-like opening. According to Lima one of the beings was hairy, with claw and long like a sloth, and it was still alive despite its injuries. The other was similar to a newborn child, only on meter high and was apparently dead.

The farmer rescued the two creatures and the object, which even though it was the size of a car, it was very light, and took the creatures to his house. At first Lima contacted a local television station "Subae TV" and offered to sell the creatures. (!) Apparently at this point the military authorities were contacted. According to some of the soldiers, the strange object had a cloaking device that reflected the landscape around it, thus hindering revealing its location.

There were other witnesses to UFO activity in the area including several students who watched a large ball of light overhead that seemed to emit flashes. Two days later others saw what appeared to be metallic objects flying low over the area. There was also unusual helicopter activity reported.

HC addendum.
Source: Donald Ware, Filer's Files #21-2001.   Type: H

Location: Kadima, Israel.
Date: January 13, 1995.
Time: Unknown.

Ufologist Zvi Bighest took several photographs of mysterious circles found on the ground, along with shards of a shiny material found to be pure silicon. Some shards weighed over a pound.

When the shots were developed, several tall bald, round faced figures wearing silvery suits could be seen standing at a distance, apparently observing the proceedings.

HC addendum.
Source: Barry Chamish, FSR Vol. 41 #1.   Type: D

* * * * * * *

Location: Boynton Beach, Florida.
Date: January 17, 1995.
Time: 5:10 a.m.

The witness was at the corner of Congress and Gateway when she saw on the side of the road, a seven-foot tall brownish being with long stringy arms and legs, an elongated head, and dark eyes.

At the same time, a transparent craft, shaped like a multi-sided crystal form with two other beings inside, "tumbled" across the road about 60 feet in front of the car. The witness slammed on her brakes and turns to see the object and humanoid gone.

HC addendum.
Source: Skyscan August, 97.   Type: C & A

* * * * * * *

Location: Novi Beograd, Serbia.
Date: February, 1995.
Time: 5:00 a.m.

A female witness living on Arsenij Carnojevic Boulevard was returning home from work at the customs office in Horgos and was in front of her building's entrance, when she saw above her, a man in a black cape, hovering in midair. He looked at her with "amazing glassy eyes."

She lowered her head, looking away and when she looked up again she saw the figure flying above the building. She said, *"He was very real and was not a doll."* After losing sight of him, she rushed into the building and woke her children, but by the time they got to the window there was nothing unusual to be seen.

HC addendum.
Source: the_paladin@myway.com   Type: E

* * * * * * *

Location: Near Chiquihuitillo, Mexico.
Date: February, 1995.
Time: 8:00 p.m.

Rafael Garcia Arias was driving his truck near Lake Chapala, when he saw a flash of light emerge from the nearby mountains and disappear into the distance. Immediately next to him, in the passenger seat, a small man about 30 cm in height appeared. Surprised, he asked the little man where he was from and was told, *"From Lake Chapala."*

The little man then said that they had a base at the depths of the lake. The witness reportedly then saw a vision of a submerged "city" encased in a glass like case. He was told that they were descendants of a crashed UFO that went down in the area thousands of years ago.

HC addendum.
Source: Contacto Ovni, Mexico.   Type: E & F

* * * * * * *

Location: Near Aloha, Oregon.
Date: Spring, 1995.
Time: Night.

Driving along a lonely stretch of road, James saw what he believed to be UFOs following him. That night James heard a voice in his head that told him to go to a certain street not too far from where he lived. This street is on a big hill that is just south of 185th and SW Farmington Road.

When he got there he parked in the cul-de-sac, which had some houses around it. His girlfriend waited in his truck. Over in the shadows of the trees he could see someone standing there. He went over to the trees. There he saw up close a being, which he described as looking more bug-like than anything else. It was about five feet tall and had orange eyes. He said it had a fluorescent yellow mane of hair but not really hair.

Off to each side were two more identical beings but a little shorter and no yellow manes. And off sitting in the trees were the small Ewok type creatures.

James carried a conversation with the creature using mental telepathy. He "heard" what the creature was saying through pictures in his mind and then he would speak back to it.

He had a bible with him and asked the creature if it was true or not. The being said something to the effect *"Yes there is a God."* James was later involved in other strange incidents.

HC addendum.
Source: UFO MAN, Portland UFO Stories.   Type: E

* * * * * * *

Location: Afula, Israel.
Date: March, 1995.
Time: Unknown.

Four astonished young women watched an oversized hairy, hovering and floating head in their apartment garden for twenty minutes before the appearance of a seven foot giant in the adjacent parking lot sent them scurrying in terror. All witnesses felt the giant was a female.

HC addendum.
Source: Barry Chamish, FSR Vol. 41 #1.   Type: E

* * * * * * *

Location: Chernihiv area, Ukraine.
Date: March, 1995.
Time: 3:30 a.m.

A local farmer, Nazar Kopov, was awakened by a strange rumbling sound in his ears. The sound was like the 'whistling of a whip,' as the sound became shrilling, Nazar had the impression that he was at the verge of death. His heart began to beat furiously, he blacked out and when he came to, he seemed to be hovering in the air at an altitude of 300 meters and gradually descending. However he felt no fear, only a sense of calm. At a distance of about 8-10 meters from the ground, Nazar began to swing like a pendulum, as if someone was guiding his trajectory.

The next moment he saw a group of beings standing in a semi-circle. Their outlines were barely discernible in the darkness, but even in the dim light, he caught a glimpse of their impressive size. When he was only about two meters from the ground, Nazar again lost consciousness.

The first thing he saw when he came to was the group of creatures standing in front of him still in a semi-circle, he was lying on the ground. Each of the humanoids was at least two meters tall. One of the humanoids standing on the left side appeared to be the 'leader.' The glow coming from the body of the leader allowed Nazar to see him in more detail, the being had a powerful torso, broad shoulders and powerfully built, with a 'bull neck.' He had long arms with thick, claw-like fingers. The body was covered with scales, like a reptile, from which proceeded a very foul smell resembling rotten eggs. In the place where the head should be, Nazar could see a 'hologram' of a human face, shining like a curious mask. Suddenly the 'mask' moved its lips, but not a sound broke the tense situation.

Suddenly Nazar heard a telepathic voice *"We are bringing a message to humans, your planet is dying, your air and waters are poisoned, your forests and plants are dying out, the continued use of nuclear energy is poisoning nature, your planet is overpopulated and is running out of resources. We warn you, if mankind does not change his way of thinking today, tomorrow might be too late. There are effective and safe methods of energy and food extraction that are not harmful to your planet. Those could be used today, however we know that there exists on Earth forces that will do anything to prevent this. They will do anything possible to prevent the emergence of clean energy production and the safe production of abundant food to become part of humanity, because it's not in their interest."*

There was a pause; apparently the aliens were waiting to see if Nazar had understood what they had just said. *"The authorities are corrupt and seek to bring knowledge to their advantage without caring about the interests of humanity."* The stranger continued, *"We chose the tactic of working with ordinary people from all parts of the world so one day Earth will be able to establish a harmonious world order. We will guide your steps, when the time comes you will know what to do."*

While the stranger spoke it began to rain, a powerful downpour. However the strange creatures surrounding Nazar did not even move. And after a few minutes, Nazar realized that even though he was out in the open, not a single drop of water fell on him and the creatures. They were apparently protected by some kind of invisible protective shield, as Nazar could hear the drops fall and could see a clear distinction between the realm of the rain and dry space.

Seconds later the stranger said, *"We must go."* Nazar then heard a click and felt again that he was being carried by a mysterious force, again he lost consciousness. Later Nazar learned that he had come in contact with the 'highest caste' of aliens known as the 'Guardians' and was told that the shorter gray ones were the 'workhorses.'

HC addendum.
Source: Yaroslav V Sochka, UFODOS, and Anton Anfalov.   Type: G

Location: Near Skrunda, Latvia.
Date: March 2, 1995.
Time: Unknown.

After being shot at by another UFO, a craft reportedly crashed into a forest 100km southeast of Riga. The craft was almost intact and crashed into an isolated area of woods and bogs close to a military reservation and was recovered by a Russian military communications unit possibly working at the Skrunda radar station. According to a 1rst hand eyewitness, soldier V Verkhorubov, who accidentally caught a glance of the disk while it was in a surface hangar, the craft was a dome-shaped disk about 7-8 meters in diameter, with a vertical slit opening on one side. His commanding officer noticed him near the disk, observing closely the many details of the disk. Suddenly, his commanding officer yelled at him, *"Radiation, get away!"* After that, all the soldiers of the unit were locked back again in the barracks.

The disk was already opened when the military found it. Three dead humanoids were found onboard, all killed by the hard impact, including two bio-robots and another conscious alien. The three dead aliens were of the gray type, their skin was green-grayish, and they were dwarf-like with big hairless heads, huge eyes, Asiatic looking faces, hands with four webbed fingers and hoofed feet.

The bodies were extracted from the disk and moved expeditiously by a military airplane from a nearby Latvian military aerodrome to Moscow by a special recovery team. The bodies were transported in cryogenic containers. Inscriptions found inside the disk resembled Sanskrit. The disk was moved to a surface hangar in a military industrial complex in Korolyov, in the vicinity of Moscow just north of it. There it was dismantled into six segments. The segments of the disk were then eventually moved to the island of Novaya Zemlya, a top-secret military installation build inside a mountain code-named "Glacier."

The autopsy of the alien bodies and their preservation was performed in an isolated top-secret underground bunker located under building on the territory of a military biomedical research center east of Solnechnogorsk.

HC addendum.
Source: Anton Anfalov list, quoting Lev Melnikov, Larissa Chora, and clairvoyant Lenura Azizova.   Type: H

Location: Ammon, Idaho.
Date: March 10, 1995.
Time: 5:45 a.m.

Witnesses observed a circular metallic object with lights hovering over the area. One of the witnesses reported receiving a telepathic message from the craft. No other information.

HC addendum.
Source: UFO Intelligence Newsletter June, 1996.   Type: F

* * * * * * *

Location: Petange, Luxembourg.
Date: March 12, 1995.
Time: 10:00 p.m.

Three witnesses watched a large green sphere on the ground. Three humanoids wearing silvery coveralls were seen walking around and in front of the sphere. After a while the scene vanished. No other information.

HC addendum.
Source: Raoul Fischer, La Circulaire 4-1995.   Type: C

* * * * * * *

Location: Saltos Cabra, Puerto Rico.
Date: Middle of March, 1995.
Time: Night.

Two anonymous police officers responding to a call in reference to some lambs found mutilated at a local ranch, saw standing on the side of the road, a strange four foot tall creature, described as humanoid in shape, orange-yellow in color. The officers did not see any facial features since it was dark. In a quick sudden move the creature ran to its left and into the thick brush disappearing from sight. When one of the officers attempted to follow the creature he was overcome by a sudden headache & severe dizziness & had to be assisted by his companion.

HC addendum.
Source: Jorge Martin in Evidencia, OVNI #6.   Type: E
High Strangeness Index: 8
Reliability of Source: 9

Comments: This case appears to have been the beginning of the so-called Chupacabra epidemic. Also the January 1995, Pitahaya case was significant. The dizziness experienced by the witness is very significant also since it appears that the humanoid exerted some type of "control" over the witnesses, indicating the very interesting display of intelligence by the bizarre creature.

* * * * * * *

Location: Fort Lauderdale, Florida.
Date: April, 1995.
Time: Evening.

Maria Bone and her younger sister were walking along a local park when they noticed a small child-like creature that appeared to be chasing a similar smaller creature at an incredible rate of speed. Upon noticing the witnesses the taller creature ran behind a tree and began making strange sounds apparently directed towards Maria. According to Maria the creature had a long neck, was gray in color and was about 4-½ ft tall.

Its face resembled that of a bird with large black reptilian eyes. She observed the creature for about 15 minutes until it disappeared into the woods. The creature's back resembled that of a normal human being. She informed the police about the incident but she was ignored. Mrs. Bone holds the opinion that the earth is going through changes of an evolutionary nature creating new species and creatures.

HC addendum.
Source: Jorge Martin, Conspiracion Chupacabras.   Type: E

* * * * * * *

Location: Sogea, Zanzibar, Tanzania.
Date: April, 1995.
Time: Night.

There were numerous reports of encounters with dwarf-like creatures with a Cyclops eye, small pointed ears, bat wings, and talons that attacked persons while sleeping.

One supposedly attacked a peasant farmer Mjaka Hamad, who was dragged from his bed while he fought and screamed. He apparently got away.

HC addendum.
Source: Fortean Times May, 1996.   Type: E

Location: Emmelshausen, Germany.
Date: May 7, 1995.
Time: 6:00 p.m.

Two witnesses were trekking through a forest when they suddenly heard a sort of a swishing noise. They looked around and soon after saw several "non-material" humanoid figures walking through the forest.

The figures appeared to be made out of numerous multicolored "dots" that you could see through. It seemed as if they were looking for something. The shocked witnesses went back to their car and then heard a mechanical "hovering" sound over the area but could not see anything.

HC addendum.
Source: NUFORC   Type: E

* * * * * * *

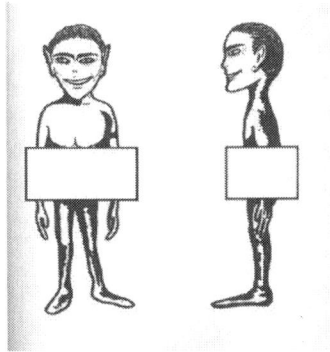

Location: Near Pasiano, Italy.
Date: May 19, 1995.
Time: 11:15

A professional stopped his car to watch a metallic, top shaped craft with a transparent section hovering over the road. Inside he was able to see a large number of apparently naked, smiling humanoids standing around. These were about four-foot tall with large elongated heads, topped with short-cropped dark hair.

The humanoids appeared to be smiling and had normal looking eyes and noses, and large pointed ears. They had long dangling arms with large hands. The craft took off after a few minutes, that same evening witnesses watched moving lights in the sky in the same area.

HC addendum.
Source: Dario Bortolini, ITUFOR Vol. 2 #2.   Type: A

Location: Cascade County, Montana.
Date: May, 1995.
Time: Unknown.

A lone hunter reportedly came across an 8 foot tall, reddish brown hair creature with glowing red eyes. The hunter shot at the creature and it disappeared in a flash of light. No other information.

HC addendum.
Source: Linda Moulton Howe, Art Bell Show, June 18, 1995.   Type: E

* * * * * * *

Location: Near Eilat, Israel.
Date: Summer, 1995.
Time: Morning.

Reportedly a man named Pyetr, a millionaire visitor from the Ukraine, was driving his BMW to the famous Red Sea resort of Eilat. He was alone in the car, listening to music. Suddenly, according to the witness, the engine of the car stalled amid the scorching hot desert. He pulled over to the side of the road and went outside to see what had happened. But suddenly he became very weak at the knees, his legs gave way and cold sweat appeared on his forehead. Bathed in sweat and terrified he fell to his knees and began crawling on all fours in the hot sand.

Suddenly he saw a bright orange-crimson colored sphere that was hovering in the air, at an altitude of about 30 meters. The sphere was about 2-3 meters in diameter and emitted bright light, similar to that of a halo depicted around the heads of Saints.

The silent UFO changed colors from green to red, to yellow, and from yellow to green again. This sequence was repeated on numerous occasions. The witness became terribly scared and wanted to scream, but suddenly his whole body became numb and stiff, he thinks he succeeded in screaming something but incredibly did not hear the sound of his voice.

Minutes later, three humanoid figures appeared from inside the spherical UFO. All figures were no less than 2.5m in height. The aliens had long arms and hands with numerous fingers that seemed to move in synchronicity. Their skin was brown-green in color; their heads were relatively small, pumpkin-shaped and emitted a bright light from their eyes.

He understood that the creatures were two males and one female. Soon the creatures began emitting strange sounds resembling abrupt staccato whistle-like sounds. Then they allegedly telepathically transmitted this message to the witness, *"In seven years and seven months, when the era of Aquarius arrives and God's blessing will be upon the three Slavic territories, Russia, Belarus and Ukraine, you will begin to cure people. However you will have to change your life completely."*

Reportedly, aliens from another planet had chosen him to cure people and after this contact he was able to establish telepathic contact with them. Then the alien "woman" approached him and touched the back of his head with her hand (reportedly strange marks remained where the alien woman had touched him).

After that one of the alien males said to him, *"You were chosen by us quite a long time ago, but we didn't inform you about it, we wanted to see how far down the abyss you would fall. You must save the world, to heal people we will give you the necessary energy and knowledge for that, but all that will be later, in time."*

All of a sudden and very quickly, the extraterrestrials returned to their craft and as unexpectedly as it had appeared, the mysterious sphere easily ascended in a beam of light and disappeared behind the clouds.

When Pyetr looked around, he noticed that at the location where the UFO had hovered there was now a huge crater apparently left behind by the departing UFO. He slowly rose from his knees and dragged himself back to his car. To his amazement the car now started.

The witness claimed that he changed after the contact, ceasing contact with all his previous unsavory friends and began immersing himself in UFO literature. He claims that there were subsequent alien contacts and that he was abducted on several occasions.

HC addendum.
Source: Boulevard newspaper, Ukraine #4 January, 2003. Type: B or F?

Location: Near Kiev, Ukraine.
Date: Summer, 1995.
Time: Evening.

A local man was returning from an outlying village on foot, about a 15 km walk when he stopped to rest under a birch tree. He sat down smoking a cigarette and looking at the night sky. Suddenly a bright red star caught his attention. It was very large and at first he thought it was the planet Mars. Suddenly the "star" began to grow in size right in front of his eyes. Soon the supposed star turned into a large cylinder or barrel-shaped object, bright red hot in color.

A bright beam of light from the object suddenly surrounded the witness. The strange beam enveloped his body, penetrating every cell and next a feeling of unearthly love filled him. It was a feeling of complete bliss or ecstasy. He now felt weightless, as if he was floating. Overwhelmed, he almost burst into tears.

Suddenly he found himself amid an incredibly white room with columns resembling marble. He looked around but could not see anyone. The room was oval-shaped, the columns were positioned in a circle and he was directly in the center. His attention was drawn to patterns drawn on the columns; these resembled unknown ornaments or plants. For some reason he thought they were lilies, and imagined how the ornament would look with lilies intertwined in it. To his amazement, lilies suddenly appeared intertwined in the pattern.

He then heard a loud male voice, *"Not too bad"* from behind him. He turned around and noticed a male and a woman standing there. They wore ancient style robes, the man in a white one and the woman in a violet-colored one. Both were tall and very beautiful in appearance. *"They are Gods,"* the witness thought. The humanoids apparently read his mind, and both man and woman smiled and he heard, *"We are the same Gods as you."* The alien man pointed at the intricate pattern of lilies and said, *"You can also become a God if that is what you really*

30

want." He then pointed to the floor and the columns disappeared; now a huge "hatch" appeared on the floor. The witness came closer and looked down into it. There he noticed crowds of people walking, men and women. The people appeared confused and walked aimlessly. They were holding children and walking without direction (this was obviously an alien hologram made especially for the witness to watch).

Suddenly the witness felt an urge to help the hapless crowd and yelled at them, *"You are walking in the wrong direction, look up, you hear me, look up!"* There was no reaction from the crowd. *"We are also not heard,"* said the alien man.

The witness looked up and the columns had returned, and he noticed two men with long beards wearing white clothing seating on benches along the oval wall. The witness then heard the man's voice say, *"You can become one of them. Purify yourself."* But the witness said that he had to return. After that was said, both bearded men got up from their bench and walked to the center of the room.

The next moment, a huge book appeared out of nowhere on a pedestal in the middle of the room, the bearded men opened the book somewhere in the middle of the book and one of them began reading in a strange language.

The witness listened attentively to the unknown words, but could not understand anything that was said, and later he could not remember anything that was said. After that the witness then found himself sitting under the birch tree again, and the red star above him blinking as if saying goodbye, it disappeared into the night sky.

HC addendum.
Source: Bogdan Duma, 'Interesnaya Gazeta,' #4, 1998.   Type: G

* * * * * * *

Location: Near Lexington, Kentucky.
Date: Summer, 1995.
Time: Afternoon.

In a farm area, a man looked outside to see his young kids playing on a field and standing near them, two short man-like figures that appeared to be wearing white smocks.

Startled he yelled at his children who apparently had not seen the intruders. The two little men then ran up a hill and behind some farm buildings and were lost from sight. A search failed to find anything.

HC addendum.
Source: Haunted Stories of the South.   Type: E

31

Location: El Yunque, Puerto Rico.
Date: Summer, 1995.
Time: Night.

Frank Bourness and a friend had gone camping in the area. Later as they waited for the bus in the visitor's center next to state Road 191, they suddenly heard loud grunting noises coming from behind them. Turning around they were startled to see a formidable creature standing about 15 ft from their location. The creature seemed to have been attacking a dog. It had huge luminous eyes, and it was about ten foot tall, "resembling Godzilla, except that it was covered with hair" and with huge hind legs.

Bourness and his friend threw rocks at the creature and this one just grunted at them. Terrified they ran inside the empty visitor center and locked themselves inside. Through an open window they heard the loud grunting noises for a short while. Later they could find no sign of the creature or the dog.

HC addendum.
Source: Jorge Martin, Conspiracion Chupacabras.   Type: E

* * * * * * *

Location: Camden County, Missouri.
Date: Summer, 1995.
Time: Afternoon.

The witness had decided to explore a cave which was part of a fairly large system in the area. From what he could tell, this particular cave had not been explored for a long period of time. The entrance was very narrow and well hidden.

After squeezing through the opening, he descended another fifty feet or so before the cave began to open up into a series of chambers. He moved through several of these chambers, taking his time to examine the area for possible artifacts and formations. He finally reached, what he thought was the end of the cave.

At this point he began to hear a rustling sound that was echoing from a small opening near the top of the chamber. He assumed the sounds were bats and didn't pay much attention to it. But after a while he heard motorized sounds and talking. He stood up and listened for several minutes, wondering what was on the other side of this chamber. The opening was about ten feet above him. He maneuvered his way up to the opening which was flat and narrow but large enough for him to get a decent look into it.

As he positioned himself to the front of the opening, he started to see light at the other end. The passageway was only a few feet long but it was just too narrow for him to move through. As he looked through the opening there was a very warm draft of air hitting his face. As well, the air had a very acrid vinegar like odor. There was a very large and well-lit 'room' with limestone walls.

He noticed a small vehicle that looked like a golf cart but was very low to the ground and without wheels. He continued to observe until he started to hear voices that were getting louder and nearer. Something was making its way toward the vehicle. He had to rub his eyes because he didn't believe what he was looking at.

This 'creature,' because it was not a man, stood about seven foot and had brown scaly skin. The face and head were shaped like a human with a flat nose but there were no ears or hair. The top of the head had a slight scaly ridge that extended down the back of the neck. From what he could see, it had lips and regular sized eyes. The arms were very long and muscular with human-like hands. It also had a massive 4-5 foot tail that tapered to a point. It was dressed in a gold metallic outfit with long pants and shoes. It also carried an oval-shaped bag attached to its back.

This creature was looking at something on the vehicle. The witness had a camera which he used to obtain a few distorted images of the being. Suddenly while he was taking the photos, the creature stopped and turned, looking in his direction. It then made a terrible "hissing" sound as it continued to look in his direction. That was enough for the witness which quickly made a bee-line out of the cave. When he reached the entrance he was shaking and hyperventilating. He finally reached his vehicle and drove home.

He continued to explore caves in the area and has heard stories of people encountering strange underground beings, but he had never disclosed his experience. A few years after his experience, he went back to the cave but was unable to get near it since the area is now government property.

HC addendum.
Source: Lon Stickler, Phantoms & Monsters, October 28, 2011.   Type: E

Location: Near Boscobel, Wisconsin.
Date: June, 1995.
Time: Daytime.

Daniel Klemsrud was walking with a girlfriend in a wooded area near town when they suddenly were turned around and lost. Although it had been in a clear and sunny day, it now suddenly seemed as though the sky was dark and cloudy, and consequently the wooded area in which they were walking became shadowy, murky, as if night were about to fall. A heavy mist also appeared that made it extremely difficult to stay on the trail. Suddenly from all around them they could hear the sounds of giggling, like small children laughing and playing. The laughter was almost musical. Klemsrud walked toward a clump of bushes that were shaking as if they were sheltering some little eavesdroppers.

As he pulled back the branches, he caught a glimpse of two smallish, yet perfectly proportioned, men in greenish jumpsuits scurrying into a hole. They were only about three feet in height and he saw a shiny buckle on the boot of one of them as he dove into what appeared to be a tunnel. That was when he noticed that they were standing at the base of a rather large mound of earth that was completely barren of vegetation.

Responding to an inner message, Daniel reached in his pocket and found some loose change. The moment he tossed the coins into the opening of the mound, the sky became clear, the dark mist lifted, and he could now easily see the path he had missed just minutes before.

HC addendum.
Source: Brad Steiger, Out Of the Dark.   Type: E

* * * * * * *

Location: Almendra De Aliste, Zamora, Spain.
Date: June 15, 1995.
Time: 7:15 a.m.

While numerous locals observed mysterious lights maneuvering low over fields, Maria Corcero and Rodrigo Martin stood next to a field observing a series of lights that formed a straight line. As they walked back to their house, they had the impression that the lights seemed to possess intelligence of their own.

As both stood just inside the entrance to their home, they watched dumbfounded as the lights appeared to fuse together and form into a heavy set humanoid body made out of pure light. The figure formed itself only down to a little bit below the waist. It had a wide torso and a small elongated head and long thin arms.

Before running into their home both witnesses observed the figure dissolve into a mass of light and disappear.

HC addendum.
Source: Iker Jimenez, Historia de Los Ovni En España.   Type: E?

* * * * * * *

Location: Versailles, Missouri.
Date: July 9, 1995.
Time: 11:00 p.m.

Near this location, two Air Force officers and a dozen other witnesses saw five very large UFOs, a triangular craft and four discs, each as long as a football field, hovering over an empty field.

On the ground were twenty to twenty-five extraterrestrials moving about. Three different races were present; some short ones with purplish skin and large ears, another type described as luminous energy beings, and a third group of tall humanoids in jumpsuits. No other information.

HC addendum.
Source: National UFO Reporting Center.   Type: C

* * * * * * *

Location: Varpasalo, Raakkyla, Finland.
Date: July 19 or 20, 1995.
Time: 3:00 p.m.

An old farmer's wife went out to see if there were any strawberries at a familiar spot in the forest. Walking towards it she heard three faint shot-like noises, but ignored them. When she came closer to the spot she noticed something blue in the forest. When she came closer she saw something resembling a giant blue "umbrella," which rose and then descended about half a meter. She heard two "sigh" like noises when the "umbrella" descended to some 20cm above the ground. Under the blue surface of the object some kind of ribbing could be seen, hence the image of an umbrella.

To her astonishment she now saw that a man was standing, stooped over, about a meter from the blue object. He seemed to be picking something up and throwing it into his vessel, which made a "ping" like noise every time he threw something inside. She assumed the man was collecting pieces of ore, as there were many mines in the area. The man was clad in a dark green overall with possibly a broad belt. Once he stood up and then stooped back down again.

After observing the man for some 5-15 minutes, she felt a compulsive urge to leave, so that she would not disturb the man's work. She went home (the man and the object were still there when she left), and on her way looked around for any cars in the forest but did not see any.

When she got home, her daughter in law noticed that something had happened to her, and after they discussed the event, they decide to go to the site two hours later. When they came to the spot, a faint impression could be seen on the ground.

During the next several months, the elderly witness often felt a compulsion to visit the site and could see the ground vegetation withering away, turning almost black at the end. UFO investigators visited the site the following spring and found five black spots still visible on the ground. The area on the ground was still lifeless as of 1996.

HC addendum.
Source: Heikki Virtanen, Finland.   Type: C

* * * * * * *

Location: Nikopol, Dnepropetrovsk region, Ukraine.
Date: August, 1995.
Time: Daytime.

Several young men had gone to the local beach on a hot August day and after swimming for a while, they returned to the shore. There they were stunned to see four beautiful young naked women coming out of the water. The young men asked them if they were nudists, but silence was the answer. Their impression was that the girls did not understand their speech at all, but one of the men knew three languages and asked the same question in German, French and English, but the reaction was the same. The girls then returned to the water and when they began to swim the young men noticed that the girls' movements were unnatural, they seemed to be "gliding" in the water. It also appeared that when they

36

dove into the water they seemed to remain dry. Between them the strange females were exchanging strange whistle-like sounds (like Dolphins?).

One of the men decided to approach one of the women and touch her but as he did, he was struck by what felt like an electric charge of such strength that he was almost repelled ten meters out of the water. The strange woman then turned around waved her hand and then easily dove over several large waves, her friends did the same. Soon they had swum to the center of the Kahovskoye water reservoir.

It began to drizzle, and the boys returned to the shore when suddenly a huge luminous globe of light appeared out of the clouds. It descended over the waters and began to hover directly over the location where the strange females floated. Moments later, all four women ascended into the globe or were absorbed into the globe. And then the globe quickly zoomed up and vanished amid the clouds.

HC addendum.
Source: RIA 'Novosti' (Russian news agency) and 'Fourth Dimension and UFOs,' Newspaper of the Yaroslavl UFO Research Group, 1995 #11.
Type: B

* * * * * * *

Location: Dorado, Puerto Rico.
Date: August, 1995.
Time: Night.

Local residents reported seeing disc-shaped objects descend and drop off several bizarre Chupacabra-like creatures accompanied by two taller beings.

They allegedly descended from the objects in single file formation. Others reported that when the creatures approached nearby lagoons, the waters bubbled strangely. No other information.

HC addendum.
Source: Scott Corrales Chupacabra & other Mysteries.   Type: B

Location: Siuna, Atlantico Norte, Nicaragua.
Date: August 9, 1995.
Time: 9:00 p.m.

Years after his first encounter, Eduardo Salgado Castro, former Nicaraguan Army soldier, receives "a telepathic invitation" giving him instructions to visit an area near the above locality alone and wait "for his older brothers." Despite his previous military training Eduardo was apprehensive as he arrived at the location indicated by the 'aliens.' As he stood alone on a field suddenly a large cloud began to form above him, he saw what appeared to be lightning but he heard no thunder.

Moments later a lightning bolt seemed to strike the ground near them and from the light, two beings emerged. The two beings were human in appearance and quickly approached Salgado placing their hands on top of his head, immediately erasing his fear. At the same time Salgado felt a tremendous surge of energy entering his body.

The beings were about two meters in height and wore tight-fitting one-piece divers' outfits, knee high black boots and a black belt, curiously according to Salgado both beings had on their chests a symbol resembling the hebrew "Star of David." The beings claimed they were from Ganymede, Jupiter's largest moon.

Suddenly according to Salgado, he was 'teleported' to an isolated coastal region of the Atlantic in Costa Rica, allegedly across from an alien submarine base at the bottom of the ocean. There the aliens spoke to Salgado about his future as a "missionary" and the necessity to initiate changes, and transformation in the human race, messages which according to the aliens had been passed to humanity for years. They told him that humanity must prepare itself for the events which were about to occur in the not too distant future.

According to Salgado, the contact seemed to last at least three hours, but upon returning to the original meeting site, only ten minutes had transpired. He would have a further contact in 2005.

HC addendum.
Source: www.nicanoticias.com/2012

Type: G

Location: Arzamas-16 (Sarov) nuclear military center, Nizhniy Novgorod region, Russia.
Date: August 16, 1995.
Time: 2:15 a.m.-2:30 a.m.

A duty military serviceman named Pavel was on guard duty at the sentry box, when the commander of the guard reported that something like a UFO was hovering in the region of the industrial area, over a facility called Zh-H-385/3. The commander's words were, *"If you want to see a miracle come out quickly."* The witness ran out with the others and ran beyond the sentry box and saw something that resembled a "flying saucer" but quite afar (maybe 5km away or closer).

The group of soldiers gathered around and began talking about what they were seeing as beams of light descended over the forest from the UFO. Parts of the forest were also lit from the ground by a bright but not blinding light, also a bright beam of light was pointed towards the sky from a point before the horizon, the beam seem to pulsate, becoming broader and then narrowing until almost becoming a straight line.

After watching the scene for about 2-3 minutes, the witness mentally asked the following question, *"Who are you and what do you want?"* Incredibly the witness received the following answer, *"If you're not afraid, come closer."* It sounded like a very polite invitation from the uninvited "guests." Nervous, the witness lit up a cigarette and thought, *"Where do I look for you?"* Immediately he received the telepathic answer, *"Come straight."*

Taking into account of his previous experience with anomalous phenomena, the witness was sure that the aliens would not harm him, so unafraid he calmly walked forward. His commander asked him, *"Pasha where are you going?"* the witness answered, *"I will return soon."* He heard the other men commenting about what he was doing as he walked on.

After about 100-150 meters, Pavel descended to the embankment and began walking on the railroad tracks, facing a very strong wind. Looking behind him he saw two figures carrying flashlights at about 300m behind him, he was convinced that these were other soldiers that had followed him. At this point the witness heard another telepathic message, *"Hurry or they would run after you."* Pavel walked for about 5-6 minutes and suddenly felt the air ahead of him become "condensed," or glutinous, it became harder for him to walk.

Soon he understood that he could not walk any further. He could literally feel the invisible barrier with his bare hands; it seemed resilient but not sticky. Pavel then stopped, turned around and saw the same "flying saucer" of a solid red color but not shiny, though quite bright. He distinctly could see several yellow colored windows or portholes around the disk-shaped craft, lighted from inside.

He pulled out a cigarette and was immediately asked telepathically *"What is that?"* He explained what it was and what it did, *"Why do you need that?"* was the next question inside his head. His answer was, *"because I just like it"* apparently satisfied the aliens asked him to show them a cigarette, he took one cigarette and raised it up in the air, suddenly the cigarette suddenly vanished in plain sight.

Still nervous, Pavel took out another cigarette and asked the following question, *"So who are you and what do you need?"* The alien answer was confusing but it resembled the following, *"We are hunting for contrabandists that supply to us the proto plasma that you use for uneconomical purposes."* (!)

Pavel's next question was, *"From what planet are you from and how can we enter in contact with you?"* but he received another absurd answer, *"We live in the same planet as you, but we are from another dimension, so contact with us would be impossible without special preparation."* They then exchanged several more nonsensical questions and answers and then the witness turned around and quietly started walking away from the saucer, nothing hindered him now but the road back somehow seem longer now.

When he returned to the sentry box he was met by the agitated company commander, and other officers. They told him that they were about to go out searching for him. After having a cup of tea with the commander, Pavel and the commander went outdoors and the "saucer" was still hovering and pulsating over the region but with less intensiveness. The time was now 4:45 a.m.

The object was estimated to have been 50-60 meters in diameter and 10-12 meters high with 8-9 illuminated ellipse-shaped windows positioned along the lower part of the saucer. On top of the saucer there was an additional hemispheric structure with an additional four to five lighted windows.

HC addendum.
Source: Mikhail Gershtein, 'UFO Adventures over Nuclear areas' in: 'Anomalia' newspaper, Saint Petersburg #1, 2000.   Type: F

Location: Puebla, Mexico.
Date: August 16, 1995.
Time: Night.

Farmer Victor Morales, encountered a bizarre creature that bit him on the arm. The creature was described as half female, half fish, with wings and a long tail.

The farmer had confronted the bizarre creature as it apparently attacked his farm animals.

HC addendum.
Source: Ruben Manrique.   Type: E

* * * * * * *

Location: Piracicaba, Sao Paolo, Brazil.
Date: August 26, 1995.
Time: Night.

A witness encountered three 50 cm tall humanoids wearying white coveralls and helmets with antennas. One carried a pen-like instrument, which he pointed towards the witness who fled in his motorcycle.

While he looked back he saw the humanoids walking towards a landed luminous round object.

HC addendum.
Source: GEPUC Brazil.   Type: C

* * * * * * *

Location: Vasilkov, Kiev region, Ukraine.
Date: Late August, 1995.
Time: Evening.

Marina, a local student at Kiev's T. G. Shevchenko University, was staying at a home at the northern end of town and one day was drawing pictures in the verandah when she suddenly felt as if she had come under a state of hypnosis (mind control?). Someone then opened the closed verandah door.

When Marina turned around to look, she saw two male humanoid figures. One was about 2 to 2.5 meters in height reaching the ceiling; the second was about 1.5m in height. Both were dressed in turquoise or blue shiny coveralls. They had large eyes without pupils. The tall humanoid wore a small cap on his head; the smaller alien was absolutely hairless,

41

wearing a tight-fitting skullcap. Extremely fearful, Marina was unable to utter a word.

The strangers could obviously read her mind, so they began to answer her questions by using telepathy. She heard a voice in her head, *"You want to see our ship? It is beyond the forest."* The smaller alien stretched his hand toward her, his hand was very thin and delicate, and fearfully Marina retreated back and sat on the chair. Then the two humanoids walked out the closed verandah doors. After they left, Marina regained control of her senses; she felt an unusual energy within her body. She decided to follow the aliens.

She went outside but could not see the aliens anywhere. But she remembered that they had mentioned that their ship was beyond the forest and she then followed the only narrow road into the forest. She hurried down the path and at about 500 meters into the pine forest she noticed flashes of light and when she passed by a small copse she came over a large gully and in the gully she saw the spaceship. She described it as a large disc-shaped object, resting on a tripod-leg landing gear. The craft had round windows that gave off a black and white light from a television set.

The tall alien was standing close to the disk. As she watched, no one noticed her. She stared at the scene as if hypnotized or charmed. In about five minutes, the lights on the craft dimmed and it became dark. Suddenly, Marina felt an immense fear, an uncommon fear apparently generated by the aliens themselves (for protection?).

In a state of horror she rushed home. The next morning she visited the landing place and noticed an area of matted down grass but did not dare descend into the gully. After the incident Marina began drawing pictures of space or alien themes; however she was never able to duplicate the alien object that she witnessed.

HC addendum.
Source: 'Interesnaya Gazeta' D-Block #8, 1997.   Type: C

Location: Tanjung Sepat, Selangor, Malaysia.
Date: September, 1995.
Time: 7:30 a.m.

Rosli Kadir, 36, claimed that he had encountered a small green being in his plantation. The incident occurred early in the morning when the witness was attending to his oil palm trees. While bending down to pick up the leaves of the oil palm, he suddenly caught sight of a green, bi-pedal creature about 2.5 feet tall staring at him, just about twenty feet away. He was so shocked by the sight that he left whatever he was doing and immediately ran away. He told his friend about the presence of the green creature.

When they returned to the site, the strange being was gone. Rosli described the being as greenish in color, without clothes, and the body was covered with scales, the head of the being appeared normal as compared to its body. It was bald headed and had a pair of large pointed ears. The eyes were described as reddish and a bit slanted at the sides. The nose and mouth were small.

HC addendum.
Source: Ahmad Jamaluddin.   Type: E

*   *   *   *   *   *   *

Location: Tanjung Sepat Laut, Selangor, Malaysia.
Date: September, 1995.
Time: Daytime.

Crowds gathered at the village and apparently reported seeing a UFO as large as a soccer pitch land.

Two, two-foot tall humanoids with long ears and red eyes briefly emerged from the object. No other information.

HC addendum.
Source: Marcus Day in, 'Aliens: Encounters with Unexplained.' Type: B

Location: Undisclosed.
Date: September 3, 1995.
Time: 12:15 a.m.

Mark Andrews was at home when the phone rang. A female voice advised, *"We have some students here from another planet. Would you be willing to help in their earth orientation?"* (Mark is a teacher). He was a little stunned but said *"OK."* She returned, *"We have one standing in your driveway. Follow her."*

At the end of the driveway stood a very beautiful, petite Mediterranean looking girl with ornately "woven" hair, dressed in a burgundy, wrap around robe. He followed her around to the side of the house where a soft but brilliant flash of light somehow transported them into the receiving area of an enormous starship far beyond earth's orbit. The young girl was not quite five feet tall and appeared to be possibly around 17 years of age. The only words she spoke to Andrews were following their "beam up" was when she very nonchalantly turned her head back in his direction and informed him, *"We are going to take a shower."* He was somewhat relieved to learn that the "shower" was actually a bathing (disinfecting?) light, no disrobing necessary. He then quickly caught on to the fact that despite her obvious advanced intellect and training, her English skills were not quite 100%.

He then found himself standing in front of a viewing portal that looked out toward deep space. He had no way of knowing where the ship was in relation to earth, but the view that grabbed him was so magnificent that it caused his stomach to drop and his knees to begin to buckle. It was the sight of multiple, pure stellar brilliance expanding into infinity. He was asked to keep his eyes on a screen just to the left of the viewing area. He was shown a diagram of several objects (apparently asteroids, comets, meteors, etc.) in their projected movement toward earth. He was informed by his charming companion or guide that the ship's presence in the solar system at this time was to help humans to deal with the objects that would soon threaten the earth.

The witness asked where they were from. She responded, *"We call our world "LELARI."* Then there appeared on the view screen a projection of what looked to him like the "Big Dipper" as viewed from earth. He was guided from one room to another. The rooms were really areas that had been partitioned off by movable walls that served to localize one activity from another so as not to allow interference. He then encountered a tall, blond, very beautiful, "nordic" and somewhat older looking, young woman that was to perform a medical examination on him.

She asked Andrews to lie down on a table, she looked at a monitor, and then said (with a smile) *"Your exam is finished."* His guide then took him to another area where several members of their group were gathered. It had the feel of a "break room." A very pleasant, short, nordic, "high school aged" looking male quickly pointed at him and laughed, *"I am assigned to be your baby-sitter!"*

He was then brought before one of the commanding officers of the craft. He sat at a small table, keeping his eyes fixed on a hand held view screen. He did not acknowledge Andrew's presence for what seemed 10 minutes. Andrews was beginning to get a little "insecure" due to the lack of attention, so he decided to break the ice and blurted, *"You know, I'm very grateful that you have been using English with me, but I would like to hear your language as it sounds when spoken"* He had always had a fascination with languages. The commander had not quite shoulder length brown hair, olive skin texture, large brown eyes and Native American facial features. He looked up at Andrews for the first time. His eyes projected a marvelous sense of compassion and intrigue toward the witness.

He then thought-projected a sentence from his language directly into the witness mind, it had the sound of "Finnish/Latin." Andrews then asked for a souvenir that he could keep and was told that it would be arranged later. Feeling powerful emotions, Andrews began to weep and his guide then took him by the arm and led him back through the "teleporter."

His composure was so battered at this point that his guide had to literally walk him up the steps to his front door and into the living room. She then let herself out without any more exchange of words. Andrews remained awake for the rest of the night.

HC addendum.
Source: http://ufoexperiences.blogspot.com   Type: G

Location: Coweta, Oklahoma.
Date: September 5, 1995.
Time: 3:00 p.m.

The witnesses heard the sound of a jet passing low above their country home. The man went outside in the rear of the house, facing the pasture opposite of where the noise went. At that time, something with an approximate wingspan of ten feet flew from east to west, twenty meters from the ground above the elm trees next to the house. It had a large head and a thin humanoid body, wings like a moth or insect but it did not flap them. This entity landed. His wife saw it too. It was ten to twelve feet tall, with a red oily skin, and emitted ammonia like odor.

The creature then spoke in a strange manner. The man demanded that it speak "English" of which it spoke in an older European accent. (!) It did not do any harm but the witnesses fled inside their home. According to the witness the entity claimed its name was *"Ivan Cole."* (?)

HC addendum.
Source: NUFORC   Type: E

* * * * * * *

Location: Rocchetta Sant Antonio, Italy.
Date: September 11, 1995.
Time: 5:45 p.m.

A 20-year-old woman was taking her sheep to a pasture in a valley, when she noticed something shiny standing nearby. She got closer to the object and it suddenly turned towards her. She could now see that it was a small smiling humanoid wearing a brown coverall within a sort of transparent "space suit." It stood about 50cm tall and appeared to have no arms or a nose. It had a silver half sphere with an antenna on top, on its shoulders.

She stared at the figure for about five minutes then began walking back home. The small being apparently began following her. The witness panicked and she called out to a neighbor, who attempted to approach the small being. This one then began to trot quickly away, then it took off into the air emitting a noise like a motorcycle motor. Two others saw the humanoid flying over a field.

HC addendum.
Source: Italian UFO Reporter.   Type: E

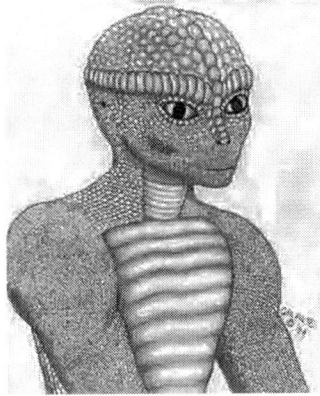

Location: Kissimmee, Florida.
Date: September 24, 1995.
Time: 8:00 p.m.

The witnesses spotted a "classic" disk shaped craft, silvery metallic in appearance, about 35 feet wide surrounded with a slight green glow except for the very bottom which had a protruding sphere and had a red glow. The craft moved very quickly as it hovered above a cow and then it lifted it up into the craft's middle hatch.

At this point the witnesses became excited at what they were seeing and began to shout and jump up and down, unwittingly attracting the attention of the craft and its occupants. A second later it was over the witnesses, the beam used on the cow was now on the witnesses as both were paralyzed but still were able to scream (and they did). The light beam looked like a white laser light; they could see sort of thick light particles in it.

Both then blacked out and awoke later inside the craft, they were on two clear tables, two foot by five foot and were paralyzed from the neck down. The room was all white and round. It had drawers or square rectangles along every part of the walls and uniform in appearance, appearing to be man-made like molded plastic. There was a window all around, five inches or so at the top of the ceiling, which was plain and white.

The witnesses do not remember the floor but saw two four foot tall lizard-reptile like beings. The beings wore collarless one piece silvery foil one-piece suits, flexible in appearance with a diamond cross pattern like a sun shield for a car. There was a hole for their tails (!) which went through. No shoes, ornaments or jewelry was evident. One carried a clipboard of sorts in his left hand about a half inch thick. One of the beings was very green in color like a tree snake, smooth and thin the other was rougher, darker brown, and bigger in muscle build, both were

47

less than five feet tall. The eyes had no slit for pupils and had a "pretty" yellow starfish pattern and the iris was surrounded by reddish browns.

They did not communicate either verbally or telepathically but the witnesses could hear them breathe at times. They both had three foot long tails, which did not drag on the floor. The heads were like typical lizards, with pointed snouts, tiny teeth and no visible hair. As the witness was suddenly able to move, he attempted to become aggressive towards them, one of them swung its tail knocking him down, he then blacked out and his next memory was being back on the ground and the UFO and aliens were gone.

HC addendum.
Source: NUFORC also UFO Casebook Forums.   Type: G

* * * * * * *

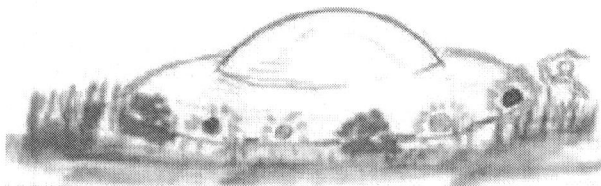

Herbst 1995, Breitbrunn am Chiemsee
(c) MUFON-CES

Location: Near Obendorf, Germany.
Date: October, 1995.
Time: Evening.

Two young girls riding their horses on a field noticed some multicolored circus like lights coming from a nearby glade. Upon investigating, they encountered a landed silvery, disc shaped object with an egg shaped cupola on top.

Next to the object, to the right stood a man like figure wearing a silvery outfit and what appeared to be an oversized raincoat. At this point the horses became frightened and stopped. Soon the craft rose up and hovered five meters from the ground and then shot away at incredible speed. Farmers in the area apparently saw the object flying away.

HC addendum.
Source: Mufon-CES.   Type: C

Location: Crestone, Saguache County, Colorado.
Date: October, 1995.
Time: Night.

The witness, Michael, suddenly woke up onboard a flying saucer. He was looking down through a large window. To the right was a panel of raised buttons, they were shaped like diamonds and squares and they were in primary colors. He kept looking around and saw three alien beings standing toward the back. They had dome-shaped heads and slanted eyes. They were wearing white robes and they were of different heights. The witness received the distinct impression that the aliens did not want him to look at them.

He then decided to look at the controls. "As I looked over to my right at the bank of controls, it was almost as though, hidden to my left behind the wall, there was a plastic covering in the shape of the control panel. It went around (covering the control panel) just slightly faster than my eyes, so, I was looking at a shiny white, curved panel. I imagine they covered the controls as a containment procedure. I thought boy, this is interesting, they're either handling my mind, or this is really a real phenomenon. So what am I going to do now?"

As he looked at the window and thought if the window was able to do anything, there was a flash and the window was suddenly covered in not only letters and numbers but also hieroglyphics in orange color. The witness had the impression that the machinery and the object reacted to his thoughts and somehow he was able to control some of the movements and maneuvers.

At about three thousand feet up, he was looking down at an angle at some mountains. He saw a ray of light going down, and it lit up this huge gold aura at the base of the ray. The witness suspected that he was being shown the location of a long lost wagonload of gold, lost hundreds of years ago. "The ship was interacting with my mind. I asked the beings, *"So, are there any more locations of lost gold?"* And suddenly another six to eight miles north he was being shown another one.

He remembered being over a particular hill and the object tilting over at an extreme angle and him looking down at this rather large amount of 'something' in the ground that emanated a golden aura. The witness then asked the beings about the major canyon treasures (gold) in this area. Very quickly he was suddenly looking down at a mountain full of gold, he noted where it came up close to the surface, where a crevice might be located for a person to find something. The aura around this gold was about a quarter mile out. The aura seemed relative to the amount of gold he was seeing.

Suddenly he heard a kind of voice or thought that seemed to come from the back of the ship, which was kind of gravelly, kind of

49

commanding. It said, "That's enough." The witness said thank you and woke up in his bed.

HC addendum.
Source: Christopher O'Brien.   Type: G
Comments: According to the witness there are numerous stories in the area of lost and hidden treasures in inaccessible mountains and hills.

* * * * * * *

Location: Anones, Naranjito, Puerto Rico.
Date: Middle of October, 1995.
Time: Evening.

Rosa Jimenez was coming back home from a nearby ranch when she noticed a round greenish luminous object slowly descend over the area. The object quickly descended and now she could see that it was an oval shaped craft ringed with large square windows. The craft hovered about three feet from the ground.

The witness then noticed several figures looking out the window. She saw the short child-like being that she had encountered before and also a tall man-like figure with dark skin, and hair sticking up on his head. He wore a tight fitting silvery outfit.

The object hovered for a few more seconds then lifted up and left at high speed. Soon after that the witness saw two bizarre bird-like creatures with oval shaped heads, red eyes and pointed ears. Their beaks were long and thin and their feet ended in black claws.

HC addendum.
Source: Jorge Martin Evidencia OVNI #8.   Type: A

Location: White Mountains, Arizona.
Date: Late October, 1995.
Time: Night.

The witness and his family were looking for a good camping spot in an isolated area, when the road became narrower and narrower. The trees curled over their heads, and soon the road became so rocky and narrow that they decided to turn back.

However before they could turn around and had the car turned halfway around they saw a little girl. She was in tattered clothing, and she looked up at the witnesses. Her eyes grew wide with fear, like she had seen a ghost. The witness's father rolled down the window and asked, *"Are you alright?"* The little girl trembled in fear and said, *"You shouldn't be here, please go back!"* The father froze in confusion. The little girl continued to say the same phrase over and over again. The mother was scared and finally said, *"Let's go back."* So they turned around and ignored it. They turned out of the narrow road and found a camping spot about 30 minutes later. They weren't very tired when they got there and the witness felt as though he had been "refreshed." The family set up the tents and made a campfire.

They relaxed around the fire, confused and scared, talking about the strange girl. Soon the father said, *"Shhhh!"* His wife laughed at him because he always joked around. But this time he was serious. His face went white, and then they knew something was watching them. The witness looked around the forest, his heart pumping fast. He didn't hear anything but he was scared. Soon a spine-chilling roar came from the woods. Then the bushes moved, and something bolted out of the forest into the light of the fire. It had sharp teeth and no fur. It was the size of a bear, but its eyes were yellow.

The witnesses were frozen with fear. It stood there for ten seconds in the light, and then galloped off into the forest. Their dog was whimpering and it curled its tail between its legs. The creature was further described as extremely thin, it looked like skin and bones; it was indeed a "disturbing" image. According to the witness he heard of other witnesses who had seen the same or similar thin creature that night in the area.

HC addendum.
Source: Your True Tales, March, 2007. Type: E
Comments: Who was the strange little girl that apparently warned the witnesses of something untoward in the area? Was she some type of apparition or guardian angel? This case has a lot of intriguing features.

Location: Vega Baja, Puerto Rico.
Date: November 12, 1995.
Time: Night.

Young Oralis Gonzalez and her mother reportedly watched from their balcony a metallic disc shaped object descend and land on their farm. The craft had multi-colored flashing lights.

Undescribed occupants exited the craft and approached the house, somehow floating up to the balcony and communicating with the young girl, as her mother remained paralyzed with fear. The extraterrestrials allegedly marked the girl's left arm with a strange tattoo: "OJO-10-OJO." The meaning remains unknown.

The father attempted to photograph the mark but each time he tried the film was mysteriously exposed. As the humanoids re-entered their craft, the mother began screaming. The father ran up to see the UFO rise up and leave at high speed. Several hens were found mutilated at the same location on the same night.

HC addendum.
Source: Jorge Martin, La Conspiracion Chupacabras.   Type: B

*　*　*　*　*　*　*

Location: Boleslaw, Poland.
Date: December 23, 1995.
Time: Midnight.

A dozen witnesses reported seeing a flash and seeing a round object maybe the size of a car, standing in the middle of a field. Two small humanoids wearing metallic outfits emerged from the object and began "strolling" around the field and apparently talking to each other. Later after the object left, landing marks were found, a possible hull impression about 8m long and small footprints without heels on the soil. Their space was smaller than that of a normal human.

HC addendum.
Source: woe_@vp.pl quoting Gazeta Wyborcza and local researcher Stanislaw Koziol.   Type: B

Location: Near Harker's Island, North Carolina.
Date: Late December, 1995.
Time: 10:45 p.m.

Rex Silverwood was out one cold winter night when he was drawn to the presence of a strange grouping of lights flying slowly, high over the property. The lights seemed to outline no discernible shape; simply five irregularly grouped white lights. His wife observed the lights also but went back inside the house. Two of the lights will fly repeatedly over the area back & forth making an odd vibrating humming sound, which was difficult to hear. Soon the witness attempted to obtain psychic impressions of the pilot. After about a minute, he received the distinct impression of a non-human intelligence and he tried to convey a friendly mental hello. He was rewarded with a definite feeling of a mutual connection with an alien mind, which acknowledged his mental and physical presence and conveyed a feeling of friendship and a wonderful sense of peace. He lost sight of the craft and watched the second one flying back and forth as he walked further into the darkened field.

Suddenly three luminous figures appeared clearly right in front of him in a V-shaped formation. Startled he stopped in his tracks and noticed that he could see right through them, yet they had definite outlines. A fourth figure seemed somewhat hazy but was also visible to the left. They appeared as short humanoid beings with two arms and two legs each, with one large bulbous head graced with two extremely large lidless black eyes and pale gray skin. Small mouths and nose less nostrils were apparently on their pale gray faces. There was no apparent visible clothing.

The witness and the beings stood there regarding each other when the being closest to him lifted its arm and pointed into the darkness toward a part of the clearing. He went walking in the direction where the being had indicated, hoping to make contact with them. As he continued to walk he heard the mental command of "stop there."

He stood there for about twenty seconds then looked around realizing the images (figures) had vanished. He then heard a sound like a high-pitched electronic vibration like he had heard earlier, but louder now, came into his ear. The sound kept getting louder and seemed to come from all around him. The sound abruptly ended and the witness saw what appeared to be the possible source. A huge dark circle silhouetted against the clear sky. On the object's outer rim, he could see a dim circle of red lights. Despite the cold he felt warm and experienced a feeling of well-being. Later back in the house he realized that he could not account for a period of three hours.

HC addendum.
Source: The Black Vault Forums.   Type: C or G?

53

1996

Location: Anapa, Black Sea, Russia.
Date: 1996.
Time: Daytime.

B. Borovikov was hunting sharks in the area and on that particular day, had descended to a depth of eight meters. He then saw giant beings rising up from below. He described them as milky white, but with humanoid faces, and something like fish tails. The being ahead of its companions noticed Borovikov, and stopped. It had giant bulging eyes. Two others joined him. The first one waved a membrane hand at the diver, and then all of them approached him and stopped a short distance away. Then they turned around and swam away.

HC addendum.
Source: Paul Stonehill.   Type: E
HS Index: 6
ROS: 7
Comments: Date is approximate; report (if true) indicates possibly underwater civilizations in some of the earth's bodies of water.

* * * * * * *

Location: Near Tijucas, Brazil.
Date: 1996.
Time: 7:00 p.m.

Driving late at night on Route BR-101 near a local bridge, Maria Marlene Carvalho, 27, saw a light in the distance and felt the car suddenly being pulled towards it. The vehicle began to shake, and she lost total control of it as the car slowed to a crawl. Marlene suddenly found herself in a wooded hill surrounded by trees. A tall dark skinned humanoid figure suddenly appeared in front of her. In a deep grave voice the creature introduced itself as "Dakon." The tall humanoid had large green glowing eyes. She seemed to black out and her next recollection was of walking into a police station near the capital. Police later searched the area but were unable to find anything.

HC addendum.
Source: Diario Catarinese.   Type: G
High Strangeness Index: 6
Reliability of Source: 3
Comments: Possibly an abduction case, but not investigated by researchers, only source is media.

* * * * * * *

Location: Kuznetsky Alatau Mountain, Khakassia Republic, Russia.
Date: 1996.
Time: Night.

At this location it was reported that five amateur speleologists disappeared without a trace. However one young man, who somehow managed to get out of the cave could only rave wildly about some furry 'monsters' and a 'flaming doorway' on a stone wall which they could not go through.
The lone survivor was exhausted and was taken to a local hospital where he died after a few weeks due to an unknown 'illness.'

HC addendum.
Source: Sergei Kozuszko,
http://wszechocean.blogspot.com/2013/03/zagadki-kaszkuakskiej-jaskini.html?spref=fb   Type: X

* * * * * * *

Location: Miami, Florida.
Date: 1996.
Time: Midnight.

The witness was sitting on her couch when she became aware of a small rectangle of light that came in through the closed window, rotating as it moved towards her, edgewise. As she looked into the rectangle she knew that she was somehow looking into another universe.
Suddenly from out of the rectangle sprang a being dressed in a bronze or amber suit, wearing a tight helmet. Although she was unable to recall any facial features, she did remember the being's eyes, which

were huge and looked directly into hers as it bent over her. She was terrified and unable to move. When she became conscious of her surroundings again it was 5:30 a.m.

HC addendum.
Source: Miami Skyscan.   Type: E
HSI: 8
ROS: 8
Comments: Are we dealing with other dimensions here? Similar case in 1994.

* * * * * * *

Location: Irkutsk, East Siberia, Russia.
Date: 1996.
Time: Various.

A local woman named Alla Yesperova reported that "aliens" were terrorizing her on a regular basis since her first encounter nine years ago. Everything began one night when she experienced a very vivid and colorful dream in which she encountered a flying saucer and humanoids dressed in red spacesuits.

Soon the aliens began "controlling" her and ordering her what to do, but they also cured her ailments and in general improved her health. But she eventually became tired of living under constant alien control and soon the aliens began feeding her tablets which slowed down her mental capabilities and also feeding her a strange liquid substance.

She became ill after those contacts and one time forgot the English language for a month which she was fluent with. Apparently the visitors were ardent "Christians" (!) Attempting to impart her to love the Church and demanded that she visited the local monasteries. She obeyed and actually lived at the Troitse-Sergieva lavra (Russian Orthodox Monastery) for three years.

One time Alla awoke in the middle of the night to find several humanoid entities in her bedroom. The humanoids were of thin features including faces and lips. And then the aliens told her telepathically that they were leaving and incredibly began kissing and hugging her. Alla felt very disgusted and hoped that all would end soon. But apparently the aliens did not leave and kept testing her nerves.

In total the witness reported that she encountered three types of aliens, small dwarf like humanoids, huge humanoids about 2.5m in height that had to bend over when they walked around her apartment, and a third type which were very similar to humans. Alla reported that all the aliens were cunning, sly, mean and cruel.

HC addendum.
Source: 'Anomalous News,' (Anomalnye Novosti) Saint Petersburg, Russia, #34, August, 2005.   Type: G or F?
Comments: Maybe this witness was a victim not of "alien visitations" but of some kind of mind control experiment which are said to occur in those remote areas of the former Soviet Union.

* * * * * * *

Location: Zacapa, Guatemala.
Date: January, 1996.
Time: 1:00 a.m.

Twice, cattleman Vicente Sosa reported seeing a strange bipedal, black hairy creature with a very long tail. One time it stood in front of the witness staring at him with large glowing red eyes. It was apparently winged.

Others saw a flying creature shiny black in color with bat-like wings & sky blue eyes. Shots were fired at the creature without apparent effect. A wave of animal mutilations was occurring in the area at the same time.

HC addendum.
Source: Jorge Martin Evidencia OVNI #12.   Type: E

* * * * * * *

Location: Near Bishop, California.
Date: January, 1996.
Time: Night.

On two occasions a group of men driving a pick-up truck on an isolated road near their ranch, spotted a small green colored humanoid figure that had the ability to float in mid-air, and hover over the roadway in front of the approaching vehicle.

The driver of the vehicle attempted to chase the entity, but it was unable to come near it, as the small figure flew away at incredible speed.

HC addendum.
Source: Rick Grootveldt, Skip Richards.   Type: E
HSI: 7
ROS: 9
Comments: Source is personal friend and I had a chance to interview witness. I seem to recall similar cases from California.

58

Location: Jardim Andere, Varginha, Brazil.
Date: January 20, 1996.
Time: 8:00 a.m.

Hildo Lucio Galindo opened his bathroom window to see a creature with oily dark brown skin crouched in a nearby alleyway. It had very small hands with three extremely long fingers, ran away when Hildo cried out. The creature had no hair or clothing and was about 4-5 feet tall. Later several calls came into the local fire department about some "wild animal" on the loose in the northern area of the park. When the fire department arrived, they found the military already on the scene.

According to other witnesses, some children had thrown stones at a strange creature that emitted a soft buzzing sound like a bee. This creature was apparently captured by the military and put in a wooden box with a white plastic canvas cover and transported away by an army truck. Around the same time, local residents heard three shots and saw soldiers come out of the woods carrying two campaign sacks, one motionless, the other moving. Sources revealed that the soldiers had shot a creature on the chest and it had died instantly. Others saw army trucks near the woods and others saw two F-5 aircraft moving at a low altitude over the area. It was reported that a total of eight creatures were captured at the time. One dead, two injured, and five unhurt and living.

Earlier that same day, around 1:30 two farm workers in the same general area had spotted a group of agitated animals running away from a location. Upon closer investigation, they saw a gray, metallic submarine-shaped craft that appeared to be trembling like a curtain and emitting smoke or fog as it descended to at least five meters above the ground. Military witnesses later admitted that it had crashed.

HC addendum.
Source: Ubirajara Franco Rodrigues.   Type: H
Comments: This was an apparent recovery of aliens that were either intentionally shot down by US or Brazilian military forces. There were many independent witnesses to this event. Encounters in the area continued well into 1997.

Location: Varginha, Brazil.
Date: January 20, 1996.
Time: 1:00 p.m.

Three girls were walking past a plot of land when they spotted a bizarre looking creature, described as man-like but only about 80 cm tall. It had brown skin, bulging red eyes, bulging veins, enormous feet, and three protruding lumps on its head. The being was apparently unclothed and its body seemed covered with oil. The girls panicked and ran away from the area to obtained additional witnesses. Soon units of the local fire department arrived and took the creature into custody. Apparently a similar creature had been captured earlier. The creature emitted a strange buzzing like sound. Others saw strange cigar-shaped objects flying low over a field.

Later the military apparently took the creature to the nearby city of Campinas. A doctor who refuses to reveal his name, reported that the body of the creature presented injuries of different kinds and grades. He said he was urgently called by the military staff responsible for keeping the creature and described his astonishment in front of something never seen or reported before. His statement regarding the appearance of the creature is not different from many other descriptions of other witnesses, but he said the creature was surely alive when he saw it.

The doctor also said that he could not understand the physiological constitution of the body he was examining even though it was an anthropomorphic being, with head, trunk and members. The doctor did not hear any sound made by the creature neither mentioned the famous "thin" bifurcated tongue," reported by other medic and military witnesses. He said he had seen its slow movements, proving it was still alive, but refused to say if it was breathing.

HC addendum.
Source: Brazilian UFO Report #6.   Type: D

Location: Ariege region, France.
Date: January 22, 1996.
Time: Late night.

The witness a local farmer named Quentin, was on his way home in his Renault 25 when suddenly the engine began to sputter and the vehicle stalled in the middle of the road. He stepped out of his car and apparently fainted. When he woke up he was in a room that seemed to have no doors, no windows, or light but nevertheless it was perfectly lit.

Shortly after, a portion of the wall began to 'slide' open and two individuals about 5ft tall each entered the room. The figures wore a very tight-fitting black suit which looked as if 'liquid had completely covered their bodies and dried up.' Behind them stood a female humanoid which was completely naked, then the two black garbed humanoids left the room leaving the naked female and the witness alone behind.

The naked humanoid was very much like a human female, but with a quite different face with pale hair, almond shaped eyes and a highly stretched triangular-shaped face. Smiling seductively she approached the witness and then engaged in sexual relations with him. After the deed was done, she left the room. However before she exited, the witness called to her, she turned around, pointed to her abdomen and then to sky, smiled and left.

After that the witness awoke in his garden, dressed and confident that it had all been a dream. Later that evening he was told that his car had been abandoned on the emergency lane on the N20 road near Foix.

HC addendum.
Source: GREPI Switzerland, http://www.ovni.ch/home/frame4.htm
Type: G
Comments: Obvious similarities with the famous October 1957, Antonio Vilas Boas case.

*   *   *   *   *   *   *

Location: Near Romatambo, Peru.
Date: January 31, 1996.
Time: 8:00 a.m.

At a remote mountain village several Quechua Indian shepherds tending their flocks watched six objects flying over the area. According to a witness, Silvia Bedoya, 40, the objects apparently emerged from nearby Lake Cococha. The objects formed what seemed a protective circle around a larger mother-ship type object. The flight of the objects illuminated the whole valley in an eerie deep purple type of light. The "mother ship" landed upriver from the village. Soon two occupants

61

emerged from the object. These were described as 3 feet, 3 inches tall, with large oversized heads, long spindly arms and short bandy legs. They wore gunmetal gray helmets and matching one-piece coveralls. The humanoids took out transparent containers and, ignoring the shepherds, collected many samples, like soil, grass, mountain weeds, & water from the nearby river. Soon the humanoids entered the large object and all the objects shot away into space at high speed.

HC addendum.
Source: UFO Roundup Vol. 1 #15.   Type: B
HIS: 6
ROS: 6
Comments: Peru has always been a hotbed for UFO contacts and encounters.

* * * * * * *

Location: Barretal, Tamaulipas, Mexico.
Date: Early February, 1996.
Time: Night.

During the same time period that numerous witnesses saw a large disc-shaped craft that emitted a loud humming sound, flying at a low altitude over a river, other witnesses encountered a strange being described as short, ape-like, that walked hunched over on two legs, with three large claw-like protrusions on its feet, brown color hair, and huge bright red colored eyes. The strange being gave out a peculiar odor resembling "burnt wood." There were also reports of animal mutilations in the area.

HC addendum.
Source: Marco A Reynoso.   Type: D

62

Location: Kijal, Terengganu, Malaysia.
Date: February, 1996.
Time: 3:00 a.m.

A witness was driving along the Kemaman-Dungun Road, and while passing an area at Kijal, he saw a small being measuring less than a meter in height, standing in the middle of the road. He described the being as having a big head and with a pair of large and elongated eyes.

According to the witness, the being appeared naked and its skin looked dark in color and scaly, the being seemed to have been moving slowly to the side of the road when his car passed by it. There was a very foul odor in the air and the witness sped off as fast as he could.

HC addendum.
Source: Ahmad Jamaluddin.   Type: E

* * * * * * *

Location: Thurso, Quebec, Canada.
Date: February 6, 1996.
Time: 7:30 p.m.

The same night that witnesses saw a large triangular vessel hovering over the town of Buckingham, Quebec, farmer Louis Boisvert, 19, saw a very large metallic triangular craft with a set of red lights hovering over a barn, while plowing snow on his tractor. The craft seemed to very slowly fly over the barn. The light coming from the triangle did not illuminate the ground or even the roof of the barn. The craft then suddenly left. After the craft left Boisvert and his father, noticed that their electric water pump would not function.

Troubled by recurring dreams, Boisvert underwent hypnotic regressing. He was then able to remember that he had hopped off the tractor and ran to the barn where his father was working. As he rushed into the barn, he saw his father standing there with a blank expression on his face. Besides him stood two reptilian looking creatures, with long faces, scaled leathery skin, black eyes, clawed hands, and gaunt arms and legs. Both Boisvert and his father were taken onboard the triangular object by the humanoids.

HC addendum.
Source: CEIPI Quebec.   Type: G
Comments: Abduction by reptilian type humanoids.

Location: Huon Valley, Tasmania, Australia.
Date: February 10, 1996.
Time: 2:00 a.m.

The witness woke up to find the room lit up, & had an overwhelming feeling to go outside. From the verandah she saw the source of light to be a bright long elliptical shape about 50 m away on the paddock. There was a brilliant blue/white light and a metallic smell you could almost taste. Standing in the garden was a tall thin figure over 2 m tall. The figure beckoned the witness with its left hand. She walked down the verandah steps then suddenly became alarmed and returned back home. She threw some furniture outside, and then everything went dark.

A week after the previous encounter, the witness woke up with the same feeling that she had to go outside. Again she saw the tall figure in the garden, but no object present. The same metallic smell was in the air. A bright mist surrounded the tall figure. It wore a one-piece silvery suit with a band around the waist. It seemed to have long wrap-around eyes and pointed ears. Also present were two smaller stocky figures to either side of the tall figure. These were fat in the body with small arms & legs. They moved in a jerky fashion. One had a trowel-like instrument that it kept pointing at the ground. The witness fell compelled to follow the beings, but retreated into the house and locked the doors.

HC addendum.
Source: TUFOIC

Type: E

* * * * * * *

Location: Sherman Oaks, California.
Date: February 18, 1996.
Time: 9:30 p.m.

A man named Marcel and a friend were driving on the 101 West Road when they spotted a bizarre creature running alongside the road next to their car. Attempting to avoid hitting the creature they skidded and ran the vehicle off the side of the road.

Two other vehicles apparently stopped nearby. Marcel now noticed two similar creatures that were apparently running towards a bright light that hovered above a nearby field. The light was very bright and silent.

The two creatures ran on two legs and were very fast. They appeared to have scales along their backs and a band of sharp spikes that ran down from the back of their heads along the back. Seen in profile they resembled bipedal goats with short snouts and a tail. They also had bright red, teardrop shaped eyes.

Apparently the police filed a report on the incident.

HC addendum.
Source: Jorge Martin, La Conspiracion Chupacabras.   Type: C?
Comments: This report apparently describes a direct connection between UFOs and Chupacabra type creatures.

* * * * * * *

Location: Nuevo Centro, Abasolo, Tamaulipas, Mexico.
Date: February 23, 1996.
Time: 10:00 p.m.

Irasema Margarita Cuevas and other witnesses in the household heard their dogs barking outside and went out to investigate. Outside they saw a red-orange dome shaped craft floating a few feet from the ground, near some nearby trees about 50 meters away.

Soon from the craft a small humanoid emerged, about one meter in height. It began floating up and down in peculiar movements. From a belt around its waist, a bluish beam of light emerged. The being appeared robotic in nature, somewhat resembling "Alpha" from the well-known children's show, "The Power Rangers." After a few minutes the being re-entered the object, which rose up to join a similar craft. They both then flew towards the nearby swamps. Several witnesses then followed the objects and were able to see a brilliant light emerge from behind some trees and a huge column of gray smoke.

Upon seeing this, the head of the household, Guillermo Serna Marquez, told his family to return to the house and went into the woods to investigate alone, on the way there he ran into a farmhand, which accompanied him into the woods. As they watched, they saw a luminous craft fly over the trees in the direction of the swamp, then a two meter tall humanoid appeared, seemingly floating above the trees and accompanied by the small robotic "Alpha" like entity. They watched the beings float around and then enter the dome shaped object, after a while the witnesses grew tired of watching this spectacle and went back home.

The next day a large section of the ground was found scorched in the form of three enormous circles. Strange foam like substance was also found at the site, purplish white in color. Numerous other strange incidents were reported in subsequent days. Small flying red spheres, more animal mutilations, and a large orange sphere that followed some of the investigators late one night.

HC addendum.
Source: Marco A. Reynoso.   Type: B
Comments: Translated by Albert S Rosales.

65

Location: Potrero, Veracruz, Mexico.
Date: February 24, 1996.
Time: 11:00 p.m.

Mr. Anselmo Huerta Martinez, his wife, Irene Flores Ramirez and their two sons, 8 and 9 years of age respectively were walking through a sugarcane field near their home when suddenly they felt a strong gust of wind and at the same time the area around them became brightly illuminated. Looking up they saw a disc-shaped object surrounded by beautiful blinking and rotating multicolored lights.

As the object hovered over the sugarcane field, an opening became visible and a man-like figure wearing a white doctor's smock was seen standing at the "door." Next to the first figure stood a female figure which the witnesses assumed was a "nurse." Suddenly the door closed and the craft vanished into the distance creating a strong "whirlwind" like wind over the cane field. The witnesses described the craft as big as a house and aluminum in appearance. The beings were further described as short in stature and with "handsome" features.

HC addendum.
Source: Rossana Tejeda Lopez, Mexico.   Type: A
Comments: Translated by Albert S. Rosales.

* * * * * * *

Location: Cuscatancingo, El Salvador.
Date: February 29, 1996.
Time: 10:00 p.m.

On March 2, 1996, at 6:30 a.m. police found a 17-year old boy wandering confused at the edge of Ilopango Lake. Later under interrogation he related a bizarre story.

During the night in question he had been walking towards his home during a local "black-out." Suddenly there was a bright flash of blue light from behind him. Thinking that it was the police he turned slowly around. Then his next memory was of being in a completely white "space" or room. He could not distinguish any walls or furniture of any kind. He then realized that he was lying prone and unable to move in some sort of "bed." He noticed numerous "cables" that appeared to be connected to his chest area, and on his right arm he had an object resembling a blood IV machine.

He then saw several humanoids, about 1.2 meters in height. They had extremely large heads, huge eyes and in the forehead area he could see what appeared to be another "protuberance" resembling another eye. They also had sparse beards around the mouth and chin area. In a horrible state of confusion he noticed other humans in the room but could not tell if they were also prisoners or not. He remembered seeing a terrible scene in which he saw several of the humanoids apparently operating on a woman, seemingly cutting her in half. Then they took the upper half of the human female and somehow inserted it on top and back of a "hump-like" area of one female humanoid that had apparently was being prepared on another bed.

The humanoids wore white tunics on which they had a strange "symbol" on the right side of their chests. He was then taken to the shores of Lake Ilopango where they told the witness that their race "was in a state of war and could not reproduce in their original normal manner." He then had the sensation of falling towards the lake. This part was very confusing and could not be remembered in detail. The beings also told the witness that on the bottom of the lake they had their reproductive "eggs." Several strange scars were found on the witness body.

HC addendum.
Source: Y Files, Dr. Luis E. Lopez.   Type: G
Comments: Again a rare abduction report from this other Central American country and very bizarre in nature.

* * * * * * *

Location: Dorado, Puerto Rico.
Date: End of February, 1996.
Time: Late night.

A local family heard a loud racket coming from the animal pen and their three fierce Doberman guard dogs apparently fighting with something. Looking out the window they were terrified to see several "Chupacabra" type creatures fighting with the dogs while others, which levitated over the ground, entered the hog pen killing several of the animals.

After killing the hogs the creatures levitated up again, carrying the dead hogs out one by one. Immediately after, the creatures deposited the

67

dead hogs in a perfect straight line on the ground. There was no doubt to the witnesses; the creatures were apparently behaving in an intelligent manner. After killing all the hogs and laying them out on the ground, the creatures departed. After a while, the family went outside and found all the hogs dead, apparently bloodless and also two of the dogs. The third dog survived but later died of its injuries.

HC addendum.
Source: Jorge Martin, Conspiracion Chupacabras.   Type: E
Comments: Apparently these bizarre so-called Chupacabra type entities have different abilities and demonstrate a clear intelligent behavior and purpose.

* * * * * * *

Location: Alfenas, Minas Gerais, Brazil.
Date: March, 1996.
Time: Early morning.

Antonio Candido de Moraes, who lives near Varginha, was cycling to work along a dirt road when he saw a strange creature. Thinking it was a monkey he stopped the bicycle.

The creature resembled a little man covered all over with dark hair; it had a big oval head and protruding eyes that stared at him. Scared, he rode away and looking back, he saw the creature still staring at him while walking into the jungle.

HC addendum.
Source: Varginha Diary.   Type: E

* * * * * * *

Location: West Dade County, Florida.
Date: March 6, 1996.
Time: 11:00 p.m.

Teide Carballo De Trinidad, a nurse's aide at a local boarding home for the elderly looked out the window to see a six foot tall creature, tan in color with a large head, walking swiftly around the yard. She panicked and lost sight of the being as it disappeared behind a wall.

The creature was bipedal and appeared to walk hunched over. No other details were noted. The next day goats and chickens were found dead and mutilated at the house and at other locations in the area. Strange tracks were also found.

HC addendum.
Source: Personal Investigation.   Type: E
Comments: I remember being at the scene of the encounter and finding
two round holes on the neck of the one of the dead goats, after a while a
greenish liquid began oozing out of the holes. Soon after that a man
claiming to be from a local University came along and took the dead
animal away in a pickup truck.

*   *   *   *   *   *   *

Location: Near Moundhouse, Nevada.
Date: April, 1996.
Time: 11:00 p.m.

The 25-year old witness was driving his Dodge Rampage on Highway
50 east of Moundhouse. His window was down, the air was blowing on
his face and the radio was on fairly loud. As he passed the Virginia City
turn off on his left, he noticed some lights on the hills at the mouth of the
Canyon there. There were four lights. They were a whitish blue and very
bright. They were lighting up the sagebrush on the hillside on the west
side of the Highway. They were about 50 to 100 ft off the ground. As he
drove away he thought that it must have been a low flying jet or plane
coming from Reno. He looked back at the lights and they were still in the
same spot. They were not moving, he could see the brush on the hill
bright as day.
      He then saw some "things" moving in the brush, little objects
scurrying about very quick like some type of animal like a coyote or
something. His heart began to thump, his adrenaline kicked in as he
realized that it was something different from the ordinary. He slowed
down so he could see more of it. He then began to think it was a UFO,
and said out loud, *"Haha, yeah you know I can see you."*
      As soon as he said that, the lights began to turn, they were no longer
shining on the bush. They span approximately 100 yards apart with two
on top about 30 yards apart and the lower ones at the sides about 100
yards apart. They resembled the lights in a stadium; they were very big
and bright. There were no other cars behind him. Frightened he no
longer watched the road; the lights had his total attention. The lights
turned around and began slowly hovering over the Canyon towards the
Highway, as the witness kept driving on. There were smaller lights below
the larger ones that were blinking in succession. That's when he realized
that it was a round object. He kept driving towards the lights and his
radio became fuzzy and then silent. Soon he came upon an embankment
on the side of the highway that separated the lights from his vision but
he also knew that the object was moving down the canyon at the same
speed he was.

He came to the hill and as soon as the embankment receded, there he saw something that he claims he will never forget. It was on the top of the hill to his left, right there as the ground cleared away he was gazing into the middle of a set of windows, mesmerized he stared. The windows were long draping all the way across and around. He saw tiers or stories, he saw walls. Everything inside was white. On the left bottom story in the window he saw several aliens, all wearing white robes; he saw a female figure with a bracelet and a necklace on, either gold or silver with makeup on her cheeks. Her arm was on the shoulder of a younger one, a boy, and they were looking right at the witness. She nudged herself to the boy and spoke to the other younger children along the window maybe ten or so more. They were all smaller than a 5-year old. She was talking to the older boy without apparently speaking. At the same time the witness felt a joyful feeling as they gazed into his eyes and she then smiled and pointed at him as to show them that he understood them. She had three long fingers and a thumb.

He then had a terrible feeling and looked up to the second tier or story. Two beings were there in the middle of the room. The being he first saw had a long draped back skull like that of the move "Alien" and large black eyes, his skin was chocolate brown and he too was wearing a white robe. His skull was maybe two ft long behind his head draping down. The one with the draped skull on the second story was standing and holding a clipboard against himself in his white robe, he seemed to notice the witness, his mouth dropped and his eyes bulged as the alien realized that the witness was looking at him, he seemed frightened that the witness had seen him. He was definitely surprised, his eyes were white with huge blue irises and pupils, the witness estimated that he was 20ft away from this alien. He immediately turned to the other one in the room in front of him. The one in front of him was sitting. The witness saw a side view of him but only his head at the time. He had a human-like head, with wrinkles all over his head, which made him look very old, no hair whatsoever was evident. He appeared to be wearing a black suit; he then turned his head to face the witness. At this point the witness became frightened, the alien's face was wrinkled and old and his eyes beady, and pure black.

As the witness stared at the alien he realized that it was a human, and that he must have been thousands of years old. The witness was petrified. The "human" alien gave him a snarling look but at the same time displaying an immense intellect. There appeared to be a large screen in front of the alien which appeared to be blinking. Then looking directly at the witness he raised his hand up with a very long finger and smiled or smirked as he hit a button on some kind of panel in front of him.

Instantly the windows covered themselves with a fanlike shell that resembled a Chinese fan descending from the top. Corrugated riffles about one foot high each descended from the top to the middle. They sparkled with different colors and were sharp-looking like razor blades. The bottom sealed up and lights began to blink in succession. Then the craft began to spin, emitting a slight humming sound like the blades of a giant fan. The object tilted at about 45 degree angle and as it spun faster and faster the witness could only see the outline of it, like it was suddenly cloaked. It then shot up into the sky leaving a small white trail behind for a split second. The witness seems to have experienced a period of missing time.

HC addendum.
Source: NUFORC and http://www.ufosnw.com   Type: A & G?

*   *   *   *   *   *   *

Location: Tonto Hills, Arizona.
Date: April 16, 1996.
Time: Unknown.

A couple that had observed a large diamond shaped craft land in the same area back in February, observed a large craft landing nearby. It was white, diamond shape, and had green and red lights around it. Three entities (not described) walked around it as if searching for something. The sighting lasted for 15 minutes.

HC addendum.
Source: Jim Ossipov, Myron K. Olson.   Type: C

*   *   *   *   *   *   *

Location: Belem, Brazil.
Date: April 17, 1996.
Time: 1:00 a.m.

Alfredo de Oliveira Mendes, 27, a sacristan at a local church witnessed a UFO land in the backyard of the mission. There was a period of missing time. Under hypnosis the witness recalled being abducted by eight beings, described as silver in color with long eyes and what looked like a fin on their foreheads.
The beings wore silver coverall type outfits with an emblem containing a pyramid and a wing. A burnt circle was found on the ground at the site. No other information.

HC addendum.
Source: Brazilian UFO Report.   Type: G

71

Location: Zapata, Texas.
Date: April 20, 1996.
Time: Night.

Rachel Tolen was driving alongside a dark roadway when she stopped to see a strange creature that appeared to be eating something on the side of the road. The creature turned to look at her and she could see large glowing red eyes. She approached the creature with her car and this one suddenly flew up into the air and vanished.

She described the creature as about 4 ft tall, with dark brown hairy skin, with what appeared to be feathers covering part of the body and a line of sharp spikes that ran along its back starting at the nape of the skull.

Others in the vicinity reported seeing a similar creature and there were reports of bizarre goat and chicken mutilations in the area. The animals were usually found bloodless.

HC addendum.
Source: Jorge Martin, Conspiracion Chupacabras.   Type: E

*   *   *   *   *   *   *

Location: Varginha, Brazil.
Date: April 21, 1996.
Time: Evening.

Teresinha Galo, age 67, reportedly saw a strange short creature, with bulging red eyes, brown skin, a large head with three oval protrusions, on the grounds of the local Jardim Zoologico.

The creature apparently hid behind some bushes. It reportedly wore a golden helmet.

HC addendum.
Source: Brazilian UFO Report Issue #6.   Type: E

Location: Near Boyle, Sligo County, Roscommon, Ireland.
Date: May, 1996.
Time: Night.

Several residents reported seeing a large silver saucer-shaped object plunge from the sky, clip some treetops on a hillside and crash in a lake just north of Boyle.

According to some accounts, several occupants of the craft survived the crash and were taken into custody by the Gardai (Irish Police). A NATO task force then reportedly moved into the crash zone and remained there for several months.

HC addendum.
Source: Dr. Anton Anfalov, UFO Crash list.   Type: H
High Strangeness Index: 8
Source reliability: 10

* * * * * * *

Location: Texas, (exact location not given).
Date: May, 1996.
Time: Night.

Sharon (involved in other encounters) woke up during the night to strange bumping sounds in her house. The mysterious bumping sounds woke her up periodically during the night. She was afraid to get up and investigate on her own. Finally she woke up again to see a strange humanoid hovering in the hallway directly across from her bed.

She described the humanoid as a small Negroid being about three & a half feet to four feet tall. He wore a complete astronaut's suit with a helmet, dark blue gloves, and boots. The helmet had a clear visor, and she could see his face through it. She described his complexion as being a reddish or dark pink color with two vertical folds of flesh across the side of his cheeks. His lips were large and fleshy, and his nose, broad and flat. His eyes looked totally human and his expression was that of "complete boredom."

He was holding a round, black device that seemed to her like an old style radar gun used by the police. He pointed the object at the window in her bedroom and floated there as though waiting for something to happen. She also observed a white glowing light around him that reminded her of an aura.

After a few minutes he disappeared, and the hallway and bedroom became dark again. A minute or two later, the room and everything in it was suddenly brightly illuminated. Then to her surprise everything abruptly went completely dark again. The next morning she found all the

73

grass and tree leaves on the side of her house near the bedroom window were yellowed and clearly dehydrated.

HC addendum.
Source: C. L. Turnage, Sexual Encounters with Extraterrestrials. Type: E

* * * * * * *

Location: Rio Parana, Buenos Aires, Argentina.
Date: May, 1996.
Time: Night.

Several locals reported that while fishing in the River Parana they spotted a strange creature half-man, half reptilian that apparently damaged some of their fishing nets.
It disappeared from sight beneath the waters. No other information.

HC addendum.
Source: Fabio Picasso quoting Cronica de Buenos Aires.　　　Type: E

* * * * * * *

Location: Near Varginha, Brazil.
Date: May 12, 1996.
Time: Night.

A truck driver was turning a curve when the headlights illuminated a short humanoid creature standing on the roadway. The creature resembled one of those reportedly captured by the military in the area back in January.
The driver slammed on the brakes to see the creature raise its hands and protect its large red glowing eyes, the creature then ran into the woods and disappeared. The witness noticed that the creature had only four fingers on each hand.

HC addendum.
Source: Graham Birdsall, Evidencia OVNI #12.　　　Type: E

Location: Pettorano sul Gizio, Italy.
Date: May 26, 1996.
Time: Afternoon.

Claudio Pettine and his wife, Angela Santilli spotted a bizarre spherical robotic figure resembling an animated "puppet" hovering over a nearby field. It had a rudimentary "face" with large eyes.

As Pettine attempted to approach the figure it oscillated rapidly and shot up vertically disappearing from sight at very high speed. The strange figure was first seen hovering over Pettine's dog pound. The same or similar humanoid was seen in the area three years before.

HC addendum.
Source: Antonio Manerra, Ovni Domus.   Type: E

* * * * * * *

Location: Near Tocopila, Chile.
Date: Summer, 1996.
Time: Afternoon.

A family of four was driving on their way to Tocopila but halfway there, the father, (driver) changed his mind and decided to return, explaining that by the time they arrived to Tocopila everything would be closed. On their way he took a secondary road that past by an empty airfield, located in an isolated plain. As they drove near the airfield they all noticed a strange triangular-shaped mark on the ground; however they did not stop to investigate. Soon they began hearing bizarre screams resembling those of a woman being attacked.

Immediately after that they all saw a brilliant humanoid figure at least three meters in height, it shone like brilliant metal. Its face was oval-shaped and its eyes almond in shape, emitting a brilliant light.

Astounded, the witnesses watched as the shiny giant creature stepped in front of their car and signaled them to stop. The mother began screaming as the creature turned its head towards them and emitted a brilliant beam of bluish light from each eye.

The whole time the driver slowed the vehicle down until it was going a minimal speed. They were able to notice that the creature had extremely long arms; it was of thin build, and was wearing a one-piece shiny silvery outfit. It was totally hairless. As the mother screamed hysterically, the creature disappeared in plain sight and everything returned to normal. The witnesses quickly drove away from the area.

HC addendum.
Source: Ramon Navia, 'La Verdad Oculta' Chile.   Type: E

Location: Beverly Hills, California.
Date: Summer, 1996.
Time: Afternoon.

A Mr. William Silverstone had seen the shadow of a human figure above the swimming pool he was using. He only saw it briefly but said that it was a man in a tight-fitting yellow suit, wearing a helmet. Its arms were stretched out and it was flying at an altitude of around 150 feet.

Another family also reported seeing it, making a total of seven witnesses. They also reported that they hadn't seen any kind of mechanical device helping it to fly.

HC addendum.
Source: http://www.kithra.com/flyinghumanoids.html   Type: E

* * * * * * *

Location: Near Ust-Kut, Irkutsk region, East Siberia, Russia.
Date: Summer, 1996.
Time: Around 5:00 p.m.

Helicopter pilot Denis Voronin was flying over this vast deserted forest in Eastern Siberia onboard a Mi-2 helicopter based out of Ust-Kut airport north of Irkutsk. He was part of the local air civil aviation squadron that delivered post, food and supplies to remote settlements, and prospecting teams of geologists. He was the flight navigator assisting the pilot. They were the only crewmembers onboard the helicopter on that day as the helicopter flew over the banks of one of the many tributaries to great Siberian Lena River. The Sun was still blinding that afternoon so Denis was wearing his polarization glasses and was looking through them at the dense pine forest in the direction of their flight at about 1km in altitude.

Suddenly Denis distinctly and clearly saw a strange "city" positioned far in the horizon, "What the hell is this" he thought knowing that there were no such cities in this remote area of the taiga, only small and scattered wood settlements. Denis took off his glasses and gave them to the pilot who clearly saw the strange city, confirming that Denis was not insane or delirious. They had enough fuel onboard so both men decided to approach the strange city and investigate.

After about 15 minutes quite suddenly and unexpectedly their engine began to "cough" (misfiring) without any apparent cause. Both the pilot and Denis hastily began checking the helicopter's instruments in attempt to find the cause of the malfunction. They could not locate a cause since every instrument appeared to be operating normally and they still plenty of fuel. They then tried to make radio contact with their base at Ust-Kut airport by only heard static over the radio. And then something quite unbelievable occurred both men clearly heard a loud voice inside the cabin, telling them: *"Turn Back!"*

Denis couldn't tell where the voice had come from, seemingly to him the word sounded inside his head. They turned back and the engine stopped malfunctioning and returned to work normally. Upon returning to their base, mechanics could not find any mechanical problems in the engine. Both pilots then began talking about the strange city they had seen and soon Denis was fired from his job without any apparent reason.

When Denis asked some of the locals about the mysterious "city," some told him that if he flew at night and high in the air and using night vision goggles he would be able to see "roads" or lines (reportedly located underground) which originate from the mysterious city. Denis added that most probably he had only seen a small portion of the city. From afar it looked like a giant snowflake about 2 km in diameter that could only be seen through the special night polarization goggles. Once the goggles came off, the viewer could now only see a dense pine forest.

HC addendum.
Source: Letter from the witness in: 'Taynaya Vlast' (The Secret Power) Newspaper Moscow #16, 2001.   Type: F?
Comments: Did the men see a top-secret Russian installation, an underground city, or an interdimensional portal or a mirage?

* * * * * * *

Location: Near Asuncion, Paraguay.
Date: Summer, 1996.
Time: Evening.

89-year old Julio Pedroso was outside working on his garden when suddenly a bright light from above illuminated him, concerned he hastened home. After taking several steps a bright beam of light was directed towards him from the light. Having heard of similar events he immediately lay prone on the ground.

The beam of light became increasingly more brilliant and suddenly Julio felt he was being torn from the earth. After struggling a bit he looked and noticed some kind of four pronged hook that was being lowered from the hovering UFO. The object was cigar-shaped, with large brightly lit openings. In one of them Julio noticed three women dressed in green and a man with a long beard. One of the women was pointing down at Pedroso, as if urging the others on.

Meanwhile one of the hooks had lodged into Pedroso's shirt and was rising up into the object. Thankfully his shirt ripped and he fell back into the vegetable garden. The craft then circled around over the witness and

77

without making further attempts to abduct him they flew away into the distance. Terrified Julio stumbled into his house. He never worked alone at night in the garden again.

HC addendum.
Source: NLO #14, 2002.   Type: G
Comments: Abduction attempt using definitely unorthodox means.

*   *   *   *   *   *   *

Location: Ay-Petri plateau, Crimea, Ukraine.
Date: Summer, 1996.
Time: Evening.

Three tourists, including two doctors and one worker, at an area, Dolphinarium (recreational pool for dolphins) were vacationing in the "Orlinyi Zalyet" tourist's camp (Eagle's Nest) near the hamlet of Sokolinoye. One evening while walking on the Ay-Petri mountainous plateau south of the village, they stumbled upon a strange humanoid entity, completely covered in grayish fur and about 2-2.5m in height. The hairy entity was bipedal, walking on two legs like humans and exuded an odor similar to a mixture of ammonia and iodine.

Stunned, the tourists hid behind the bushes, wanting to run away but soon seized by curiosity decided to stay and contact the entity. When they tried to approach the entity, which was still hiding on the plateau, all three felt strong dizziness and nausea. In 15-20minutes after the distance between them and the entity had decreased to only several dozen meters all three felt strong fear and in the next several minutes they all lost consciousness, just like falling into "a black hole" and remembering nothing of what happened next.

When they returned back to their senses, to their outmost amazement they found themselves on the other side of Mt. Ay-Petri (1234m above sea level) in a completely different location. It appeared that their faces and parts of their upper extremities (the hands and palms) were covered with strange red itchy spots. When they went to the nearest town of Yalta, southeast of the plateau for medical help doctors found slight 1st degree burns on those areas.

After an investigation it was revealed that 24 hours before the humanoid encounter, several at the tourist camp had also felt a strange discomfort and giddiness which they could not explain and also their radios would not work as well as the telephone at the tourist base. Radio receivers were also not operational during the contact as a result of a strange interference.

Witnesses further described the entity as definitely a hairy female since they saw what appeared to be breasts. The grass on the place where the alien entity sat later became wilted and brown.

Other local residents observe numerous anomalous phenomena in the area of the Ay-Petri plateau. One local resident remembered of a similar case and possible abduction which occurred to a group of tourists camped at the plateau in 1967.

HC addendum.
Source: Anton A. Anfalov personal investigation.   Type: E or G?

* * * * * * *

Location: Sussex, New Jersey.
Date: Summer, 1996.
Time: Night.

J. D. Grant and another person had been walking on Layton Road when they encountered "a tall shaggy creature with red eyes," which stood near the edge of the road and watched them from approximately ten feet away. Grant was quoted as saying, *"I knew it wasn't a bear, it was too lean and upright, it was humanoid."*

HC addendum.
Source: Loren Coleman and Bruce Hallenbeck, 'Monsters of New Jersey'
p. 46.   Type: E

* * * * * * *

Location: Adirondack Mountains, Northern New York.
Date: Summer, 1996.
Time: Night.

On the last night of their camping trip, three boy scouts, Juarez, Mike and Bobby were restless and decided to sneak out and investigate a trail they had found earlier in the week that led up into the mountain. With flashlights in hand, they set out on the path. It was a very dark night with no moon, and the woods on both sides of the path were thick. The path went on for quite a while and seemed to get steeper and steeper as it wove higher into the forest. Bobby began to feel spooked and suggested they turn back, but Juarez and Mike felt drawn to keep going higher up into the hills. They continued on for what they determined was a very long time, when finally, up ahead they saw a warm orange glow. A campfire. As they drew closer, they realized the fire was massive, a raging bonfire. In the middle of a circular clearing in the forest, they saw someone

79

standing next to the huge bonfire, but it was still too far away to see it clearly.

They crept closer, sneaking up behind a large oak tree. To their horror, they saw very clearly not who, but what it was. There in the middle of the clearing, stood what they could only describe as a "deer man."

Juarez recalled that it was huge, at least ten feet tall, probably taller. To Juarez, this creature appeared to be towering over the fire, it was so big. It looked like a typical whitetail deer buck, except it stood on its two hind legs like a human. Upon its head was the biggest rack Juarez had ever seen. Its forelegs were not hooved like a deer's however, they were hands like a person's. It held a twisted wooden staff in one hand and a skull in the other. Needless to say they were speechless as they stared slack jawed from behind the tree. Just when they thought it couldn't get any stranger, it did. The strange creature actually began to sing and dance. It sang horrible words, they couldn't understand and didn't want to. They remember its voice was high-pitched crackly and they were instantly reminded of an impossibly old woman. It gyrated and shimmied in a fashion they found so horrifying Juarez felt his heart sink. It leapt completely over the fire several times, prancing about like a deer would. Juarez remembers looking at his friends and seeing the terror in their eyes.

Despite the fact that they had not made any noise, the creature stopped and whipped its head in the direction where the boys were hiding. It pointed its staff at them and let out the most blood-curdling scream. Terrified, the three turned and charged off down the path and down the mountain too scared to stop or look back. They ran all the way to the lodge and stormed through the door. In between crying the boys managed to tell a concerned scout leader about what they saw. While he doubted them, he did put a call out to a forest ranger stationed nearby asking him to investigate a strange man hanging out near the lodge. They boys watched as the forest ranger's Jeep drove up the path into the hills. About 15 minutes later the ranger returned. He entered the cabin, informing them that there was no one up there. He told them that he had driven all the way to the clearing but there was no one there.

The next morning after they had all packed and were waiting to go, the scout leader agreed to drive up there and check it out if only to put the boy's minds at ease. To his surprise, they found the clearing and a large fire pit that was still smoldering. They also discovered a number of deer tracks around the pit that seemed to weave around in impossible patterns. The scout leader and the boys couldn't get out of there fast enough.

HC addendum.
Source: GameFaqs, Paranormal section.   Type: E?

Location: Vidra, Romania.
Date: June, 1996.
Time: Unknown.

The entire population of this remote village in the Carpathian Mountains reportedly saw a saucer shaped object land. A group of humanoids emerged from the object. These were described as small, gray colored, with large ears and huge eyes. Most witnesses became afraid then ran and hid.

HC addendum.
Source: UFO Roundup Vol. 1 #38.   Type: B

* * * * * * *

Location: Near Twain Hart, California.
Date: June 15, 1996.
Time: Afternoon.

A woman reported seeing "a type of UFO that looked like a huge bubble" near Twain Harte, a small town east of Sonora, just across the Stanislaus River. She described the "bubble" as looking like "a gelatinous mass that is covering a large area," transparent but "sort of an opaque gray color." Within the bubble she could make out a number of occupants. The occupants appeared only in silhouette and left no features that she could identify.

She also reported that about a month earlier, about one mile northwest of Tuolumne City, a small town located in the Stanislaus National Forest, hikers reportedly saw a disc-shaped UFO descend slowly to the forest floor, and then "it just vanished instantly." Curiously enough, a few minutes later, a helicopter with the white letters "UN" on its side hovered over the forest meadow, as if "searching for something" and then turned about and flew away to the west.

HC addendum.
Source: UFO Roundup Vol. 1 #19.   Type: A

Location: Near Flexeiras, Minas Gerais, Brazil.
Date: June 21, 1996.
Time: Night.

The witness, 64 year old, Cesar Miglioranza, was in his car coming back from work when he noticed a strong light at a nearby field. He stopped the car and decided to investigate. As he approached the area, he saw near some trees a large object on the ground. Suddenly he felt paralyzed and was unable to move.

Next to the object were two short beings with large heads and helmets, long arms and wearing silvery tight fitting suits. The two beings seemed to be collecting samples from the ground. After a few moments they conversed among themselves in an unknown language then boarded the object, which quickly took off at high speed. Cesar was unable to move for about five minutes afterwards. The witness felt very tired and sleepy for two to three days after the incident.

HC addendum.
Source: Victor Lourenco.   Type: B

* * * * * * *

Location: Near Medford, Wisconsin.
Date: July, 1996.
Time: Unknown.

A warden traveling down Highway 13 just south of the city, saw a figure standing in the middle of the road. He slowed down his vehicle as he approached it. He could not believe his eyes as he saw a shiny, green scaly, large figure staring at him. As he got within several yards of it, wings suddenly popped out from behind the creature's back. The creature went vertical, zooming straight up and passing over the vehicle.

It landed on the road behind the warden. To the witness it resembled a winged, reptile man.

A group of highway workers also had a similar encounter along the same stretch of highway. They too saw a shiny, green scaly figure standing on the road. As they approached the figure, wings shot out from behind its back. It took off, and to their utter amazement, flew away into the trees.

HC addendum.
Source: Weird Wisconsin Files.   Type: E

* * * * * * *

Location: Area 51, Nevada.
Date: July, 1996.
Time: Unknown.

A man reported having being stationed at the Groom Lake, facility known commonly as 'Area 51,' as a security guard with a high clearance. He said that he was once called into a room where people were dissecting Bigfoot type creatures. There were several complete corpses in vats of liquid similar to formaldehyde. There were body parts, hearts, livers, and such, scattered all over the tables.

Once he got to peek into another room he was passing when the door opened after a retinal scan of another guard, there he saw more vats, only containing "little white aliens with big black eyes."

HC addendum.
Source: IBS Report #2798. *"Caller wants to remain anonymous. Continuing conversation, my caller said he had a friend that had a son that was stationed at Groom Lake, NV, as a security guard with a high clearance, fairly recently."* http://www.mid-americabigfoot.com/forums/viewtopic.php?f=167&t=4097   Type: X
Comments: Date is approximate.

Location: Coates, Minnesota.
Date: July, 1996.
Time: 2:00 a.m.

The main witness and his friend were on their way home to Rochester. It was around 2:00 a.m. and they were driving past the town of Coates. Suddenly he heard a humming sound which got louder. He could feel a vibration all over his body. He looked out of the passenger window and saw a bright light at tree top level about 200 feet away. He told his friend to stop the car and he started to get hysterical. He got a tire iron from under the car seat and he was going to check it out. He got to the ditch and that is the last memory he had.

Later after undergoing hypnosis he was able to recall being hit by a blue beam of light which carried him to a craft where a ramp opened, and he was brought inside. A door opened and a tall grey with a normal sized grey entered. The tall grey had on a black jumpsuit. Then a human entered, also wearing a black jumpsuit. He was smiling and said there was no reason to be afraid. *"This is going to be a pure learning experience."* And he brought him into the cockpit area and told him to look outside the windows. The windows were one way, were you could see out, but the craft looked like it had windows. The man showed him the control panel and how to operate it. He took him into another room where there were an assortment of monitors on the wall. He said to follow along with the images and they would teach him "what he needed to learn."

He watched the images for about two hours and somehow he was able to understand what he was watching. When the alien man returned he told the witness that it was vital that he understand these things because there may come a time when they will not be here to teach him. He would have to continue the 'big plan' in their place. He told the witness that he didn't know when that time would be as there are many factors involved that could change the outcome.

Then the two greys came back in the room and the ramp opened up. The smaller grey escorted him out of the craft and to his car. He put a small device on the side of the witness' head and he became paralyzed and his vision went black.

The next thing he remembered was he and his friend pulling into a restaurant. They were both in a daze and couldn't figure out how the time got to be 5:30 a.m. They had a large chunk of missing time. Since that time his friend has received flashbacks but doesn't want to get involved in any way.

HC addendum.
Source: Mufon CMS.

Type: G

Location: Buenos Aires, Argentina.
Date: July, 1996.
Time: 4:00 a.m.

The witness, Miguel Villegas, (involved in other contacts) was asleep on his bed when he was suddenly awakened by a brilliant blue light that seemed to come from the dining room next to his bedroom. He attempted to speak and move but was unable to move or say a word.

Suddenly two beings entered the bedroom, a man and a woman, both wearing white coveralls, with gold embroidery in the waist and wrist areas. Villegas then heard a telepathic message telling him not to be afraid and that if he so desired he could visit their ship. One of the beings then approached and placed a hand on Villegas' forehead and he fell asleep. When he woke up, he was onboard a huge ship, apparently a mothership. He was greeted by a woman wearing the same type of clothing who gave him her name. He was given a tour of the ship which had beautiful white walls and emitted a soft glowing white light. The floors were metallic and he saw many other aliens who paid no attention to him as they seemed very busy with different tasks.

They came up to a large storage area which opened up in front of Villegas. Inside he saw numerous species of different plants and trees from Earth. He was told that they kept this in case of any catastrophic event that might occur on Earth. He was then taken to a laboratory which Villegas was told was used to develop the human "Chakra" and permit greater human development.

HC addendum.
Source: http://www.astroufo.com/entrevistamv.htm   Type: G

* * * * * * *

Location: Near Sisters, Oregon.
Date: July, 1996.
Time: Afternoon.

A lady was camping with her family near the area of Panther Springs Campground when all of a sudden, she smelled a terrible smell. She walked outside her tent, and about 20 feet away, she saw a tan colored, hairy creature with its fist in the air. She said it didn't seem threatening, more like a greeting. She said it had a peaked head, and large brown eyes, and it "looked highly intelligent." She said that it "talked in her mind" and told her that they called themselves the "Meikoy," and that they were a race of benevolent creatures from a different dimension. They were here to study humans and to find out why we were so emotional, etc.

85

They were apparently interested in how we humans reproduced and wanted to remain hidden and not found out. As her family returned, the creature ran off into the woods.

HC addendum.
Source: Nathan Peak, Western Bigfoot Society Newsletter #64.
Type: E or F?
Comments: One of the growing number of incidents describing definitely intelligent and paranormal abilities on the part of the so-called Bigfoot type creatures.

* * * * * * *

Location: Yvelines, Paris, France.
Date: July, 1996.
Time: 3:00 p.m.

The main witness was playing football (soccer) with five friends all about his age (eight to ten years old). The field was across a beautiful forested area. At one point the witness struck the ball too hard and it went close to the nearby forest. He was looking for the ball when he came across saw two strange 'persons' with brown skin tight suits, with long arms, long legs and necks. They were standing about ten yards away from the witness.

The strange pair suddenly scurried into the forest and the witness remained frozen in place. The witness was finally able to snap back to his senses and then warned his friends to go home, telling them what he had seen, some stayed behind to search but did not find anything. Around that time there was also a report of a missing juvenile from the same neighborhood that was never located.

HC addendum.
Source: http://www.ovni.ch/temoign/   Type: E

Location: Togliatti region, Russia.
Date: July, 1996.
Time: Night.

The witness was staying at a lake side cottage and was doing laundry late one night, when she happened to look up and saw a slow flying triangle-shaped object. It was very bright and about the size of a full moon. It had three angular flashing lights in its center.

A week after, she was at her suburban home and in the middle of the night got up to look out her second floor window. The object then descended at high speed, frightening the witness who tried to hide behind the window. The object passed by but then returned and hovered in front of the window in which the witness was hiding behind.

Curious by now, She looked out and saw a sort of 'door,' open on the object. Inside, she did not see the normal contents of a supposed spacecraft but a "glimpse of their world." (?) She then saw a tall man, about two meters in height, accompanied by a tall woman that stood a little behind him. Her features were difficult to discern. The man was of athletic built. He had black hair combed back, with deep set eyes that seemed to stare into space, not at the witness.

Before the astounded witness could utter any questions they were automatically answered in her thoughts (telepathically):

Witness: *"Why are you so similar to humans?"*

Man: *"This is the most perfect form in the universe for intelligent beings."*

Witness: *"Why did you return?"*

Man: *"We saw a very interesting structure, and we stopped to see what it was. We have no time to answer your questions. We are in a hurry."*

The aperture on the UFO closed and the object departed. Before it did the man told the witness that they might return to see her. Apparently the witness experienced another encounter in 1997 in which a disc-shaped object landed close to her residence, however for some reason she did not wish to 'meet them' and attempted to hide. However she heard the following words in her mind before the object left, *"Do not hide, you will work with us."*

HC addendum.
Source:http://svitk.ru/004_book_book/4b/853_makarovahroniki_ya
vleniy.php
Type: G

Location: Fayetteville, Arkansas.
Date: July 4, 1996.
Time: 7:35 p.m.

The witnesses had just finished firing off fireworks and had entered a patch of woods away from the pasture to enjoy the warm night for a few minutes. In the woods they noticed a light about 100 yards away. Thinking that it was somebody shooting fireworks in the woods, they walked towards it.

As they approached, they saw in a clearing, three triangular shaped objects hovering just above the ground. Lights were pointing down off each point of the triangles. Three strange beings, stood around speaking among themselves in gruff voices. The beings were described as tall and covered with very thick hair that covered their bodies completely.

The beings seem to sniff the air, and glared in their direction. The beings then quickly ran into their ships, which shot away into the sky emitting a bright burst of light, knocking the witnesses to the ground. The crafts seem to elongate as they accelerated.

HC addendum.
Source: NUFORC   Type: B
Comments: Another incident describing UFOs in direct connection with Bigfoot type entities.

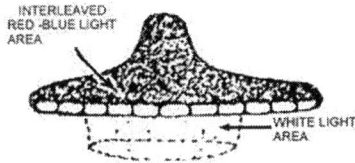

Location: Certesti, Romania.
Date: July 9, 1996.
Time: 12:30 a.m.

Police sergeant Marian Mancu and volunteer police officer Marcel Rusu were patrolling on the main road passing the village in front of the police office. Between the road and the sidewalks, there are deep ditches, with small bridges across them. Mancu lived in the area and told Rusu he was going to eat something at his home. The moment the sergeant passed the corner near his house, he heard a whistling sound from the street and sensed a current of air. He turned immediately back, seeing on the road something, which "splashed blue and red lights, making a sound like voom-voom."

At first Mancu thought it was a police car from the district that had arrived on a routine patrol. Getting closer, he realized that the object was hovering half a meter above the paved road and a small and very strange figure was moving around it. He yelled for Rusu that was now hiding behind the ditch, observing the strange spectacle. Rusu declared that immediately after Mancu had left and disappeared behind the apartment house, "a fluttering from above appeared." The neon lighting in the street seemed to change in intensity.

The object descended slowly, without noise, behind him. He became frightened when he noticed that the object remained suspended above the ground and three small human like creatures were moving around it. As both witnesses agreed, the object had the form of a flat hut, 5-6 meter

89

across and 2 2.5 meters high, and was hovering and balancing at about ½ meter from the ground. Around the edge it had a continuous girdle of light "like a rainbow." The colors, red, and blue changed from each other and flared. At the bottom of the object was a bright white light. None of the witnesses saw doors, portholes or other details. After about two minutes, the UFO rose vertically. At that moment its lights became much brighter, but the neon streetlights went off. The object then rose to about 30 meters and then disappeared towards the east at high speed.

Rusu saw the humanoid creatures better as Mancu noticed only one and only from behind. Their height was estimated to have been around one meter, maybe less. Rusu said he heard some noises made by the humanoids, "as the rain in the drain pipe." Both described the creatures as "abortions" or ugly. They had large heads, very elongated behind and covered with bumps, with no hair, and large ears. Their faces were white and they had big eyes. Gray metallic shiny scales, resembling fish scales, covered their bodies. They also had large limp protruding bellies. They had thin spindly arms and no noses or mouths were visible. The witnesses thought that the creatures floated just above the ground and moved around "as if they were drunk."

A huge sweet cherry tree nearby had around 15% of its leaves affected as by an extreme heat. Other witnesses in nearby villages reported strange lights over the area on the same night.

HC addendum.
Source: Dan D. Farcas, Romania.   Type: C

*   *   *   *   *   *   *

Location: Deschutes National Forest, Oregon.
Date: July 13, 1996.
Time: Afternoon.

Hav Tranh had been hiking up a steep slope when he slipped and fell, breaking his leg, a compound fracture with the bone sticking out. He passed out, and when he regained consciousness, there were two huge hair covered creatures hovering over him.

The larger one was 7-8 foot, a gray white color, eyes black with no whites, large sloping forehead, and peaked head-domed, very big feet. The second creature was about the same height, sandy colored gray with a white ruff on top of its head. They were very hairy and he could not see any sex organs. They were jabbering at each other with their small mouths, but not using "words" but indistinct noises.

He passed out again, and did not reawaken until his wife, Gioking, shook him awake, and said two ape-men had carried him out of the forest and deposited him near her. She said they were horribly ugly and added that they had very long hair except on the face, heads and feet. She then took her husband to a local hospital.

HC addendum.
Source: Nathan Peak, Western Bigfoot Society Newsletter #69. Type: E

* * * * * * *

Location: St. Patrick's Chair, County Moneghan, Ireland.
Date: September, 1996.
Time: Evening.

46-year-old Lawrence John and his dog were exploring a rock formation in an isolated area when they were suddenly enveloped in a blinding white light. John suddenly found himself standing outside a huge object with several humanoid figures standing in front of him.

The beings were about 5-feet tall, gray in color, & appeared to be floating just above the ground. They wore something resembling a caftan. He was apparently taken inside the craft; there he saw at least 50 other similar beings. The beings communicated by using telepathy. Later he suddenly found himself outside with his dog & the craft and beings were gone.

HC addendum.
Source: United Kingdom UFO Bulletin August, 1997.   Type: G

* * * * * * *

Location: Iporanga, Sao Paolo, Brazil.
Date: September 2, 1996.
Time: Night.

Three local police officers watched an object land near Serro das Mottas. They approached the area in order to obtain a better look when suddenly the object emitted two bright flashes of light and two small humanoids suddenly appeared. The humanoids had human-like faces with large luminous eyes. These approached to within 50 meters of the officers using quick lateral movements. A strange malaise seemed to overcome the officers that quickly left the area and did not see the object or humanoids depart.

HC addendum.
Source: Ivan Carlos Anker.   Type: B

Location: Piracicaba, Sao Paulo, Brazil.
Date: September 8, 1996.
Time: Unknown.

Several people saw a triangular shaped craft land. A hatch opened, and three occupants floated to the ground. These were described as 1-foot, 10 inches tall, wearing a coverall garment, with very large heads, far out of proportion to their bodies. No other information.

HC addendum.
Source: UFO Roundup Vol. 1 #29.   Type: B

* * * * * * *

Location: Cabeca da Penha Mountain, Portugal.
Date: September 15, 1996.
Time: Unknown.

A young backpacker, Ricardo Machado Oliveira, was exploring a remote mountain cave and while in it, apparently blacked out. When he came to, he found himself in a vast underground hangar surrounded by "three distinct species of aliens." Nearby were several ovoid silvery craft. The aliens told Ricardo that they were part of an alliance of interstellar worlds engaged in observing Earth. Their base under the Serra da Guardunha was one of four such bases. Immediately after hearing this Ricardo blacked out again. When he opened his eyes, he was lying on the ground right outside the cave.

In the 14th century, at the same cave, a little girl from a nearby village vanished for three days. When she was finally found, she told the search party that she had been cared for by "a lady in white," who had offered her water to drink from a bell. Some have attributed this to a visitation by the Blessed Virgin Mary.

HC addendum.
Source: UFO Roundup Vol. 1 #32.   Type: G

Location: Nazareth, Israel.
Date: September 16, 1996.
Time: Evening.

62-year old Uri Sakhov was walking to a local post office when suddenly he heard a loud whizzing sound and felt hands grab his hair and shoulders. In an instant he found himself being pulled into an egg shaped object. Inside he found himself in a strange crystal chamber surrounded by several small humanoids. These were described as two to three feet tall, with heads shaped like light bulbs and skinny limbs that made unintelligible noises. The leader was described as taller and green colored wearing flowing robes. He was very slender and had a narrow vertical head, with eyes located on either side of it. One of the small humanoids stepped up to the witness and sprayed his face with a yellowish powder.

Soon they conducted numerous medical tests on Sakhov, which made him feel "horrible" and very uncomfortable. Midway through the tests the witness blacked out. When he came to he found himself lying flat on his back in the middle of a soccer stadium half a kilometer from his house. Feeling dizzy he went home and noticed that he still had some of the yellow powder on his face. The powder was analyzed at a local hospital and it was discovered that it was about 60 percent aluminum and different from any soil found in the area.

HC addendum.
Source: Barry Chamish.   Type: G

*   *   *   *   *   *   *

Location: Ojen, Malaga, Spain.
Date: September 26, 1996.
Time: 9:00 p.m.

The well-known "humanistic" sculptor Marino Amaya was staying at his farm when he noticed a bright light shooting across the skies overhead. Later on, accompanied by his two dogs, he heard strange sounds coming from behind some nearby trees. He suddenly felt the earth tremble beneath him and a blinding light illuminated him and his dogs, completely paralyzing them.

From the bright light, a thin humanoid about 90cm in height appeared. The humanoid had very long arms, its feet were very flat like those of amphibians, and its eyes were very large and intense blue in color, the rest of its body was brick red in color. Amaya immediately assumed it was an extraterrestrial as the being moved floating just above the ground. The humanoid finally descended on top of a large rock and stared intently at Amaya's eyes.

The humanoid seemed to exude peace and tranquility. Stunned the witness asked the humanoid, *"Why come to me and not to others more qualified than me?"* The humanoid answered, *"Because you are good, love life, love the Earth and nature and love the animals, that's why I come to you to give you a message of good and love."* The humanoid added, *"Talk about me to the world, so the Earth, the mother of life is respected, since she is the reason that humanity exists. Tell the world that I am here on Earth to protect Earth. If that wasn't so, everything will change; there will be great earthquakes and huge floods that will destroy entire cities."*

Marino listened to everything the humanoid said. After 30 minutes the humanoid lifted its arms and rose up and to the sky telling Marino, *"Good bye my friend, we will see each other again."* The witness ran to his studio to reproduce the image of the humanoid in clay, which later he made into a bronze statue.

HC addendum.
Source: http://es.geociteis.com/casoovni/Ojen.htm   Type: E

* * * * * * *

Location: Punta Palma, Puerto Rico.
Date: September 27, 1996.
Time: 1:30 a.m.

Nelson Cortes had been unable to fall sleep that night when his younger brother Josue alerted him to a strange-lighted object that had apparently landed in a field behind Cortes house. Upon investigating the site they saw a large rounded object that had landed on three leg-like supports. The object was surrounded by a brilliant red glow.

The craft was silvery metallic in color. The two witnesses then saw a ramp like protrusion extend to the ground. Several short green humanoids then exited the object via the ramp. These were described as thin, with long skinny arms, potbellies, large heads, huge pointy ears, and large dark oval shaped eyes. They all wore tight fitting metallic helmets on their heads. The beings began to walk around the field.

At that moment both witnesses panicked and began screaming. Immediately the beings ran into the object, which then closed the ramp, became brighter, tilted to one side then shot away at incredible speed. Neighbors heard the boys scream and also saw the object and lights.

HC addendum. Source: Marleen Lopez de Martin, Evidencia OVNI #13.
Type: B

Location: Cordillera de Tajsara, Bolivia.
Date: September 27, 1996.
Time: 7:00 p.m.

While hiking in the rugged mountainous region, Roberto Suarez Molina, 28, became lost. During the search, air rescue units reported strange glows around the snow-covered peak of Nevado Chorolque, at the western end of the Tajsara Range.

On the Friday, Roberto saw a light with a weird appearance; it crossed the sky, stopped for a moment in mid-air, and then became a red light before disappearing. Later a bright light lit up Roberto's campsite. Looking up he saw a "tube of light" of incredible brilliance. The tube of light turned from the horizontal to the vertical, then slowly descended, landing on the mountain trail near his campfire.

He suddenly found himself face to face with a luminous humanoid form that "told him things." The entity predicted that Roberto would be rescued by the Bolivian air force around noontime on Saturday. The humanoid was right; on that day Roberto was spotted by a Cessna aircraft and was picked up by a helicopter.

HC addendum.
Source: Luis Pacheco, UFOZONE,   Type: C

*   *   *   *   *   *   *

Location: Moscow, Russia.
Date: October, 1996.
Time: 6-7:00 p.m.

A first year student at Moscow's Lomonosov's State University Alexander noticed that his close friend, also a student, Andrey had been missing classes and had been absent almost daily from the University. He decided to go to Andrey's home and after a few minutes of banging on the door and yelling, a haggard Andrey answered the door. He looked like he hadn't slept in days, and with trembling hands he spoke in a weak voice. Concerned, Alexander asked him what had happened.

According to Andrey he was returning late as usual from the University walking through an empty dump and waste land when he suddenly noticed a strange light ahead. Curious he went closer to the light. As he came upon the location of the light he was shocked to see standing among a rubbish heap within a circle of light a beautiful naked young female figure. According to Andrey she was very beautiful, adding that he had never seen such amazing beauty before. The girl then looked at Andrey and he heard the following words inside his head, *"You should not have seen me. Now is too late. I must take you with me!"* Terrified he ran to his apartment, hardly venturing out for days. Visibly afraid Andrey then told Alexander that lately he had been having some unusual "dreams" in which he would find himself in a strange orange-colored planet with huge mountains, with stones frequently rolling down the mountains. According to Andrey he was sure that this was the place that the aliens intended to take him. Alexander left, but soon as he attempted to contact Andrey by phone, he could not get an answer. Concerned, he called the local Militia and when they arrived and entered Andrey's apartment, they found it empty. He has not been seen since.

HC addendum.
Source: 'The Secret Doctrine' (Taynaya Doktrina newspaper) Simferopol, Ukraine #10, May, 2001.   Type: G
Comments: Sounds like a permanent abduction to the orange planet.

* * * * * * *

Location: Tulkarem, Palestine, Israel.
Date: October 6, 1996.
Time: Unknown.

Several local inhabitants reported seeing a creature, its size larger than a man, with green scaly skin and frog-like eyes. It apparently approached several terrified farmers before zooming up into the sky and disappearing from sight. According to Palestinian authorities the creature "is probably a highly technological product" from the state of Israel.

HC addendum.
Source: UFO Nieuwsbrief Jaargan 2 #1.   Type: E

* * * * * * *

Location: Near Sao Paulo, Brazil.
Date: October 7, 1996.
Time: Night.

Two witnesses sighted a creature that resembled a large dog walking on its hind legs. The beast had large black eyes, long fangs, and a body covered by dense yellow fur. A local farmer found strange claw-shaped footprints, thirteen inches long, "deeply edged into dry, hardened soil." Subsequent analysis of the footprints indicated that the beast "weighed some 440 pounds."

HC addendum. Source: Brad Steiger, 'Out of the Dark.'   Type: E

Location: Near Snoqualmie Pass, Washington.
Date: October 15, 1996.
Time: Early afternoon.

Dr. Jonathan Reed had been hiking for about an hour and a half when his 7-year old Golden Retriever ran ahead of him and disappeared over a rise. He began barking frantically. Dr Reed dropped his backpack and ran up the slope where the dog had disappeared. He picked up a tree branch on the way, thinking that he might need it to rescue her from some kind of animal. Topping the rise he saw that Suzy (the dog) had a strange creature by the left arm. The creature was shaking violently in an attempt to dislodge the dog. The dog released the creature and backed away. At the same time the creature extended a "fleshy pseudo pod" around the dog's muzzle and severely wounded her. Suzy's tissues seemed to "flow" into this wound. She was consumed in a matter of seconds. Later, Dr. Reed could find no trace of her except for a fine white powder on the ground.

The creature turned to look at Reed with an expression of what seemed to be pure rage then turned its head back to look at Suzy. Reed ran forward at this point and hit the creature with the branch with all the force he could muster. He knocked the creature back about four ft. The creature lay dead on the ground covered in its own blood.

Shocked, Reed fell to the ground, attempting to compose himself. Finally he remembered the camera equipment he usually carried on his frequent hikes ran back for his backpack and began taking pictures and videotape footage of the creature. A short time later, Jonathan became aware of a strange, low frequency vibration. He surveyed the area and discovered a black (craft like) device floating above the ground nearby. He approached the object and touched it. It was freezing cold and burned his hand. He took pictures of the object. After several hours, Jonathan felt very sick.

He decided to wrap the creature in a survival blanket that he had with him. He decided to take the creature with him back to Seattle. He put the creature in a small freezer he had at home. The creature was described

97

as about 4 ft. tall that was capable of moving incredibly fast. It had large bloated eyes, which it was able to open and close light in color. He also said that the creature emitted a horrifying scream or "shriek" as it fell to the ground.

Around the fourth day Jonathan heard noises coming from within the freezer. He opened it and the creature was alive. In a panic he slammed the freezer shut, and then called a friend over.

Over the next few days he attempted many times to communicate with the creature and did so. He tried to feed it but it refused all food. It did, however drink water.

Apparently unknown government agents broke into the house and removed the creature.

HC addendum.
Source: World of the Strange & Unsolved UFO Mysteries, William J. Birnes & Harold Burt.   Type: E or H?

* * * * * * *

Location: Acre, Israel.
Date: October 15, 1996.
Time: Night.

Several residents watched a semi-circular object with bright red lights descend low to the ground. Soon three short creatures, wearing orange-metallic suits and with what appeared to be short wings on their backs floated towards the witnesses home and attempted to enter the house on several occasions.

The occupants of the house screamed in terror and threw sticks at the creatures which then apparently left. No other information.

HC addendum.
Source: Gil Bar UFOs in Israel Timeline.   Type: C

Location: Madre De Dios, Peru.
Date: November, 1996.
Time: Daytime.

In the Amazon Jungle area Ricardo Gonzalez reported encountering a tall, man like figure with perfect features that communicated with him and told him he was a member of an underground civilization that thrived nearby, apparently near the famed lost Inca City of "Paititi."

Gonzalez was to have further encounters.

HC addendum.
Source: Cristian Riffo, Ovni Terra. Type: E or G?

* * * * * * *

Location: Near Swindle RAF, Wiltshire, England.
Date: November 14, 1996.
Time: Night.

Joseph Carpenter and four other men were traveling by car when they spotted a huge black triangular shaped object descending over the road. The men appear to lose consciousness at this point.

Later under hypnosis Carpenter recalled encountering a humanoid creature with a triangle-shaped head onboard the object. The creature had an olive complexion. He also recalled being exposed to a strange scenery and environment and of seeing a creature resembling a "dolphin."

HC addendum.
Source: Denys Breysse, Project Becassine. Type: G

Location: Surrey, British Columbia, Canada.
Date: Winter, 1996.
Time: 10:30 p.m.

Two witnesses were returning from a visit to the United States when the car, as it was proceeding north on 184th, suddenly came to a stop. The passenger looked up and was shocked to see a group of tall stick-like beings gliding across the road approximately 30 feet in front of the car. The group of beings glided across the road from a clearing on the right side of the road to a clearing on the left hand side of the road. The car then began moving. The two witnesses did not speak to each other until much later.

HC addendum.
Source: UFO BC.   Type: E

* * * * * * *

Location: Surrey, British Columbia, Canada.
Date: Winter, 1996.
Time: 10:30 p.m.

Two witnesses were returning from a visit to the United States when the car, as it was proceeding north on 184th suddenly came to a stop. The passenger looked up and was shocked to see a group of tall, stick-like beings, gliding across the road approximately 30 feet in front of the car.
The group of beings glided across the road from a clearing on the right side of the road to a clearing on the left hand side of the road. The car then began moving. The two witnesses, in shock, did not speak to each other until much later.

HC addendum.
Source: UFO BC.   Type: E

Location: El Verde, Rio Grande, Puerto Rico.
Date: December, 1996.
Time: Night.

Luis Torres Cruz reported seeing several huge cigar-shaped flying objects that appeared to release smaller disc shaped craft, which then descended towards El Yunque rain forest and disappeared. Shortly after that he saw a huge 9 ft tall black winged humanoid gliding over the area using gigantic bat-like wings near the area of the forest.

HC addendum.
Source: Jorge Martin, La Conspiracion Chupacabras.   Type: D?

* * * * * * *

Location: Veracruz, Mexico.
Date: December, 1996.
Time: 11:30 p.m.

Professional soccer referee Jorge Ruiz reported seeing a luminous disc-shaped craft descend over him. He attempted to scream but was unable to as he was completely paralyzed. As the craft hovered nearby, two human-like figures descended from it.

He described the aliens as very human-like except for their large pointed ears. They wore silvery combination suits. Ruiz was powerless to resist as the two aliens carried him onboard the craft. He was reportedly then strapped to a kind of "doctor's bed." According to Ruiz; the aliens never "operated" on him but communicated with him by using telepathy. His mind seemed to answer their questions automatically. They told him not to be afraid. That they were here to observe and analyze him only "they wanted to know about him."

He was told that he would only remember certain things, the things that they wanted him to talk about. Later Ruiz found himself back home at 5:00 a.m.

HC addendum.
Source: http://www.telemundochicago.com   Type: G

101

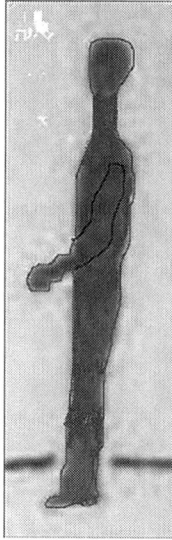

Location: Carta Blanca, near Cuautlapam, Yucatan, Mexico.
Date: December, 1996.
Time: 1-2:00 a.m.

A family of four traveling in their truck on the Ixtaczoquitlan-Cuautlapam road had arrived at a curve known as "Carta Blanca" when a very tall, thin being with very long thin arms suddenly jumped from the wooded side of the road into the middle of the road. The truck had its high beams on and the witnesses were able to clearly see the humanoid, which wore a one-piece red colored coverall and moved with impressive agility.

The driver immediately applied the brakes of the truck as the creature took another leap into the other side of the road and into a very deep embankment, quickly disappearing from sight.

HC addendum.
Source: http://www.eldurmientedeorizaba.com   Type: E
Comments: Translated by Albert S Rosales.

Location: Tblisi, Georgia (former USSR).
Date: December, 1996.
Time: 4:45 a.m.

The witness woke up late at night feeling very cold he then noticed a figure standing next to a wheelchair by his bed. The figure was man-like and wore a dark blue astronaut like suit.

Apparently he wore a visor helmet since the witness could not see his face clearly. The witness stood up and the figure disappeared. Looking out the window, he noticed a fiery moon-like object hovering over the area. It then sailed away at high speed.

HC addendum.
Source: GUFOA   Type: D?

* * * * * * *

Location: Mt. Nathan, Queensland, Australia.
Date: December, 1996.
Time: Late night.

A woman reported several very unusual occurrences, which had happened on her 20-acre property. One night she saw her husband go out through the windows, being levitated and floated out somehow.

She had seen circles of light in the paddocks and found a flattened area of grass the next day. She also saw shadowy figures in the distance, with red lights behind; the figures seemed to move very quickly, one other morning she was woken up at 3:00 a.m., to see red lights just above a shed, and a shadowy figure moving across the shed roof.

The next day she found a dam half empty.

HC addendum.
Source: Glennys Mackay, Keith Basterfield.   Type: C

Location: Near Bethel, Ohio.
Date: December 1, 1996.
Time: Late night.

Two hunters and their hunting dogs were parked on Leonard Rd, six miles south of Bethel, waiting for the right time to set their dogs loose. Soon they did and followed them into a harvested cornfield. As they approached some nearby power lines, the dogs got deathly quiet. That was very uncommon for that type of dog. As one of the hunters stepped into a clearing, he was shocked to see a silvery-saucer shaped craft with a transparent cupola, sitting on the ground. Nearby stood three humanoids wearing some kind of coverall uniform. The beings were described as "Grays." Short with slanted black eyes; one of them was slightly taller and had a much bigger head. As both hunters and their dogs watched, the three humanoids ran to their saucer and disappeared through an open hatch, then the object rose into the air straight up and vanished.

HC addendum.
Source: UFO Roundup Vol 1 #41.   Type: B

* * * * * * *

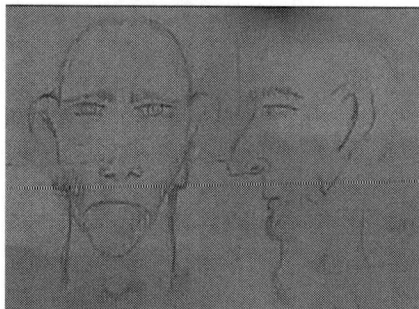

Location: Governador Valadares, Mina Gerais, Brazil.
Date: December 9, 1996.
Time: 6:30 p.m.

74-year old laborer, Plinio Bragatto was on his way back home after a day's work, when he made a brief stop to buy some beers. He proceeded on and stopped to sit on a rock in order to drink one of the beers. He then heard a loud sound coming from behind him. Turning around he saw a large metallic oval shaped craft landing on a field close to him. The object landed on several leg-like protrusions. Once the object landed a door opened, and a sort of ladder or escalator was lowered to the ground. Then a two meter tall humanoid figure stepped out.

The humanoid approached Bragatto and in a peculiar language that sounded like Spanish invited the witness inside the object. The witness agreed and was escorted inside. Once inside he noticed that the inside of the object had a metallic bluish sheen to it. Still speaking in the peculiar language, that the witness was somehow able to understand, the humanoid told Bragatto that they were going to take him to their "native planet." He was given the impression that the planet was "Mars."

Inside the object there were a total of three humanoids, two men and a woman, described as closely resembling humans, wearing loose fitting gray outfits, with several golden medallions hanging around their necks. According to the witness, the humanoid's hair grew from the middle of their heads back, and they had large ears and mouths, making them somewhat ugly. Before leaving, Bragatto was given a medical examination by the beings. His stomach area was probed with several needle-like instruments.

On the way to the humanoid's home planet the witness was given a fruit resembling a "Mamey" (known tropical fruit) and something resembling an empanada. He was also given a bitter beverage to taste that seemed to contain alcohol. In turn he offered the humanoids a beer, which he apparently had taken inside the craft with him. They immediately accepted.

Arriving, the witness was greeted by many similar appearing beings. He noticed that the "planet" was beautiful in appearance and saw numerous buildings that appeared to be made of a nylon-like material. When his time was up, one of the beings approached him and told him that it was time to go, that eight hours had already passed.

On his way back to the object, the witness saw a huge television screen which showed strange holographic like images, that included dinosaur like animals. The witness then asked the humanoids when they were returning to Earth, he was then told *"We will return when the storms are less intense, since we have already lost five of our aircraft as a result of lighting."*

Around 4:00 a.m. the witness was returned to Earth, he found himself in an unfamiliar field. He then followed a nearby path and reached a village where he discovered that the humanoids had dropped him off more than 800 kilometers from his hometown.

He went to the police and told them what had happened. A police officer conducting an investigation found a circular ground mark at the field where Bragatto was dropped off by the humanoids.

HC addendum.
Source: CIPFANI   Type: G

Location: Cruz do Incio, Lugo, Spain.
Date: December 12, 1996.
Time: 11:00 p.m.

A local man (name not given) was sleeping when he suddenly woke up and remembered he had to retrieve some fishing lines he had left hidden by the nearby river. Armed with a flashlight, he went to retrieve the property. However, at about fifty meters from the river, he noticed a greenish light that descended from the sky and landed close to him.

As the light dimmed he noticed that it was an object shaped like a 'telephone booth' and in it he could see two men dressed in black and at least three meters in height. He watched stunned as the green light illuminated its surroundings, soon he also saw a door open and the two men from the 'booth' exited and began walking in his direction, taking huge strides without bending their knees. He could not see any facial features or their arms.

Terrified he ran home and locked himself inside. In the morning accompanied by his wife they inspected the area where the strange object had landed, but only found a small area of flattened grass.

HC addendum.
Source: Lo Oculto, "Ovnis en España."   Type: B

* * * * * * *

1997

Location: Near Togliatti, Russia.
Date: 1997.
Time: Night.

Two men, M. Yumtsov and P. Stepashin were traveling by car in the area when they suddenly saw a bright light descending directly over them. Both men seem to lose consciousness.

Soon Yumtsov regained consciousness and saw his partner apparently sleeping, leaning against the door. He was surprised to see his speedometer reading 80km per hour; he felt no sensation of movement. In front of the car hovered a luminous sphere. He watched as several diffused figures descended from the sphere on what appeared to be bright threads. One of the figures floated up to the front windshield of the car and began to make hand signals, as if suggesting Yumtsov to open the door. The witness wanted to open the door but suddenly became very frightened and remained still. The figure appeared not to have a face; instead of eyes or a mouth it had slight indentations. When the witness refused to open the door, the humanoid apparently became terribly angered and emitted a shrill whistling scream, almost bursting out Yumtsov's eardrums. The figure approached the windshield further and somehow managed to insert several silvery threads into the car. The threads grabbed on to the sleeping Stepashin's arm and encircled and then began to pull him. Terrified, Yumtsov suddenly applied the brakes this somehow caused the bizarre figure at the windshield to float back and retrieve the silvery threads thus releasing Stepashin. The luminous sphere then also disappeared.

Stepashin's next recollection is of regaining consciousness again in the car, not knowing what had occurred. He did find several bruises around his wrists. Also several dents were found on the car's hood. The two men were so terrified that they remained parked on the side of the road the rest of the night.

HC addendum.
Source: Igor Tsarev "Secret Authority" #21.   Type: B or G attempt?

Location: Vyprolzovo, Bogorodskiy area, Nizhniy Novgorod, Russia.
Date: 1997.
Time: Afternoon.

Andrey Shibayev, a middle school student, saw a black-colored disk with an opening in its middle. The disk hovered closed to the ground in a tilted position near a tree. The boy couldn't remember the exact size of the disc. Several small humanoid figures were moving near the disk. The boy decided to approach but he suddenly stepped on a dry twig which gave away his location. The humanoid figures turned to look at the witness and he saw greenish lights emanating from the figures. After that he lost consciousness.

Andrey woke up about 300 meters from the location of the incident. The area was separated from the place of the encounter by a deep gully; he does not know how he got there. Returning later to the location of the encounter he discovered an unknown liquid in the place where the disk had hovered.

Researchers visited the location three years after the incident. Artur Uspenskiy, assistant to the Chairman of the Nizhniy Novgorod section on anomalous phenomena reported that the landing place distinctly displayed anomalous qualities. Researchers also discovered an unknown black-greenish colored thin coating on the surface of the tree. The chemical compound of this substance remained a mystery. A military officer equipped with a mine detector accompanied the research group. The detector behaved strangely, indicating a magnetic or metallic anomaly despite the absence of mines in the area.

HC addendum.
Source: Konstantin Gusev in KP-NN elmsomolskaya Pravda Nizhniy Novgorod" October, 2005.   Type: C

* * * * * * *

Location: Santander, Cantabria, Spain.
Date: 1997.
Time: Night.

After reporting seeing strange maneuvering lights over the area, Saretta MacPheterson was sitting alone on a beach staring out into the sea. There were few other people around when suddenly a tall, thin man-like figure approached her. He seemed to be wearing a plastic coverall suit. He had an expressionless face, gray in color. The stranger sat next to Saretta who noticed that the figure had four fingered hands. The being told her that she should not marry. Scared, Saretta got up and ran home.

Months later after getting married, Saretta was found murdered in her flat, apparently strangled with a towel. Neighbors reported seeing a strange tall, thin pale figure loitering around the apartment complex around the same time. The night of her funeral several attendants reported seeing a luminous object hovering over the area.

HC addendum.
Source: Testigo Ovni #5, 1998.   Type: D? Or F?

* * * * * * *

Location: Buryatiya Republic, East Siberia, Russia.
Date: 1997.
Time: Unknown.

A remarkable episode reportedly occurred to Klara Doronina when she was vacationing on the east side of Lake Baikal with her friend R. Slavskiy who was badly ill with leprosy. Apparently the pair spotted a UFO which landed not too far away from them. Several human looking entities exited the object and abducted Klara and her friend onboard their spacecraft and reportedly traveled to a planet located within the Pleiades star cluster, in the Constellation of Taurus. There the extraterrestrials cured Slavskiy of his leprosy they were then returned home.

HC addendum.
Source: Marina Popovich, 'UFO over planet Earth,' Moscow, 2003. Also in German K Kochin, 'UFOs and Aliens: Intrusion on Earth,' Moscow & Saint Petersburg, Sova publishing, 2007.   Type: G

* * * * * * *

Location: Pico Del Toro, Zacatecas, Mexico.
Date: January, 1997.
Time: Unknown.

A local farmer Gonzalez Cabrillo, reportedly encountered a landed UFO and its occupants who he communicated with. They were described as human like & dark complexioned with generally human like features. They allegedly told the witness that they came from the planet "Ummo." Many other sightings were made in the area around the same time, including the sighting of a flight of 10 cross-shaped objects that flew at 20,000 feet overhead.

HC addendum. Source: Colonel Steven Wilson (retired).   Type: G

Location: Chelyabinsk region, Urals, Russia.
Date: January, 1997.
Time: 8-9:00 a.m.

A soldier of a local military unit who was also a cook at the radar post deep in the dense forest, had gone to the perimeter fence of his unit in order to obtain some firewood from logs already prepared and positioned near the fence. He needed to prepare dinner for the company. The time was a little bit after breakfast. The weather was good and frosty with lots of snow on the ground and a good clear day.

Suddenly he saw two hairy humanoids, one about 2.2m in height, the second about 1.7m. Both were covered in dense fur. Kind of dirty red in color. The soldier thought that the taller entity was a female and the second shorter one, probably a child. Both entities had penetrated inside the perimeter of the unit, possibly attracted by the smell of the kitchen area. The witness was carrying an axe and for some strange reason was not afraid only curious, and walked towards the creatures in an attempt to obtain a better look. Amazingly he wasn't able to approach the pair, since both constantly seemed to move ahead of him, he couldn't make up any ground between them so he increased his pace but at the same time the entities increased theirs moving quickly away from him.

Finally, moving faster and faster the entities jumped up into the air and momentarily the witness thought that the perimeter fence would hinder their escape, but to his amazement he saw how both of the hairy humanoids simply zoomed into the air and levitated over the fence. The humanoids then flew away and vanished above the tall pine trees in the forest which surrounded the military installation. The witness then stopped his pursuit, returned back to the fence and saw two tracks of footprints which were left on the snow. The layer of snow was thick and strong, evidently the tall hairy humanoid was very heavy. However the footprints seemed to become dimmer and less deep as they neared the fence, indicating that the humanoids apparently began ascending into the air. Other soldiers reported seeing the footprints but were reluctant to report it to their commanding officer.

HC addendum.
Source: Vladimir P. Boyko, Simferopol UFO Research Crimea Ukraine.
Type: E
Comments: Flying Bigfoot/Yeti.

Location: Sao Gabriel da Cachoeira, Amazonas, Brazil.
Date: January, 1997.
Time: Evening.

At the time when several local residents reported seeing a bluish-white light that meandered over the area, a 14-year old girl reportedly saw what she described as an "angel" standing by the shores of the Negro River. It resembled a person 'enveloped in light' which then floated over the river at about thirty meters from the young witness. The young witness could see the strange figure moving its mouth very slowly but could not hear anything. It remained a few moments, floating above the water, and then left disappearing in the sky.

HC addendum.
Source: Pablo Villarrubia, "Brasil Insolito" p. 38.   Type: E
Comments: There is no mention of any wings seen on the humanoid.

* * * * * * *

Location: Prague, Czech Republic.
Date: January, 1997.
Time: Night.

Blanka Slemendova saw a shiny white human like figure standing on what appeared to be a "rainbow" in the sky. She felt telepathic communication from the figure. The witness has been involved in further encounters.

HC addendum
Source: Direct from witness.   Type: E or F?
Comments: It is interesting to note the similarity of the humanoid reported in the preceding case from Brazil, entered years later after the Czech case.

Location: Siracusa, Sicily, Italy.
Date: January 10, 1997.
Time: Afternoon.

A 39-year old police inspector was on foot patrol when he was startled to see at a nearby uncultivated field at about 80-100 meters distance a short humanoid figure about 120 cm in height dressed in a silvery suit.

The witness attempted to approach the figure in order to surprise it but he accidentally brushed against some shrubs and in an instant the figure made a tremendous leap of about 2.2 m in the air and disappeared into an adjoining field at very high speed. The witness could not keep up with it.

HC addendum.
Source: CISU Sicily.   Type: E

* * * * * * *

Location: Bloemfontein, South Africa.
Date: January 14, 1997.
Time: 8:30 a.m.

Several watched a gray spherical object with red and yellow flashing lights descend low over their heads nearly knocking them down. It had many lighted windows and inside one of them a gray face, with large dark eyes could be seen staring down at the witnesses. The craft apparently then left the area.

HC addendum.
Source: UFO Sightings in New Mexico & the World.   Type: A

* * * * * * *

Location: Anisevka, Primorskiy Kray, Far East, Russia.
Date: End of January, 1997.
Time: Unknown.

Inessa Grigoryeva, a resident from the city of Khabarovsk, had arrived in this village to have a well-deserved rest. While walking on the outskirts of the village, she noticed a weird "big bird" flying in her direction, straight towards her. She looked closely, trying to establish what it really was and was stunned when she saw two humanoid legs hanging down from the body of the weird creature. The creature descended, made a circle near the witness and then flew away. The

112

creature's wings were immovable, so it was gliding in mid-air or it carried some kind of anti-gravitational device that was concealed to the witness. It moved without a sound, totally silent. The entity had a face remotely resembling that of a human in which the witness could discern a mouth and two large eyes. Other witnesses in the area have reported encounters with a similar flying humanoid in the Russian Far East near the Pacific Ocean.

HC addendum.
Source: Alexander Rempel VAUFON (Vladivostok UFO Research) quoted by 'Inoplanetyanin' Ukraine #15, October 10, 2004.   Type: E

* * * * * * *

Location: Between Winifreda & Santa Rosa, La Pampa, Argentina.
Date: February, 1997.
Time: 2:00 a.m.

Oscar F, 45-year old was returning to Santa Rosa on National highway #35 in his truck, when in an isolated area between both communities he noticed a bright white light on the side of the road. As he approached the light, he noticed that it was an inverted cone-shaped beam of light located at about six to seven meters above the ground. At the base of the cone of light, he was able to see three humanoid figures standing next to the roadway.

The humanoids were over two meters in height, in appearance, two males and one female. They wore tight-fitting one-piece gray colored overalls, and on their sleeves they had what appeared to be fluorescent orange strips, the same color as their 7 cm belts and boots. Oscar also noticed that they had white skin and blond, shoulder length hair, and chiseled Nordic facial features. This experience was confirmed by a second witness who was driving by the same location in his vehicle and also saw the light and humanoids.

HC addendum.
Source: Raul Oscar Chaves, "Ciufoslapampa" Argentina.   Type: E

Location: Nekouz area, Yaroslavl region, Russia.
Date: February 10, 1997.
Time: Night.

A local woman named Irina O. was awakened by a bright light shining through her window. She realized that the only thing that was usually visible through her window was the forest and the sky, so it could not have been a car's headlights. The light soon dimmed out, but then gradually became bright again.

Suddenly there was a sudden flash of light which quickly extinguished itself. In total silence the witness then saw a greenish light in the shape of a human figure. The green light gradually became dense and assumed a distinct humanoid shape. At this point the beam of light outside the window began to increase in intensity and the room became lit like daytime. Irina's dog, Chuck, which had been sitting near the bed suddenly awoke and began watching with curiosity. Now instead of a greenish shape, there was now a tall woman with distinct features in its place. She had white skin, black eyes and long straight black hair. She glanced at the witness and her dog and said, *"I am Gelida from the planet UTA."*

The alien woman was dressed in a silver "spacesuit." A symbol or design shaped like the Latin letter "Z" was visible on the left breast area of her suit. Gelida noticed the witness staring at it and said that it was the symbol of "their Universe."

The witness then lost consciousness and then woke up later to find herself standing on a glassy surface. She could see a black abyss filled with many stars all around her, she looked around and noticed that all this was outside a large window which ran the whole perimeter of the round room; she could only see darkness and stars through it. There was a control panel on the floor near the witness. Opposite to Irina, Gelida was standing, wearing the same spacesuit and next to her two awkward shaped alien men resembling mannequins. Gelida explained that these were "bio-robots." Irina looked at Gelida's hands and noticed that they were white, with five fingers. Gelida then gestured to the witness and told her to take off her suit (the witness was now somehow dressed in the same type of spacesuit as Gelida's). After taking it off, Irina was left with only her nightgown on. The spacesuit fell to the metallic floor on her feet emitting a dull sound, at then vanished. The floor appeared to be glassy.

At this point the stars which were visible behind the large window appeared to suddenly increase in size. Irina understood that the speed of the spacecraft had now increased. Hear ears became numb. Soon there was total silence and Irina noticed that one of the "bio-robots" was looking intently out the window never turning around. The second robot stood to the left of the first one and turned around from time to time glancing at Gelida, which was operating the control panel. Gelida looked

114

at him intently apparently giving him telepathic instructions. The bio-robot seemed to be "calming" his leader (Gelida) assuring her telepathically that everything was going as planned.

Suddenly the stars outside the window froze in their places. Irina's head cleared and heard Gelida say, *"We are approaching our planet, here it is"* To her horror Irina now saw black ash, under her feet, through the glassy bottom of the craft; she could also see ominous red lava and the crater of a volcano. Gelida then said, *"Here is what we did with our planet UTA, we destroyed it ourselves. Now we live on another planet and we have now learned to take care of its ecology. UTA will be that way for a long time."* After those words were spoken Irina lost consciousness again.

She woke up later sitting on a bright green meadow, wearing her same nightgown, without the spacesuit or her slippers. Her dog Chuck was running joyfully around the meadow. He was jumping up and down playing and biting the beautiful blades of grass. The stems were similar to terrestrial sedge but ten times bigger. Irina also saw some very large red fruit similar to strawberries but much bigger. Her dog was eating some of the "strawberries," the pieces of the fruit resembled meat. Gelida invited Irina to taste the fruit also. She tore one of the fruits and tasted it. The taste reminded her of pineapple and strawberry combination. Red juice fell from the fruit and stained Irina's nightgown.

While she stared at her dog and at her nightgown not believing what was happening Irina suddenly woke up in her bed with her dog Chuck yelping at her feet. The red stain was clearly visible on the nightgown. She realized that it had not been a dream. She felt strange and decided to visit a doctor. After a blood test the doctor discovered something unusual, the presence of an excessive amount of leucocytes and very few lymphocytes. She was at first concerned but did not experience any aftereffects.

HC addendum.
Source: Vladimir Narcissov, deputy director of Yaroslavl UFO Center in: 'Fourth Dimension and UFOs' #3, 2000.   Type: G

Location: Nekouz area, Yaroslavl region, Russia.
Date: February 20, 1997.
Time: Night.

The local woman, Irina O. reported having another contact with aliens (see her first contact on February 10). She was again abducted into an alien spacecraft and apparently taken to another planet. There she saw an extraterrestrial city. There was absolute silence everywhere. The air was crystal clean and she saw fountains and springs with clear blue water all around her.

Everywhere serene and wise looking humanoids were walking around. These aliens were dressed in a way similar to the Greeks and Romans. The vegetation was very bright green in color. She saw numerous uncommon looking structures seemingly made out of glass and metal. She also saw small wagon-like objects that hovered just above the surface of the alien planet. Apparently other details from this second contact were erased from her memory.

HC addendum.
Source: Vladimir Narcissov, deputy director of Yaroslavl UFO Center in: Fourth Dimension and UFOs #3, 2000.   Type: G
Comments: In a telepathic society that also doesn't use noisy combustion engine technology, it would indeed be a lot quieter.

* * * * * * *

Location: Paradeseca, Orense, Spain.
Date: February 20, 1997.
Time: 4:00 p.m.

Local farmer Heliodoro Nunez was tending his sheep in an isolated pasture, when suddenly his dog began to bark. Looking back he saw three 10-foot tall entities wearing strange conical headgear. The beings appeared shiny and seemed to change colors at all times. Upon seeing these he began to pray. Apparently he did not see the entities depart. Others saw strange lights over the pasture.

HC addendum.
Source: UFO Roundup Vol. 2 #18.   Type: D

Location: Jacan, Los Arabos, Matanzas Province, Cuba.
Date: February 23, 1997.
Time: 11:00 a.m.

The witness, Jorge Luis Borges, a local heavy equipment operator was transporting a tractor through a sugar cane field when he suddenly heard a loud explosion. Frightened he jumped from the tractor thinking that something bad had occurred. He noticed that at only 30 meters from him, there was a disc-shaped object on the ground that was similar to a water tank commonly used in the area. The object was silver in color.

Moments later, on the hull of the object, a door began to open from top to bottom, and immediately a figure, human in appearance, about 1.7 m in height and wearing a sort of helmet that covered his head and face, exited the craft. The humanoid walked several meters in the witness direction, which noticed that it walked like 'a normal human being.' This caused the witness to become frightened.

Suddenly the figure stopped to pick up some plant samples, possibly sugarcane, or dirt and then returned to the object. The door on the object closed and then another powerful explosion was heard and the craft began to rise vertically at very high speed until it disappeared from sight in the sky.

Immediately afterwards, Borges screamed and ran several kilometers until he reached the town, where he contacted the local authorities. A commission from the FAR (Revolutionary armed forces) combed the scene of the incident, and reportedly conducted several investigations which included chemical analysis. The results of the investigation are unknown.

HC addendum.
Source: Hugo Francos Parrado.   Type: B

Location: Volzhskiy, Volgograd region, Russia.
Date: March, 1997.
Time: 1:00 a.m.

A local female resident named L. had just returned home from her work when she found a strange inscription on the door apparently written in chalk. It was written in clumsy Russian letters and it said the following, *"In one hour we will come."* Not knowing what to make of it she sat in her living room near the television and decided to wait it out. Soon a strong feeling of drowsiness overcame her and she fell asleep. Suddenly at about 1:00 a.m. she heard a steady increasing sound like, *"tu-tu-tu."* The front door knob then turned and clicked. Strange puffs of fog entered into the room and enveloped the witness.

Suddenly a heavy weight pushed her down into her armchair and she was unable to move. Her body felt as if it was being pierced by millions of tiny needles. She opened her eyes and saw a huge, two meter tall entity approaching her. The entity was dressed entirely in a black inflated overall. On the head it wore a rectangular helmet, shaped like a bucket. Gathering her remaining strength, the witness screamed in terror. This apparently startled the stranger, which then turned and walked right through the window, floating in mid-air and departed. At the same time the strange undulating sound vanished. The woman remained sitting paralyzed in the armchair until the morning.

HC addendum.
Source: Y. Oranskiy, 'Fourth Dimension and NLO' #7, 1997.   Type: E

* * * * * * *

Location: Los Toldos, Salta, Argentina.
Date: March, 1997.
Time: Afternoon.

Mapuche Cacique Martin Antiman (involved in previous encounters) was alone in a field, praying silently to God, when suddenly a large object or ship descended nearby and several human-like figures exited the object, and approached the witness. One of the aliens, a man that looked about 50-years of age, then told the witness *"Elio Torregiani will be chosen as leader and will grant us this place."* Elio Torregiani was indeed elected by the native Mapuche parliament in 2000 as leader. After the brief the encounter the aliens returned to their craft which then shot away at high speed and disappeared in the sky.

HC addendum.
Source: www.visionovni.com.ar   Type: B

118

Location: Magog, Quebec, Canada.
Date: March 7, 1997.
Time: Evening.

A witness encountered a humming silver disc-shaped object on the ground. Three short beings only 30 cm tall were seen next to the object. The beings wore silvery-white inflated suits, with round helmets and appeared to be collecting items from the ground around the object. Ground traces and electro-magnetic effects were reported. No other information.

HC addendum.
Source: Canadian UFO Survey 1997.   Type: C?

*   *   *   *   *   *   *

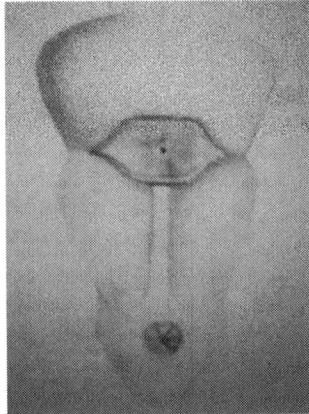

Location: Bogota, Colombia.
Date: March 10, 1997.
Time: 3:00 a.m.

After dropping off his girlfriend at her house, Juan Sudarsky was walking home alone. Suddenly he felt very cold. He then saw a purple light drop from the sky, at the same time hearing a loud high-pitched screeching sound, he also felt dizzy. He fell to his knees sweating profusely. Then an orange beam of light suddenly appeared next to him. Several bizarre medium sized creatures then appeared out of the beam.

They were described as having only one eye and with large antennae that radiated an odd blue light. They had a strange orifice where their mouth should have been. The creatures emitted intermittent screeches of varying frequencies. The witness apparently understood them in his mind. The creatures then formed a circle around Sudarsky. One of them

119

approached and touched his forehead. He then heard a mental message in perfect spanish, telling him to guard the planet against pollution, that theirs was almost totally ruined, that there were only fifty of them left.

Soon they flew back into the purple light via the orange beam of light. Before leaving, their leader showed Sudarsky a strange communicating device.

HC addendum.
Source: UFO Sightings in New Mexico & the World.   Type: B

*   *   *   *   *   *   *

Location: Uintah County, Utah.
Date: March 12, 1997.
Time: Late night.

At an isolated ranch in Northeastern Utah, barking dogs alerted a team of investigators to something lurking in a tree near the ranch house. Tom Gorman grabbed a hunting rifle and took off in his truck toward the tree. Two NIDS staffers followed in another vehicle. Up in the tree branches, they could make out a huge set of yellowish, reptilian eyes. The head of this "animal" had to be three feet wide, they guessed. At the bottom of the tree there was something else. Gorman described it as huge and hairy, with massively muscled front legs and a dog-like head,

Gorman who is a crack shot, fired at both figures from a distance of 40 yards. The creature on the ground seemed to vanish. The thing in the tree apparently fell to the ground because Gorman heard it as it landed heavily in the patches of snow below. All three men ran through the pasture and scrub brush, chasing what they thought was a wounded animal, but they never found the animal and saw no blood either.

A professional tracker failed to locate anything. At the bottom of the tree, they found and photographed a weird footprint, or rather, a claw print. The print left in the snow was from something large. It had three digits with what they guessed were sharp claws on the end. After analysis, and incredibly, the print closely resembled that of a velociraptor, an extinct dinosaur made famous in the Jurassic Park films.

HC addendum.
Source: Las Vegas Mercury & NIDS.   Type: E

Location: Faiano, Campania, Italy.
Date: March 17, 1997.
Time: 5:15 p.m.

Giovanni Domenico and his son observed a strange flying figure of humanoid form approaching from a nearby mountain at about 10-12 meters from the ground. They observed the figure for about ten minutes. They describe it as small and ungainly in appearance, about 1.2 meters in height and was flying at a low rate of speed. It had a large hairless head, disproportional to the rest of its body, which was dark gray in color. Its eyes were large and green in color and the nose was small and a little bit protruding. Its body was thin and delicate and appeared to be wearing a form fitting dark blue suit.

The humanoid seemed to be scanning the fields by turning its head slowly to the right and left. The witness noticed something suspended just above the humanoid's head that rotated like the rotor blades of a helicopter. The strange humanoid disappeared into the distance and was probably seen by other witnesses in the area.

HC addendum.
Source: Moreno Tambellini, SHADO.   Type: E

* * * * * * *

Location: Ain region, France.
Date: March 23, 1997.
Time: 11:00 p.m.

The witness, Gabrielle, (involved in other encounters) was dozing off on her couch when a white light appeared in the hallway and then she saw a figure with a round head that ended in a point (conical) with big brown, almond-shaped eyes without eyebrows. Small ears, nose and mouth. It had a "majestic" aura and it held in one hand a metallic cylinder. Her memories of the event seem to end there. The next day she found a sort of "bite mark" on her neck and one arms felt paralyzed.

HC addendum.
Source: Jean-Pierre Troadec, Daniel Robin, Laurent Merle and Bernard Jolivet 'UFOs, The mystery remains' The Frontier, 2004.   Type: E
Comments: Gabrielle claimed further encounters in 1998. One time she was in the presence of several creatures all identical to each other except for one who seemed to be the leader and who spoke to her. She believes she has an implant in her nose due to excessive nosebleeds and one in her left ear since she suffers from pounding pain in that ear.

Location: Roldan, Argentina.
Date: Early April, 1997.
Time: Evening.

Two sisters were walking near route AO-12 facing a silo factory, when they were startled by the appearance of a diminutive creature, entirely covered in hair and with shiny eyes. The younger of the sisters felt compelled to go towards the entity as if something were overcoming her will. Her older sister shouted at her and seized her arm to keep her from going any closer. The two sisters said that the creature made no hostile gestures upon seeing them, aside from the strange power of attracting one of them.

Suddenly, the creature made a surprising jump and landed on the other side of the road (over 12 meters), losing itself in the soybean fields. The younger sister suffered a nervous breakdown and was sent to a local hospital.

Days later, another witness was in her country home late at night when she felt a strange compulsion to open the door and go outside. She then saw a strange creature; she would later refer to as "a bear" staring fixedly at her at a distance of twenty meters. The witness reported feeling "mesmerized" by the entity and only emerged from the trance when her husband called her insistently from within the home. According to the witness the being resembled a dog walking on all fours, standing on its rear extremities during the encounter. The face resembled that of a "small bear."

HC addendum.
Source: Guillermo Aldunati   Type: E

* * * * * * *

Location: Deer Island, Oregon.
Date: April, 1997.
Time: Afternoon.

A witness saw a bizarre creature that ran in front of his car on the road. The 8-foot creature had a dome shaped head, and the eyes reflected in the headlights of the car. It appeared to be an albino; white fur and pink skin. It was very hairy, and they could see a flat nose and the eyes were close together.

HC addendum.
Source: The Western Bigfoot Society Newsletter #67.   Type: E

Location: New York City, New York.
Date: April, 1997.
Time: Night.

Chilean Model Christie Moller was on her way home walking along Park Avenue accompanied by a bodyguard and a private detective when from out of the shadows a short troll like little man, with greenish hair, hurled himself at her grabbing her. Terrified she began screaming, before her bodyguard and the detective could react, the little man had disappeared into a darkened alley. According to Moller this is not the first time she had seen such entity.

HC addendum.
Source: Paranigma Chile   Type: E

* * * * * * *

Location: Praia de Leste, Parana, Brazil.
Date: April, 1997.
Time: Night.

The main witness was in a field along with some of her family members, playing cards, when an object shaped like a bus appeared overhead. The craft was silent and well lit. Soon the witness and her family heard a very strong buzzing sound from an indirect source.

The witness felt compelled to follow the object to an unknown empty field nearby. The object then landed in front of her. Three strange beings exited the craft. These were described as having large red deep-set eyes, heads disproportionately large for their bodies. Their skin appeared to be wrinkled and greenish in color.

One of the humanoids communicated telepathically with her telling her; *"You are not happy here, leave this place. We will take you with us!"* In a panic she attempted to fight off the humanoids and lost consciousness. The next morning she was found wandering the fields, disoriented and confused. Five strange bruises were found next to her right eye.

HC addendum.
Source: Jackson Camargo, GEPUC.   Type: B or G?

Location: Bezhetsk, Tver region, Russia.
Date: April 23, 1997.
Time: Evening.

A local resident named Igor Utkin was in his apartment when he saw a column of blue light penetrating from somewhere in the ceiling, stretching down to the floor like a stalactite. Soon the beam reached the floor and seemed to become solid. A male humanoid and two female humanoids then descended out of the beam of light. One of the women was apparently the leader of the group. She approached the witness to within a couple of feet and began telepathic communication with him.

The witness reported that she was about 1.7 meters in height, with an elongated face, medium sized round dark eyes, and eyebrows that were outlined by narrow arcs, her head was hairless. She wore a tall hat on her head shaped like those wore by Catholic Bishops. Here skin was dense green in color, not shiny. The dress of the alien woman reminded the witness of those old style dresses wore by women, long light-green in color, with a red cloak and a tall light red collar. The claret-colored hat had a yellow "feather" on the front section. Within the feather he saw something crystal-like resembling a diamond. The alien woman was holding a stick shaped like a scepter with a double tip in her right hand. The alien female telepathically informed Igor that her name was 'Zuri,' and that she was from the planet GALEYA.

She then invited the witness to leave the earth with them in order to decrease his "sufferings." Igor declined, saying that his relatives would suffer without him. The woman then said that they could cause this to happen in a way that no one would notice and will not even suspect, because they had the ability to incarnate another soul into his body that would replace his departing soul the existence of his body on earth will continue as a bio-robot. (!)

Utkin still refused. The contact lasted for about 5 minutes and then the humanoids re-entered the blue beam or energy channel and quickly zoomed up. After that the beam of light vanished. The alien woman reportedly appeared to the witness again the next day (April 24 1997, in the evening), but then quickly vanished.

HC addendum.
Source: Pavel Hiylov and Anton A. Anfalov.   Type: E
Comments: I wonder if there have been instances in which witnesses have agreed to travel or leave with the aliens. I suspect so because there has been reports of deaths of humans which have left notes or information behind detailing their contacts with aliens and the fact that they could only travel with them in astral form or with their "souls" or spirits.

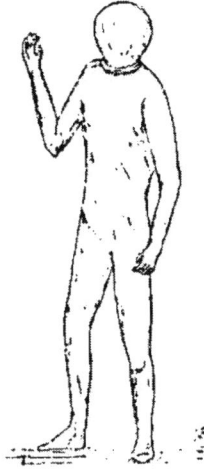

Location: El Morado Natural Reserve, Chile.
Date: May, 1997.
Time: Night.

Electronic technician Claudio Pasten was camping in an isolated area when he was reportedly abducted by bizarre luminous beings with transparent glowing faces. He was transported to different otherworldly locations. He remembering traveling inside an object surrounded by numerous luminous balls of light the size of ping-pong balls. The craft seemed to run in "light" energy. He was supposedly given numerous messages some of a divine nature. No other information.

HC addendum.
Source: Ovnis Terra, Chile.   Type: G

*   *   *   *   *   *   *

Location: Sheggia, Umbria, Italy.
Date: May 11, 1997.
Time: Morning.

Oddo Brunamonti was cutting some brush in a field when he noticed a strange figure among some nearby trees. At first he thought it could have been a horse until upon closer inspection, he noticed that it was some type of creature standing erect. Scared, he ran to his vehicle and then returned to the area along a road close to the woods. At this point the creature stepped out of the woods and the witness noticed that it was about 1.6 meters in height and completely covered in reddish-brown

125

hair. The creature then executed a tremendous jump landing in the middle of the road, about two meters away from the car. Then the humanoid raised his arms and emitted a deafening scream, opening its huge mouth. Inside the red colored mouth, the terrified witness saw a row of powerful pointy fangs.

Horrified, the witness maneuvered his vehicle around the creature, revving the car engine at high speed. The sound of the engine apparently spooked the creature which, performing another incredible jump, disappeared into the woods. Before the creature disappeared, the witness looked back to see a pair of powerful and clawed hands on the creature. The next morning another witness heard strange wailing sounds coming from the same patch of wooded area.

Soon numerous domestic pets and animals were found strangely mutilated in the area. Others reported unusual military helicopter activity and still others reported seeing a UFO over the same location.

HC addendum.
Source: Moreno Tambellini, SHADO.   Type: E?

* * * * * * *

Location: Near Clines Corner, New Mexico.
Date: Middle of May, 1997.
Time: Daytime.

A silvery disc shaped craft with a dome on top descended on a cattle field besides the I-40 highway. Motorists in both directions stopped and got out of their vehicles to see the craft. To their amazement, three reptilian like humanoids emerged from the object and walked about nonchalantly, ignoring the crowd of onlookers.

The creatures were about five feet tall and had light blue skin with dark hues and tones. The reptilians had three long, claw like fingers and toes and yellow eyes with a black, catlike split in the center.

Supposedly some in the crowd photographed the events. A state trooper came along and ordered everyone back to their vehicles. The humanoids went back inside their craft and left the area northwest bound, at a slow rate of speed.

HC addendum.
Source: C. L. Turnage, Sexual Encounters with Extraterrestrials.
Type: B

126

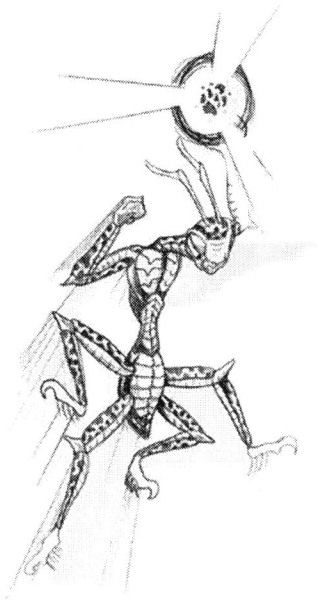

Location: Near Everglades National Park, Florida.
Date: May 15, 1997.
Time: Night.

The witness was in his RV camping when his dog, a German shepherd, wanted out that night. Shortly after, he heard a single "yelp" from the dog. He took his light, one of those million candlepower jobs, and went out, flooding the area with light. He saw a strange creature, with eyes that glowed green in and out of the light. It was almost yellow, three feet tall, about 100 pounds, bipedal, five 2-foot spines on its back, and it was sucking blood out of the dog.

It looked at him, then let out a screech, and ran off when the witness yelled at it, concerned about his pet. The dog's neck was broken, twisted to the back, and had two fang marks, and appeared to be drained of blood. He heard another scream from the distance, and hurriedly put the dog's body in his small RV bathtub, and put ice on it, and got out of there, heading to a local vet. The vet said he knew of no animal that would do that, confirming that the shepherd had been drained of blood, but admitted he had heard of other cases that were similar.

HC addendum.
Source: The Western Bigfoot Society Newsletter #68.   Type: E

Location: Redmond, Oregon,
Date: May 15, 1997.
Time: 8:00 p.m.

A man and his wife were at the Redmond lava caves near the airport when they heard a howl out of one of the caves during the early evening. Suddenly an immense creature came from one of the caves only 50-60 ft from them. It just walked out of the cave, and then walked quickly away, apparently not noticing the couple.

It left 22-inch tracks in the sand, and was really ugly, they said. The 8 foot tall creature was sandy colored with a peaked head, very broad shoulders, and no hair on the face, hands or feet.

HC addendum.
Source: The Western Bigfoot Society Newsletter #67.   Type: E

*   *   *   *   *   *   *

Location: Sao Paolo, Brazil.
Date: May 17, 1997.
Time: Night.

A man named Anisio Cacheta encountered a huge simian-canine combination like creature that was apparently being followed by a horde of normal appearing dogs. (!) It had more of a simian appearance and had spine-like formations running down the length of its body. No other information.

HC addendum.
Source: Carlos Machado, CIPEX.   Type: E

Location: Ponte A Mensola, Italy.
Date: May 18, 1997.
Time: 10:30 a.m.

In a hilly area east of Florence a local merchant watched a tall human-like figure suddenly descend slowly from the sky onto a nearby field. The figure was about 1.6 meters in height, human like and totally covered in a black tight-fitting diver's suit. It wore a red belt around its waist and a black helmet with wide dark goggles.

It landed on a vertical position on the high grass. A few minutes later it rose up, again slowly and vertically and disappeared from sight. Others in the area saw bright red lights flying in a zigzag fashion over the area.

HC addendum.
Source: Federico Rosati, CUN.   Type: D?

*   *   *   *   *   *   *

Location: Roswell, New Mexico.
Date: Summer, 1997.
Time: 5:30 a.m.

The witness had gone outside with her cup of coffee to a picnic table in the backyard. Her Chihuahua, Bella, followed her. At first she thought her neighbor had bought a dog, a little Schnauzer. Taking a better look, she noticed it was not a dog but a "little man." Bella also ran to the fence to get a better look.

They both then noticed a little man about 12 inches tall, stocky built with bushy eyebrows (gray) and a beard. He was wearing a gray woolen type shirt (no buttons) and gray pants with a rope for a belt. He had brown boots that looked like socks. Bella ran back into the house and under the bed and remained there most of the day. The little man had a funny walk from side to side and quickly ran into a Chinaberry tree and

129

disappeared. She could not see a door or entrance but the little man disappeared into the tree.

HC addendum.
Source: Robert A. Goerman (Paranormal Florida).   Type: E

* * * * * * *

Location: Bay of Finland, Saint Petersburg region, Russia.
Date: Summer, 1997.
Time: Daytime.

Officer-submariner, Nikolay M. an amateur diver had been diving in shallow water in the bay when he spotted a strange elongated object, shaped like a cucumber. Nikolay tied a rope around the object and tried to pull it to the surface. However he was not successful and decided to attach some slings to the strange "cucumber" and connect it to his automobile bumper to pull the thing out of the bay. He came to the surface and obtained the necessary equipment in order to perform that task. He brought a pneumatic drill with him for the purpose to drill holes on the object and attach the slings. Nikolay descended to the bottom again and attempted to drill the holes on the object. Suddenly a stream of dark liquid resembling oil spewed out of the object hitting him on the face. But instead of switching off the drill Nikolay increased its air pressure in an attempt to make the hole deeper. He heard a loud crunch within the "cucumber" and noticed a blood like substance in the water. The object suddenly then split in half revealing a large cavity inside, from it a large dull bubble floated out. At this moment Nikolay encountered a strange entity, apparently human-like with unnaturally white skin and what appeared to be a wound on his back caused by the drill, the wound appeared to be bleeding. The entity's face was distorted by pain and anger. The entity looked at Nikolay with an immovable hypnotic glance, soundlessly opening and closing his mouth. The witness attempted to push away the cucumber-shaped object along with the strange entity, but the entity succeeded in grabbing his hand. The humanoid had clawed fingers, very sharp, which tore into his sleeve and cutting him deeply. Struggling, Nikolay used the drill with his free hand and stabbed the entity directly into the chest. After that Nikolay apparently lost consciousness. He was pulled out of the water and saved but he had lost part of his hand. No traces of the strange humanoid or object were found. Apparently the cucumber-shaped object had been some type of alien "cocoon" which the witness had accidentally stumbled upon.

HC addendum.
Source: 'Sekretnye Isslendovaniya' #12, 1999.   Type: B?

130

Location: Near Cape Aiya resort, Crimean Peninsula, Ukraine.
Date: Summer, 1997.
Time: Unknown.

Diesel tractor operator Vasiliy Ivanovich was sitting on the rocky coast of the Black Sea near a large sandbar below a desolate rock outcrop east of Cape Aiya. He had prepared some fishing tackles and had thrown them in the water and was keeping a close eye on them. Suddenly to his amazement at about 10 meters from the shore he distinctly saw two giants or gigantic humanoid entities with large heads. The giants were more than three meters in height. The giants were speaking among themselves in some type of unknown language. Vasiliy could hear their speech and words but could not find any similarity with any known human language.

The giants were slowly swimming along the shore and talking to each other near some rocks. On their feet Vasiliy could see some type of flippers or fins. Both giants were dressed in shiny metallic silvery suits, tight-fitting to their huge bodies. Their eyes were larger than that of humans. Vasiliy was stunned and could not move for about 15 minutes, staring with fear at the two swimming gigantic figures. The humanoids kept swimming towards Cape Aiya and finally disappeared from view. Apparently they hadn't noticed the terrified witness. As the giants disappeared behind the rocks Vasiliy came to his senses and grabbed his fishing gear and fled back to the resort area.

HC addendum.
Source: Valeriy B. Ivanov, Colonel Ret. 'Mysteries of Sevastopol,' Volume #4 in: 'Natural Mysteries,' Sevastopol, 2008.   Type: E

* * * * * * *

Location: Cubatao, Sao Paolo, Brazil.
Date: June, 1997.
Time: 9:00 p.m.

During a dance at a local club, security guard Rogerio Lascoski noticed a figure that suddenly appeared in the dance floor (no one saw the stranger come in). The figure moved in bizarre synchronized movements in the middle of the dance floor. It was described as resembling a very thin humanoid that seemed to be dragging its feet when it moved. As Rogerio approached the figure he noticed that it wore a beige colored outfit that seemed to wrap around its body. It resembled a very dark woman, about 1.5 meters in height, large dark eyes, with no whites and a small nose. Thinking that it was some type of vagrant Rogerio threatened to call the police but the stranger ignored him. The

131

visitor then walked out followed by the witness that heard a phrase in his mind to the effect of *"I come from God."* The figure then walked to a nearby curve at the end of the street and was joined by two more similar figures. They stood one on each side of the first one then walked into the darkness again using strange synchronized movements. At the club, a lot of those present expressed their concern and disbelief as to the strange visitor. Incredibly some of those present did not see the figure at all.

HC addendum.
Source: Revista Brasileira de Ufologia.   Type: E
Comments: Have we here a break dancing alien?

* * * * * * *

Location: Near Borovoye, Chelyabinsk region, Russia.
Date: June, 1997.
Time: 11:00 p.m.

The witness, a farm engineer from Borovoye, had gone on a fishing expedition to a lake located at about fifteen kilometers from the village. He was accompanied by a close friend and upon arriving at the spot they quickly set up tents and placed some fishing rods by the lake. Both men spent the whole day fishing and talking and decided to sleep early.

The witness was awakened around 11 p.m. by a bright light shining outside the tent. He awakened his friend and both stepped outside the tent to see a strange glowing object shaped like an egg with a sort of flange in the middle which appeared to be hovering about two kilometers away, at a height of about five hundred meters. The glowing seemed to alternate in strength, dimming at times to a soft red light, no sound was heard. The object then began to descend and disappeared behind the tree line.

At the other side of the forest line there was another small lake in the same area where the object had descended, located about two kilometers away. Both men were very surprised and interested, and although there was a mild sense of fear his friend suggested that it could have been a man-made spaceship executing a 'parachute landing.' So the main witness then decided to go see where the object had landed. The moon was bright and visibility was excellent. His friend accompanied him to the edge of the forest but decided to return to the tent as he felt no inclination to climb over some nearby pits. The witness then walked to a nearby hill located right before the lake. When he climbed the hill he saw in a clearing near the lake the object standing on the ground at about 400 meters away. He sat down and watched the egg-shaped object, at first there was nothing visible but soon a sort of mist appeared below the object accompanied by a sort of movement.

At this point the witness decided to approach even closer and hid behind some bushes at about 100 meters away. The egg shaped object was about 20 meters in height and dark in color, the flange in the middle of the object was shiny metallic in appearance. From the craft came a soft buzzing sound and around it and within the weak luminous haze, he could see two figures, one small, about 1 meters in height and the 2nd tall, about two meters. They were humanoid in appearance, walked on two legs and had two arms. They wore some kind of 'plain' uniform. The witness wanted to see additional details and approached to within 30 meters of the craft hiding behind a large bush.

However with each step he took, the air became stifling as if a strong wind prevented him from advancing, also the sense of fear increased the closer he got. After about ten meters, his arms and legs became numb, and there was a strong tingling sensation in the area of his temples. At this point he decided to return and watch from afar.

He had already started to walk back when suddenly a tall figure appeared in front of him, blocking his way. The figure wore a loose fitting gray suit. It raised one hand and the witness' discomfort immediately disappeared. He stood about five meters from the witness, who could not clearly see his facial features since a sort of 'respirator mask' covered the bottom half of his face. On his left hand the figure held an object resembling a piece of pie. In the area of the belt there was a dark hexagonal object. Suddenly the witness began to hear words in his head:

Humanoid: *"Why are you here?"*

Witness: *"We saw your ship, I was interested and came to see it."*

Humanoid: *"If you like and are interested, I can show you our ship."*

Witness: *"I want to see it, but would you do anything to me?"*

Humanoid: *"Do not be afraid, come follow me."*

The witness then accompanied the tall figure to the ship, walking through the misty area surrounding it. There he saw two short figures that appeared to be doing something to the ground. Before him appeared a glowing oval-shaped opening. It seemed to be located on the side of the object. The tall humanoid then walked into the object and the witness heard in his head, *"Follow me"* and he disappeared through the 'doorway.'

He followed him and stepping through the bright oval entrance, he found himself in a large room, and for a moment he thought he was floating in mid-air and was enveloped in a wave of warm air, but soon realized he was standing on solid ground. The room had no sharp corners and he could see a sort of a stool, round in shape. There was diffuse light apparently coming from the ceiling area. There were two other short humanoids and an additional taller entity in the room. According to the witness, the gender of the humanoids was impossible to determine, but were most likely masculine. The tall one sat on the chair, which swiveled in all directions and took what appeared to be any form. The tall humanoid that had accompanied the witness into the object was dressed in a sort of gray overall. The witness could not see whether he had any hair on his head since both wore tight-fitting caps and addition the one sitting on the stool had a sort of metallic hoop around his head. Their facial features were very similar, *almost like twins*. The skin on their face and hands had a grayish tint and their hands had four digits, longer than that of humans apparently without any joints. The eyes were large, gray in color and without eyelashes, with high-brow ridges. The nose was small and the mouth and lips seemed to be of normal size, gray brown in color. He did not see the ears since they were probably concealed by the close-fitting cap. Their body proportions were correct and both looked quite human but not quite.

The two shorter humanoids were about 1.2 m in height and their skin was darker than the taller ones, dark gray in color. The mouth was small, colorless with a small hole for a nose. They had large black eyes with unusual *vertical pupils*. Their heads were hairless and in place of ears there were small 'ridges' with dark spots. Their hands had three digits that were unusually long. They also moved in an unusual matter, without bending their knees, almost as if gliding across the floor.

"Sit down," he heard in his head, as one of the tall humanoids pointed to a platform. The witness walked over and sat down. He was immediately grabbed from all sides, a chair-like object had molded around him. However at any time that he changed his position on this 'chair' it would immediately change shape to accommodate his moves, adapting to his every move. It was a very unusual sensation.

"Can I ask a few questions," said the witness.

"Ask," responded the tall humanoid with the metallic hoop around his head.

Witness: *"Where are you from?"*

Humanoid: *"From another star system."*

Witness: *"And where is it located?"*

Suddenly on a nearby wall appeared a map of a starry sky, one similar to the one seen from Earth. *"Here."* A red dot appeared on the star map and pointed at a star in the southern sky. The witness was not familiar with astronomy and could not tell which constellation it was.

Witness: *"And what distance is it from Earth?"*

Humanoid: *"Its light comes to your planet twenty times in what you call a year"*

Witness: *"Can your ship move at the speed of light?"*

The humanoid explained that they could only approach the speed of light, and it required a very large expenditure of energy. He went on to say that they were able to somehow, 'collapse space and time' in order to travel from one place to the other. He added that our scientists knew about this principle but for some reason did not attach any importance to it, preferring rather primitive principles of movement. This principle is *"Fluctuations in high-frequency properties of the plasma state of matter."* The witness then continued asking questions:

Witness: *"In our galaxy are there many planets with intelligent life?"*

Humanoid: *"Yes, quite a lot, but all of the civilizations at are at different stages of development."*

Witness: *"And why don't you come in direct contact with our planet (the leaders of our planet)?"*

Humanoid: *"We have had this experience with another planet and it resulted in the destruction of the population of that planet. To possess knowledge and technology, a corresponding society with a highly developed consciousness is necessary. Your planet is very young, your scientists have not yet discovered or identified the secret of matter and space. We have long been watching your planet, about eighty thousand years and at certain stages of development we have encouraged your civilization in the right direction. But something was lost along the way and we are trying to restore it."*

Witness: *"Have you come in contact with other highly developed civilizations?"*

Humanoid: *"Yes we have, and we know of nine of these civilizations."*

Witness: *"Why are you telling me all this (answering the questions)?"*

Humanoid: *"In the opinion of your society, knowledge and information of the individual is still very small and does not have a significant impact on the development of society. It certainly does not apply to the fundamental laws of physics and research. No one will be taken, as you put it, seriously. And also, we are able to block the memory of certain information."*

Witness: *"You will then erase the memory of this meeting?"*

Humanoid: *"Normally we do, but it does not always work, your brains are all arranged almost identically, but not quite the same and individual characteristics may be quite different."*

Witness: *"Are there any other inhabited planets in our solar system?"*

Humanoid: *"No, there exists extremely harsh conditions on the other planets."*

Witness: *"And is your planet similar to Earth?"*

Humanoid: *"Yes, very close. Our planet is older and there are no high mountains or large oceans, is much larger than your planet and our system consists of a total of five planets and they are all habitable."*

Witness: *"The small humanoid, is he from your world?"*

Humanoid: *"Yes, but he is a bio-robot of high intellect and capacity that can build its own kind. It is not afraid of many things that can threaten ours or your livelihood, for example he can go for a long time, without air is not affected by radiation or strong magnetic fields,* temperature gradients do not affect him either, of course within certain limits. It has other principles of nutrition and energy exchange."

Witness: "And why have you landed here?"

Humanoid: "We are here to obtain soil and water samples for our research and technical needs."

Witness: "How long have you been on our planet this time?"

Humanoid: "For a year."

Witness: "And your mother-ship?"

Humanoid: "Two years."

Witness: "And what is your task?"

Humanoid: "Investigations. We must tell you that your planet is close to disaster if you do not take urgent action. Your climate may change significantly and there will be natural disasters."

Witness: "Why don't you tell our governments?"

Humanoid: "We provide the information, but not directly, indirectly. We do not interfere with your rights, it is very dangerous."

Witness: "What do you eat?"

Humanoid: "The food that we produce from any biological mass, in principle it is possible to produce from non-biological, but it takes much more energy and time. By the way would you like to try some cactus or seaweed?" "What flavor would you like?"

Witness: "To taste like an apple if possible"

The humanoid smiled and said, "Well it's easy," he raised his hand and from next to the where he saw moved out of the wall some sort of control, he placed his hand on it. After a few seconds out of the wall a tray moved out, it was a vessel with a long spout. The tall humanoid took it and handed it to the witness. It was a transparent vessel filled with greenish liquid. The witness took a sip of it, the liquid turned out to be surprisingly smooth and tasty, tasting exactly like a good ripe apple would.

Witness: "Do you have disease?"

Humanoid: "Almost none, our life expectancy is practically unlimited. All organs can be replaced, but usually we have an individual average of 500 years (Earth years)."

Witness: "And if anyone wants to live longer?"

Humanoid: "It happens but rarely. This is a big responsibility for our society."

Witness: "Tell me, can you heal my leg? I suffered a knee injury and it did not completely heal. It hurts."

Humanoid: "If you like we will help you."

The tall humanoid again put his hand on the remote and on the opposite wall an oval shaped opening became visible from it floated three bio-robots carrying some instruments. The witness' seat was then turned into something resembling an operating table. He saw the complete procedure but felt nothing. They removed his clothing and poured a sort of greenish foam on his left leg (injured leg) which quickly froze, forming a cocoon around the leg. Next, he probably fell asleep because he could not remember the rest of the procedure. When he awoke he was again sitting on the same chair, wearing his clothes. His clothing exuded a strange odor, similar to that being in a forest after a thunderstorm (ozone?), he touched his leg and it did not hurt anymore. His knee was again flexible.

Humanoid: *"We have corrected your leg. And purified you from kidney stones."*

Witness: *"Thank you, but I did not have any kidney pain."*

Humanoid: *"You would have gotten sick soon."*

Witness: *"Thanks again, how much time has passed?"*

Humanoid: *"We do not understand your circadian concept of time. For you it has been four hours, if you like we will let you go."*

Witness: *"Yes, I have a friend who is probably worried about me."*

The tall humanoid who had originally led him onboard the craft stood up and told the witness to follow him. Again he stepped into the oval shaped door and fell gently to the ground.

He was now standing by the lake near the tent and ten paces from him stood his trembling friend. It was daylight. The egg-shaped object was gone. *"Why are you afraid?"* He asked his friend.

"I saw the egg shaped object fly overhead, it emitted a beam of light towards the ground and you came within the beam" said his frightened friend. *"I have been looking for you for over four hours, where have you been?!"*

The witness could only remember seeing the egg-shaped object on the meadow and approaching it and then remembered nothing. He thought it had only been fifteen or twenty minutes. He was surprised to find his leg healed, a fact later confirmed by the surgeons, only a peculiar pink scar remained. He suddenly remembered the whole incident one year later.

HC addendum.
Source: http://uffon-online.ru/file_3986.html   Type: G

Location: Forest of Sevre, France.
Date: June, 1997.
Time: Night.

On a road next to the wooded area two friends saw standing on the side of the road a tall female figure wearing a long white luminous robe. They stopped their vehicle to see the figure cross the road floating just above the ground and disappearing into the other side of the road into the wooded area.

HC addendum.
Source: LDLN #346.   Type: E

* * * * * * *

Location: Near Redmond, Washington.
Date: June 5, 1997.
Time: Night.

A Mr. Hassan saw a hovering saucer shaped object about half a mile away that glowed a white color. He had the headlights of his car on it also, so with the lights from the UFO, he could clearly see it abducting cattle. The cows appeared to be stunned, still upright, and they floated up into the object. He also noticed "little monsters." 50-60 pound humanoids with large heads, and grayish white skin. They had dark black eyes, no whites. The witness became scared and drove off. No one else appeared to be around.

HC addendum.
Source: Western Bigfoot Society Newsletter, #68.   Type: C

* * * * * * *

Location: Johnson City, Tennessee.
Date: June 18, 1997.
Time: 1:00 a.m.

The witness and his cousin were out in a hunting expedition and were sitting on the side of a wall of a rather large hollow which consisted of very thick underbrush and lots of evergreen and a larger valley leading to first, a clearing and then on to some ancient Indian graveyards. All of a sudden they heard the brush in the hollow bellow them shaking and they could tell that whatever was making the sounds was rather large.
The main witness was armed with a Ruger 10-22 rifle with approximately 150 rounds of ammo on hand. Under his night vision

scope he could see what appeared to be a man, but upon further inspection he realized that the "man" was a creature about 7-8 ft tall approximately 450 lbs.

It was covered with thick black fur. It was slimmer than the popular Bigfoot image, almost skinny. And it had a prominent neck. Protruding on either side of its head were long tapered "horns" also black in color. On the top of the head also protruded a horn pointing straight up. All horns were approximately 5-6 inch in length and were the same dark color as the creature.

The terrified witness emptied a 25 round clip into the creature and then retreated into a nearby cabin about 65 feet away. The next morning they could not find anything except for lots of spent shell casings and bullet holes on a walnut tree. He thought he had struck the creature several times.

Nearby animals traps had been sprung and all the bait extracted. On a nearby ridge the witnesses located a series of tunnels made up of brush and various sizes of tree limbs, vines and leaves. They thought it could have been "the lair of the beast." Afraid, they returned home.

HC addendum.
Source: GCBRO Weird Stories.   Type: E

* * * * * * *

Location: Lake District, England.
Date: June 19, 1997.
Time 11:30 p.m.

Shaun and his friend Simon had decided to go camping overnight in the Lake District. They did not have much money at the time so rather than pay to stay on an official caravan site they decided to camp on an open area of National Trust owned land. Unfortunately Shaun cannot remember the exact location where they set up their tents, he only remembered that it was a couple of miles away from a village. They drove to an ideal camping spot in Shaun's Ford Escort.

By the time they had set up the tents it was about 11:30 p.m. and fully dark. The weather was clear and the stars were visible in the sky. As it was getting a little cold they decided that they would sit in the front seats of the car to drink a beer and have a chat.

The field they were on gently sloped up, and in the distance was a hillside about half a mile away. As Shaun looked out into the dark through the front window, he suddenly noticed two orbs of light, one blue and one white, bobbing around near the base of the field. They appeared to be about 200 feet in the air. Shaun asked if Simon could see the two lights and he confirmed he could see them too. The men discussed what they could be.

Without warning the two glowing lights disappeared. Then they noticed what appeared to be two glowing white figures on the hillside. The figures looked thin, almost like matchstick men. They seemed to be stooping down towards the ground like they were looking for something or digging. The figures began to walk back and forth crossing one another continuously, covering a short patch of ground, perhaps 5 meters in distance. It was like they were pacing in a constant pattern. They would occasionally stop a moment before continuing to move.

Shaun first thought was that they were people trying to steal cattle. However the figures did not look human. They appeared to be self-luminescent rather than people holding torches, and were glowing a bright neon white. Also the speed they were moving at seemed odd. It was like they were scuttling back and forth much faster than normal walking speed.

After watching the figures for a short while, Shaun said to Simon that he was going to get out and go and have a closer look. But Simon said *"Don't be stupid!"* and persuaded Shaun that this was not a good idea. They continued to watch the figures for about 5 minutes, during which they did not alter their movement pattern. It felt like a recording playing over and over again.

Shaun then tried turning on the main headlights of the car to see if that made any difference. Simon was not happy about this and said, *"That's a bit stupid because now they know where we are!"*

The figures were too far away and were not lit up any more by the headlights anyway, so Shaun switched them back off. He asked Simon if he would like to just ditch the tents and get out of there. Simon thought this was a good idea so Shaun tried starting the car. At first it didn't start up but on a second attempt it worked. However he was too curious about what was taking place so changed his mind. He switched the engine back off and told Simon that he wanted to continue watching.

Things then got even stranger. The men suddenly became aware of a pickup truck filled with people in the rear view mirror. They reminded Shaun of hillbillies. The truck appeared to be on the grass, in the same field that they were camped in. It drove around the car in an arc and headed off in the direction of the glowing figures.

The next thing Shaun and Simon became aware of they were waking up still in the car seats. It was morning time, around 9am. Confused, Shaun asked Simon *"Which one of us fell asleep first?"* Neither of them could remember going off to sleep. Shaun says that he would have found it extremely difficult to drop off in the car seat, and it is not something he would have normally done. And it seemed even more implausible because of what had been happening.

They had both been completely transfixed by what was taking place. They were extremely puzzled by what had happened and neither of them could rationally explain it. It was like they had both been instantly switched off.

HC addendum.
Source: Dave Hodrien, Birmingham UFO Group Report.   Type: G?

* * * * * * *

Location: Jinki, Latvia.
Date: June 20, 1997.
Time: Midnight.

Aleksandr Khvostikov was looking out the window of his dacha towards the northwester section of the sky when he saw flying in the sky a large man-shaped figure, followed by a second then a third similar figure. The figures were bright white in color and descended towards the ground in a 45-degree angle.

Upon landing on a field near a wooded area the witness could see that the figures were three very tall (at least 4 meters) humanoids, wearing what appeared to be very bright clothing.

Soon after landing, the figures moved quickly away into the nearby forest and were quickly lost from sight. Others have seen luminous sphere repeatedly flying over the region.

HC addendum.
Source: UFO LATS, Latvia.   Type: E or D?

* * * * * * *

Location: Thossey Dans L'Ain, France.
Date: July, 1997.
Time: Evening.

A woman working alone in a camping ground cafeteria saw five strange men walk into the restaurant. They sat down and ordered drinks and began speaking to the woman. They told her that they had come from another planet and that they spoke all languages.

Since she spoke four languages, the woman tested them by asking them questions in all four, each time they answered correctly. They also spoke to her in other "strange" idioms, and without revealing their origin.

141

They had their drinks and left. Around the same time and in the same area three witnesses had seen a landed UFO. No other information on the second case.

HC addendum.
Source: GREPI

Type: E or D?

*   *   *   *   *   *   *

Location: Fayetteville, North Carolina.
Date: July, 1997.
Time: Night.

The main witness and a friend spotted a large low altitude low speed triangular shaped object. It had a red light on each corner and it made absolutely no sound. It seemed to drift over the area at about 100 or 200 feet above the tree line. They followed it around for about 30mintes until it disappeared into the distance.

Later the main witness was in his bed late at night when he suddenly woke up to see a strange humanoid figure staring at him from the window. The figure had a white luminous pearly white body, with a diamond shaped bulbous head; it lacked any nasal openings or mouth. The witness got the impression that he was looking at some sort of mask because it was very smooth. The eyes were a glassy black, but they were not slanted in nature. They were flat on the top and bottom, rounded on the inside edges and wrapped around the sides of the head like sunglasses, or more accurately like a dragonfly's eyes.

Terrified, the witness threw his head under the blanket, too scared to move a muscle or make any sounds. He left the room soon and stayed up all night clutching a butcher knife.

HC addendum.
Source: NUFORC

Type: D

*   *   *   *   *   *   *

Location: Pennsylvania (exact location not given).
Date: July, 1997.
Time: Night.

An unidentified witness reported seeing an object shaped like a spinning top but the bottom not pointy. It had lots of multicolored lights in numerous see through windows on the top. At least 15 to 20 alien beings, "unlike the standard look" could be seen. They were half-human

142

and half alien, full bodies, beautiful looking creatures all moving about and communicating. They all wore the same light-colored outfits.

All the lights and windows seemed to be moving constantly and turning separately from the bottom. The bottom of the object had a long yellow beam of light dropping to the ground. The UFO then disappeared. The witness searched the area to find it but could not. Suddenly when he reached the bottom of the hill it was daylight, it was somehow 6:30 a.m! He doesn't know where the night or time went.

HC addendum.
Source: http://mufonpa.com/   Type: A or G?

* * * * * * *

Location: Dubai, United Arab Emirates.
Date: July, 1997.
Time: Late night.

Darren who worked for a shipping company was posted to Dubai and later his family flew out to join him. While he had been living on his own, nothing strange had happened. But as soon as Tracey and the children arrived, life began to go haywire.

Marcus, his three year old son, was repeatedly telling his parents about a man who lived in one of the lights in his bedroom and who took him and his sister Georgina up into the light to talk and play. Darren and his wife were particularly worried because Marcus seemed to believe he could fly, and wanted to climb on to the villa roof. He knew, although his parents have no idea how, that there was a water tank up there. The "man" told Marcus to repeat the letters, E, R and S (no one has any idea of the meaning of this).

Georgina, who shared a bedroom with Marcus, woke in the early hours of one morning to see the light flickering violently in the hallway, and a strange fluorescent oval shaped light on the wall at the foot of her bed. In the center of the light was a thin gray figure with very long arms. It seemed to be moving towards her. The family's dog, Bibi, a cocker spaniel, began to whimper. Georgina glanced at Marcus, and noted that he was still soundly asleep.

She remembered nothing more until the next morning, when she showed her parents marks on both her knees, which again looked like fingerprints from four fingers.

HC addendum.
Source: Tony Dodd, 'Alien Investigator.'   Type: E

Location: Near Irati, Parana, Brazil.
Date: July 4, 1997.
Time: Night.

Jaime Flores and Lauri Alves, both employees for a local communications company, were repairing a micro ditch on the side of the road when they noticed a strange bipedal creature staring at them from some nearby woods. The creature had large reddish eyes, and long arms that ended in sharp claws.

As both men stared back at the creature they felt strangely attracted to it. And if not because they also felt scared they would have gone over to where the creature was.

HC addendum.
Source: Carlos Alberto Machado.   Type: E

* * * * * * *

Location: Cerro Las Mercedes, Tenerife, Canary Islands, Spain.
Date: July 7, 1997.
Time: 3:30 a.m.

Three technicians working at a local meteorological station were stretching their legs on the access road to the station, talking among themselves when suddenly the whole area was lit up by a bright white light, which moments later began to blink. Turning around, they saw at about 100 m distance, a strange object which was approaching their location silently.

Terrified, the men yell out that it was a UFO and began running down the path towards the station, the UFO following closely behind. After about 50 m, all three of the witnesses suddenly stopped after hearing a voice in their mind which told them, *"Running is futile, we will catch you."* All three remained standing by the metal wire fence watching the strange craft which was now only about 12 m away.

An uncanny silence suddenly filled the area. Minutes before, the sounds of crickets and other night sounds could be heard but now everything was eerily quiet. They could now see that the craft was metallic shaped like two saucers, one on top of the other. It was about 30 m in diameter and was encircled by a row of round lights, each separated by a distance of 2 m, gray-blue in color. From the center of the craft a white beam of light illuminated the road and its surroundings. All three now stood terrified, unable to move. Moments later, from the top of the craft, a beam of what appeared to be "solid" white light appeared. It resembled a funnel with its wide section covering the road, illuminating a circle about 10 meters in diameter.

Suddenly from inside the solid white light, two figures materialize. They appeared to float several centimeters just above the pavement and moved rapidly towards the witnesses, taking short steps but levitating in the air. The humanoids, at about three meters from the stunned witnesses, stared intently at them. The creatures were about 1.2 m in height, with dark, bumpy, wrinkled skin. Their heads were the size of a football, shaped like an inverted pear. The witnesses could not see any ears, noses or mouths, giving the faces a "flat" appearance. Their main prominent feature was two huge ping-pong sized eyes, dark blue in color, lacking pupils or eyelids. The creatures stood silently still staring at the three witnesses, who remained terrified and still unable to move. The arms on the creatures were extremely long and thin, almost reaching their feet. Each hand had four digits and their legs were very short in relation to the rest of their bodies and ended in a sort of "fist."

After a few moments of staring at the witnesses, one of the humanoids turned and looked at the other, which in turn did the same thing, without uttering any sound or speaking. Then after looking at the witnesses for a while, the creatures turned around and glided back to the white solid funnel of light. Once they reached the solid light, they disappeared into it and were seemingly absorbed back up into the hovering disc-shaped object. The white, solid beam of light then receded back into the craft and the ship began to move away, spinning around and then it shot away at incredible speed, becoming a dot on the horizon in seconds.

The three witnesses are now able to move again and run back into the research compound. There, other employees had seen the object but not the humanoids. The three witnesses are then interrogated by supervisors, separately and together and all warned not to talk about the experience.

HC addendum.
Source: Francisco Padron, Canary Islands, 'La pesadilla de una noche de Verano.'
Translated by Albert S. Rosales.   Type: B

Location: Near Los Angeles, California.
Date: July 11, 1997.
Time: 2:00 a.m.

Phillip H. Krapf awoke in the middle of the night and found himself encased in a luminous shaft of light, then involuntarily beamed aboard an alien spacecraft. Within a matter of seconds, he was standing before the strangest creatures he had ever seen, though not so different from depictions of alien beings that others have given. They were just over five feet tall, with dark, narrow eyes, nearly imperceptible noses, no visible body hair, and skin tones from grayish white to slightly tan. They were wearing satiny robes of varying muted colors. They spoke to Krapf in english even though their thin lips didn't move.

During the whole experience the witness felt at peace and fully alert. These aliens called themselves "The Verdants," and claimed they come from a planet some 14 million light-years from Earth (the name of their planet apparently translates into "Verdant" in English, which the witness interpreted to mean something akin to "garden planet"). They said that they had been recruiting hundreds of humans to serve as liaisons for an impending summit conference between representatives of the two species.

Krapf spent most of his waking hours on the ship being briefed by the Verdants in orientation sessions. During his stay, he had a personal tour guide and attendant who went by the name of Gina. The other key figure among the Verdants with whom he had contact was using the name "Gus." These names were adopted for his benefit because he was incapable of addressing them by their real names in their native tongue.

He learned in the orientation sessions that the Verdants have been space explorers for millions of years. Apparently they belonged to an Intergalactic Federation of Sovereign Planets. Currently the group has a total of 27,000 species or members in their files.

The Verdants also said that they had colonized a great number of formerly uninhabited planets making them more habitable or more hospitable.

HC addendum.
Source: Phillip H. Krapf, 'The Challenge of Contact.'   Type: G

Location: South Armagh, County Armagh, Northern Ireland.
Date: July 13, 1997.
Time: Late night.

SAS troops on an ambush patrol against IRA gunmen were stunned to see four small gray humanoids walk up from behind a hillside and cross their path.

The soldiers and the gray entities stared at each other for a few minutes, and then the gray figures vanished. Minutes later the soldiers saw a flash of light in the sky. The soldiers then abandoned their stakeout.

HC addendum.
Source: United Kingdom UFO Network #78.　　　　　　　Type: D?

* * * * * * *

Location: Bezhetsk, Tver region, Russia.
Date: Middle of July, 1997.
Time: 10:00 p.m.

Five local residents, including a young man named M. Ryapolov, were fishing in a pond between a grove of birches and some cottages with private garden plots near Kashinskaya and Zarechnaya Streets when suddenly they saw a fiery red-yellowish globe flying in the sky. The globe then descended in an inclined trajectory and began to hover low over the ground at an altitude of about one meter. The globe-shaped object appeared approximately to be three meters in diameter. The distance from the witnesses and the object was about 40 meters. The globe was smooth, with what appeared to be a horizontal belt consisting of a row of spikes or thorns (each one about 10cm in diameter and 25cm long) were circling its middle section on its even smooth surface. A rectangular shaped door was opened in the lower section of the globe downwards creating a ladder, which was installed in the inner surface of the door.

Two humanoids stepped out of the globe. Each entity was about 1.9 to 2 meters in height. They were dressed in dull gray black cloth-like tunics, but tighter fitting than those priests wear. The aliens had protruding noses, small ears, and hairless heads. Their skin was light, with round bulging eyes. One alien had red-yellow eyes, the second, lackluster bluish eyes. Both aliens had just slits instead of lips. At first the humanoids moved about as if they were "skating," but then moved about like normal humans.

They walked towards a cottage, several of the witnesses attempted to get closer but Ryapolov dissuaded them from doing that. Meanwhile the humanoids were returning from the cottage and were carrying an elderly

147

woman with them. The woman was screaming, *"Help me, save me!"* and was attempting to resist. When the aliens finally brought her to the craft, she stopped resisting and lost consciousness. During the ascent into the door of the craft the woman slipped out of one of the humanoid's hands, but they quickly picked her up and moved her inside the spacecraft. The door immediately closed after that, and the globe-shaped craft zoomed into the sky.

After that the witnesses approached the landing site but could not step into it as they suddenly experienced cramps and convulsions in their bodies and extremities as if shocked by electricity. It appeared to have a protective field or barrier around it. The humanoids left clear boot prints on the soil.

HC addendum.
Source: Pavel Hailov and Anton A. Anfalov.   Type: B and G?
Comments: There is no information as to what happened to the unfortunate elderly female apparently abducted by the humanoids.

* * * * * * *

Location: Arad, Israel.
Date: July 22, 1997.
Time: 1:00 a.m.

Several local residents including 23-year old student Tal Igur reported seeing a flying silvery figure over the area. The figure appeared to have a frozen, silver face with torso and arms. Others saw an object that was emitting flashes of light towards the ground.

HC addendum.
Source: Barry Chamish, Return of the Giants.   Type: D?

* * * * * * *

Location: Rostov-on-Don, Russia.
Date: July 30, 1997.
Time: 12:15 a.m.

A local young man named Igor V. Kolomiets (involved in other encounters), encountered a strange humanoid figure that suddenly appeared in his home out of thin air. The alien was very tall and was dressed in a black or gray loose-fitting overall. Facial details could not be discerned because it wore a hood or cowl that covered his head completely, and the room was also very dark. But Igor could see a greenish aura emanating from the alien's body. The alien also radiated fear and the witness was immediately paralyzed, but was able to retain the ability to speak. The witness had been subconsciously ready for the contact and asked the visitor who he was and where he was from. Igor then heard inside his head in a cold, chilly and emotionless voice, *"I am a representative of a civilization from the Canum Venaticorum constellation."*

Igor was not frightened and began to ask additional questions, he asked, *"How old is your civilization?"* *"Two million years. We are ahead of your civilization by 1000 years"* Igor then asked, *"Are you part of the Black League?"* (Apparently a group of negative civilizations from the Constellation Orion and others) The answer was a resounding *"Yes."* *"What do you want from humans"* asked Igor. He answered, *"We need vital space."* *"What do you want from Irina?"* (Igor's friend who had also experienced contacts with a similar entity). The alien answered, *"She is a powerful medium. We want her. We will take her soon"* (according to Igor's claims Irina is actually a reincarnated alien being, by the name of Inzeada).

Next the alien stopped answering questions and began speaking in a monologue, *"Your civilization disturbs and hampers us. We did not find Irina by accident; we pushed her to you, because we are searching for control of you."* The alien paused a minute and then said, *"Don't interfere in the alien or UFO business, or death will await you. You will belong to my race."* After hearing this Igor became upset and yelled at the alien to *"go to hell and get out."* At the end the alien transmitted a message in his brain, which the witness wrote in a piece of paper in the morning. It was purportedly a message from his "Government" directly to the witness.

HC addendum.
Source: Anton A. Anfalov.   Type: E
Comments: https://en.wikipedia.org/wiki/Canes_Venatici

Location: Glinik, Poland.
Date: August, 1997.
Time: 12:10 a.m.

Zdzislaw Komorek was walking back to the village among some low hills on a warm cloudless night, when he suddenly noticed a strange human-like figure which seemed to be made out of bright light, at a distance of 50 meters away. The figure was about 1.5 meters in height, white in color and with a large head and human like hands. Komorek was unable to see any facial features. The figure was gliding silently above the ground.

Terrified the witness quickly left the area but noticed that the figure was following him, always keeping a distance of about 50 meters. Eventually he looked back and the figure had mysteriously vanished.

HC addendum.
Source: Arkadiusz Miazga, MCBUFOIZA.   Type: E

* * * * * * *

Location: 'Varvarovka' anomalous zone, Zaporozhye region, Ukraine.
Date: August, 1997.
Time: 10:30 p.m.

A group of eleven men (mostly UFO enthusiasts and paranormal researchers) from the city of Zaporozhye headed by Vladislav Yevdokimovich Kanyuka (a participant of about thirty expeditions to various anomalous areas in the former Soviet Union) arrived in two cars to the area located in the left bank of the largest Ukrainian river, the Dnepr. Their aim was to spend the night, watching the skies and environs, hoping to see, photograph and videotape any type of anomaly (UFOs, humanoids, etc) that they might encounter. Fishermen and campers in the area have frequently reported encounters with all types of phenomena.

The area was covered by dense brush, with lots of cane and not too far from the water and a precipitous drop of the river bank. They were exactly about 50 km from the city of Zaporozhye at a location where the Dnepr makes an abrupt U-turn and near an ammonia pipeline that stretches over the river.

Besides Kanyuka, there was also Sergey Kravchenko, Yuriy (Yura) Poloz, Pyotr Bykov, Vladimir Viktorovich Sinyev (head of the Origen club), Ivan Mihnenko, (godfather to Kanyuka's son) and the driver Evgeniy. There was also two young boys, 12-year Evgeniy, Kanyuka's son, and 11-year old Tatyana, daughter of the driver.

The group soon camped out and started a fire, brought in some firewood and began to prepare dinner (fish, soup, etc). Suddenly Kravchenko began walking in circles as if performing some strange ritual, when asked what he was doing, he answered with a smile on his face, *"I'm calling them."* Then Yuriy Poloz asked from what direction would "they" come, Kravchenko then pointed to the opposite bank of the Dnepr. The men considered this to be all a joke; however they installed their video camera on a tripod just in case the aliens would appear. Half an hour later the men saw a white light on the opposite side of the Dnepr, exactly in the direction in which Kravchenko had pointed to.

The light resembled the moon but not exactly, the men then began photographing and videotaping it. Some became frightened, especially the young kids after seeing the light, so Kanyuka made his 12-year old son hide inside the tent. The frightened Tatyana ran to her father. The waters of the Dnepr reflected the strange light emitted by the object.

The men looked on the screen of the video cameras and using a zoom lens they saw an enlarged image of the object. They then took several more photographs. At first the object resembled a large star or a pea, but when enlarged it looked like an earthenware pot, flat on top and on the bottom, with curved sides. On the surface of the object they saw concentric circles of light, radiating from the central circle in the middle.

The UFO then apparently landed or hovered very low over the field on the opposite bank of the Dnepr. Then Kanyuka suddenly saw a strange "man" or humanoid entity walking towards them. Humanoid walked directly towards the video camera. The height of the entity was about 1.7-1.8m, dressed in a kind of dark cloak that hung below its knees. However some of those present didn't see the entity.

At first Kanyuka thought he was hallucinating but when the entity approached, Kanyuka realized that he was not. The entity looked menacing and unearthly and was walking towards the video camera being held by V. V. Sinyev. At the moment that it was going to apparently stumble into Sinyev and the video camera, the entity seemed to vanish in plain sight. Kanyuka then asked Sinyev if he had seen the humanoid, but this one replied no, since he was looking straight into the video monitor.

Back home while examining the film Kanyuka noticed that the image of the humanoid had been captured on the film for several seconds. The humanoid's face in general looked human, but not exactly, he had an unusual pale face, large eyes, and light hair combed to the side. More details could not be discerned. The total time of the video was 3.5 minutes and the object had remained there for about five minutes.

It then zoomed up into the air and began to hover over the ground. After that the UFO separated into two objects and in a minute or so both objects switched off and everything disappeared.

In the morning the witnesses only saw the deserted fields on the opposite side of the Dnepr.

HC addendum.
Source: Vladislav Yevdokimovich Kanyuka, Zaporozhye.
UFO/Paranormal research center, Ukraine.   Type: D
Comments: I would like to see this video.

* * * * * * *

Location: Gull Lake, Manitoba, Canada.
Date: August 20, 1997.
Time: Unknown.

Several witnesses claimed they saw a green luminous craft crash into the woods. Upon investigating they saw a huge hairy man-like figure apparently standing guard next to a crashed object. The witnesses then apparently left the area. No other information.

HC addendum.
Source: UFOROM   Type: H or C?

* * * * * * *

Location: Near Ballard, Uintah County, Utah.
Date: August 28, 1997.
Time: 2:00 a.m.

In the middle of his isolated ranch (known as the Sherman Ranch or more popularly as 'The Skinwalker Ranch') in Northeastern Utah, Tom Gorman saw a dull white light appearing out of nowhere, researcher Chad Deetken also saw the light. Gorman and Deetken were out in the pasture as part of an ongoing effort to document unusual activity on the property. Both men watched intently as the light grew brighter. It was as if someone had opened a window or doorway.

Gorman grabbed his night vision binoculars to get a better look but could hardly believe what he was seeing. The dull light began to resemble a bright portal, and at one end of the portal, a large, black heavily muscled, humanoid figure seemed to be struggling to crawl through the tunnel of light. After a few minutes, the humanoid figure wriggled out of the light and took off into the darkness. As it did, the window of light snapped shut, as if someone had flicked the "off" switch. Deetken had the presence of mind to snap a few photos of the event but would later learn that the film had recorded little of what the two men had witnessed.

HC addendum.
Source: Las Vegas Mercury, NIDS.   Type: B?

152

Location: Saki, Crimea, Ukraine.
Date: September, 1997.
Time: 2:30-3:00 a.m.

A Mrs. Sosedenko, who was very ill at the time, reported seeing the shadow of a cigar-shaped object hovering near the balcony of her apartment. Soon after that a strange man entered her bedroom through the balcony. He was dressed in a tight-fitting gray overall. He seemed to have normal arms and legs and head but his face seemed to be a blank spot. The alien then approached her bed, and the witness whispered, *"I am afraid."* The 'man' then stopped and began communicating with the witness telepathically. He said to her, *"We will help you, we will cure you, but you would need to come with us."* The witness then asked him if she would be brought back. *"No,"* was his answer.

She then refused the help proposed by the alien and told him that she had a deaf daughter, which she could not leave. The alien then proposed to take her daughter also but she again refused telling the alien that her daughter had a large family that she would refuse to leave behind. The alien then went out the balcony, disappearing into the hovering cigar shaped craft. Her daughter Viktoria Sosedenko also reported anomalous activity in her flat. Apparently on another occasion she was also confronted by another alien (no details on that).

HC addendum.
Source: Letter by Viktoria Sosedenko in 'The Secret Doctrine.' Newspaper, #20, 2002.   Type: E & C

* * * * * * *

Location: Cordenons, Fruili, Italy.
Date: September 4-6, 1997.
Time: Various.

Two young boys, 13-year old Giovanni and 15-year old Alessandro were walking alone on the Via Vittorio when they suddenly noticed a dazzling light emitting intermittent flashes. This flashing was immediately followed by a strange whistling sound. After walking for about 100 meters the two boys noticed a bizarre creature standing next to a light pole. It was described as short and white in color. The creature then moved very rapidly in a strange zigzagging motion disappearing into a nearby wooded area.

The next day the same two boys along with two other friends entered the wooded area in search for the strange creature. Soon about 50 meters away among some bushes the boys saw a round whitish head, hairless and extremely wrinkled in appearance.

Terrified, the boys left the area but soon returned to the site armed with a camera and a pair of binoculars. Soon they were overcome by a strange malaise and headache. They again saw the humanoid, which they described as about 90 cm in height, dirty white in color and with very long arms. It had three digit hands that ended in ball shaped tips. Its head was oval shaped and devoid of any facial expression, it was pointed at the top and it had a very pointed chin. Its most prominent features were its huge black oval shaped eyes. Its mouth was but a thin line and its nose, two small round holes. Its skin appeared to be gelatinous and was very corrugated. It appeared devoid of any sexual organs.

The boys left the scene. The creature was apparently seen on the next day in the same woods, but it scurried away into the brush when a witness approached it and disappeared.

HC addendum.
Source: Moreno Tambellini, SHADO.   Type: E

* * * * * * *

Location: Moscow, Russia.
Date: September 17, 1997.
Time: Night.

Kirsan Ilyumzhinov, then president of the Russian Republic of Kalmykia, revealed that aliens appeared in a transparent tube on the balcony of an apartment he owns in Moscow.

"I was reading my book, watching television and had almost fallen asleep," said Ilyumzhinov. *"Then I felt someone calling. I would not have believed it, if I had not had three witnesses, my driver, my minister and my aide."* *"The extraterrestrials put a yellow spacesuit on me. They gave me a tour of the spaceship and showed me the command center. I felt very comfortable with them."* His three staff searched the apartment for him during his absence and were unable to find him, nor explain his sudden reappearance an hour later.

Ilyumzhinov provided further details to the British newspaper The Guardian in 2006, *"They took me from my apartment and we went aboard their ship. We flew to some kind of star. They put a spacesuit on me, told me many things and showed me around. They wanted to demonstrate that UFOs do exist."* In another interview he elaborated further on his contact, *"They are people like us. They have the same mind, the same vision. I talked with them. I understand that we are not alone in this whole world. We are not unique."*

He also made a statement, explaining that according to his extraterrestrial information, the game of Chess originated from outer space. Since 1995, Mr. Ilyumzhinov has also been president of the World

154

Chess Federation. In 2014, he was again re-elected president after defeating Garry Kasparov, winning 110-61.

HC addendum.
Source: "Svoboda" (Freedom) live radio broadcast July 22, 2001. Anton Anfalov.   Type: G

*   *   *   *   *   *   *

Location: Penuelas, Puerto Rico.
Date: September 26, 1997.
Time: 10:00 p.m.

Ivan Rivero Morales and several other witnesses watched an object flying around a nearby mountaintop for about an hour and then land on the summit. The intensity of its light dwindled to a soft amber glow, which it retained during the duration of its landing.

To the witnesses surprise that were watching the object with binoculars and telescopes, a number of tall beings, described as greenish with large oval shaped heads, black eyes, pointed ears and a protruding belly descended from the object and walked around the summit for one hour.

After this length of time had elapsed, the beings re-entered the craft and its brilliance increased to previous levels, it then vanished in a matter of seconds.

The following night, local residents again watched an object land on the summit of a nearby mountain, but this time it was accompanied by another, smaller object. The large object landed on the same spot it had occupied on the previous evening, and its tall greenish occupants descended once more from within.

On this occasion, the beings, described again as having protruding bellies, long thin arms, large oval shaped heads, with pointed ears, remained outside for two hours, while the smaller object remained motionless over the location. After two hours both objects rose into the air and vanished from the location. The only means of access to the mountain top is by helicopter.

HC addendum.
Source: Federico Alvarez Frank.   Type: B

* * * * * * *

Location: San Jose, California.
Date: October, 1997.
Time: Early morning.

Joseph Firmage woke up to see a bizarre man-like being surrounded in a brilliant white light. The being had black hair and a beard. Telepathic communication ensued between the witness and the visitor. At the end of their brief communication the witness expressed the fact that he wanted to "travel in space."

The visitor then stared at him and suddenly a small blue electrical sphere emerged from the visitor and shot towards the witness who upon being struck by the sphere felt an extraordinary sense of ecstasy and pleasure. The being apparently then disappeared.

The witness felt as if had received some type of gift.

HC addendum.
Source: Enrique De Vicente, Año Cero 7-99.   Type: E

Location: Northern England (exact location not given).
Date: October, 1997.
Time: 8:00 p.m.

On a cold, stormy night, the main witness Valerie Spruce, and her husband were doing some work at home. They had just sat down when they heard clattering on the roof and just naturally thought it was the wind. Then they heard the same noise again but about 100 decibels louder. So they went outside and looked up.

What they saw they couldn't apprehend at first and thought "this is not possible." It was a large cigar-shaped craft hovering above their roof and next doors and a few houses further down. And then everything went blank and she looked down to see her husband on the ground, and then she couldn't remember anything and the next thing she can recall was lying down on a stretcher like bed in a room, completely white and not being able to move except for her eyes, and seeing strange beings dressed in white suits with what looked like gas masks on. On trying to move she could feel something across her stomach and wrist and ankles and within seconds a large metal device coming closer to her mouth and feeling very frightened and wanting so much to be able to free herself and run away.

The beings came towards her and had some strange tools in their hands which they stretched her mouth with, and then this device above came closer and went into her mouth, when she was expecting to feel the utmost pain, she thinks she lost consciousness and the next thing she knew, two of the beings were across the other side of the room and one went out the door at the bottom of the room right opposite from where she was lying and started communicating with signs and an odd language that she could not understand. Next she remembers being in her back garden on the ground and this craft above her moving away. She found out that she was naked and she had these straps around her ankles, wrists and stomach and she tried to remove them and in doing so felt very weak and exhausted and worried, when they came off she saw severe marks on her body and she felt she had very sore throat. She couldn't swallow properly. She lost consciousness again and woke up in bed next to her husband, it was 4 a.m.

The following morning when she got up, her husband told her exactly the same and some of the neighbors in the area also reported the same events and losing consciousness and time during this most painful period. Her husband had the same marks as she did. But he told her that he remembered more and felt pain in his chest also. That was something she did not feel. But in April the following year, her husband collapsed one morning and at the hospital died, through a very rare heart related virus in which the coroner at the time knew nothing about it and nor did the British Heart Foundation, he did not know how a fit and healthy 36 year old could have come in contact with it. Considering when the coroner worked as a medical doctor in Africa some years previous, he came across many heart related viruses including this one amongst the old and the dying.

And since this event the main witness had had dental problems of the severe kind. The mouth X-rays have confirmed she had something metallic in her upper jaw that unless surgery is performed, it cannot be removed. She is very much surprised that she is still alive today, but she believes it is because the abductions "are not finished."

HC addendum.
Source: http://www.iwasabducted.com/abductions/ also;
http://bufog.freeforums.org/abductee-t471.html   Type: G
Comments: Negative effects as a result of an alleged abduction.

* * * * * * *

Location: Tulkarem, Israel.
Date: October 10, 1997.
Time: Afternoon.

Muhand Faras, 16, was walking home from school when he came upon a strange man-sized figure, dark green in color, with a strange growth on its face. The figure had two tiny hands with three fingers on each with long fingernails. It made a threatening gesture towards Muhand, screamed in an unintelligible language, then flew up into the sky and vanished.

HC addendum.
Source: UFO Roundup, unknown number.   Type: E

* * * * * * *

Location: Tulkarem, Israel.
Date: October 10, 1997.
Time: Sundown.

Local engineer, Raid A'anam saw a black creature in the sky. He told police investigators, that he saw the outline of the figure and that it was human with two arms and two legs. It flew fast over the area, quickly disappearing from sight.

HC addendum.
Source: Israeli UFO Research.   Type: E

Location: New Jersey (exact location not given).
Date: October 24, 1997.
Time: 4:00 a.m.

The witness, who for more than a month had been seeing three dimensionally solid but transparent boomerang shaped objects, flying at very low altitudes over her house and yard, had invited investigator Harold Egeln over to discuss the matter. Around 3:30 a.m. they retired to bed. Soon her 5-year-old daughter abruptly woke up from a sound sleep, frightened by mysterious knocking sounds she heard in her bedroom. She went to sleep again at 4:00 a.m. when the witness heard her scream again. She ran to her bedroom nearly colliding with her, apparently the lights in her bedroom kept turning on and off. As the witness reached for the light switch, everything turned deep, dark velvet black and there was an apparent power outage in the neighboring area.

At this point Harold had woken up and was looking out the window where they noticed a beam of white light that emanated directly from above the house. After several minutes the witness and her daughter went back to bed. Soon a bright white light appeared in the bedroom window, and she noticed that her daughter was fast asleep.

Turning back towards the light she was startled to see a tall, thin grayish yellow being, standing beside the bed. She then heard the following words in her head: *"I am Dralov, I come as representative of the Sirian Arcturian Coalition for Interplanetary Defense."* The witness felt her body become very light and saw her sleeping daughter being levitated from her bed. In a trance like state they were escorted toward the hallway. In the living room they met Harold. Soon they left the house with a group of people all seemingly human, who waited in the corner, clearly illuminated by a bright white light from above the house. Someone in the crowd waved at Harold, and the three of them were led around the back of the house to a nearby vacant lot where a blue beam of light enveloped them and transported them up to a large craft that hovered just above the roof top.

Onboard the craft, Harold was surrounded by a group of small "little gray humanoids" who apparently knew him, and he walked off with them smiling. A tall gray being in a silvery white robe took the witness daughter hand and led her away, the witness stood with Dralov, and he pointed to an arched doorway that suddenly became visible as it opened. Telepathically Dralov told the witness that an Elder would like to see her, before the presentation.

The Elder was a short being with large blue eyes and a black robe. He sat near a small, half circle table in a white, domed room and gestured for the witness to sit next to him on a white step like seat that protruded from the wall. The Elder touched the witness on her right hand and she noticed that he had a small thumb and three fingers of nearly equal length. He communicated with her telepathically.

She was later taken into a large auditorium type room in a diamond shaped transparent elevator. In the large room she saw other humans, including one that resembled Whitley Strieber. (!)

Among other revelations she was told that she was onboard a starship called Ashalum and there were many different races of "extraterrestrials" visiting the Earth and that there was a struggle among certain groups for control.

HC addendum.
Source: UFO PI, SPACE.   Type: G

* * * * * * *

Location: Desert area, Arizona.
Date: November, 1997.
Time: Night.

22-year old Duane Berger and a friend Mark were camping in an isolated area, and as daylight faded, they had built a campfire and were sitting around eating. Soon they began to hear "terrible screams" that seemed to be coming from an old mine nearby. After a few moments of nervous discussions and assessment of the very eerie situation, the two young men decided to investigate the matter.

Armed with a tire iron the two friends entered the mineshaft. They had walked a dozen yards when they saw a greenish glow ahead of them. As they got closer they could make out the dark figures of two men in hooded robes. It was clear that they intended to block their progress farther into the mine. But as the two young men drew nearer to the light, they noticed that the two figures were barely five feet in height. They then boldly demanded that the hooded figures release the women or whoever they were hurting. Then a deep, mechanical voice boomed out of the hooded figures in unison and told them, *"The women are beyond your help! Leave at once or perish! Leave at once, or you shall join them in the caves."*

The robed figures then produced some type of wand-like instruments and directed a yellow light at the two young men that held them both immobile. Next, they aimed a greenish beam against a wall of the mineshaft. The wall of solid rock seemed to melt away, allowing them to walk into the wall and disappear. Within seconds, the wall was once again nothing but hard rock. After a few moments the two men were able to move again and fled the area quickly, knowing that there was nothing they could do to help whoever was being detained in the caves.

HC addendum.
Source: Brad Steiger, Out of the Dark.   Type: E?

* * * * * * *

Location: Sierra de Mariola, Valencia, Spain.
Date: November 1, 1997.
Time: Night.

A married couple was vacationing in the area and one night after dinner, the husband decided to walk their two Cocker Spaniels. He followed a path into a wooded area, while the dogs ran ahead. It was a very dark but starry night with plenty of visibility.

He had gone about 150 meters when both dogs suddenly stopped in their tracks and began to growl. He ignored them thinking that they had smelled some sort of animal, however when he try to pull on their leashes they would not budge. At this point, he noticed that both dogs were staring intently at a certain spot in the woods. The witness also became aware of an unusual silence that had suddenly permeated the area.

He suddenly heard the sounds of branches parting and immediately a very tall figure crossed in front of the witness and his dogs from behind the tree. It resembled a dark robed monk which emitted a slight green glow and seemed to float at about 50cm from the ground on top of a sort "floating plank."

The bizarre figure crossed the path in front of the witness from right to left, without making the slightest sound, even though that side of the path was covered in brush and rocks. At the same time that the figure floated out of sight, the dogs calmed down and gradually the normal night sounds of the forest returned. Terrified, the witness and his dogs quickly returned to the cabin.

161

HC addendum.
Source:http://www.alegsa.com.ar/Foro/viewforum.php?f=2&start=10
0   Type: E
Comments: Translated by Albert S. Rosales.

* * * * * * *

Location: Zhoksy-Kylysh Lakes, Kzyl-Orda region, Kazakhstan.
Date: November 16, 1997.
Time: 5-6:00 p.m.

The 22-year old witness, Vitaliy Anatolevich Karpov, a Russian Army Lieutenant at the time and member of an elite search and rescue unit (usually involved in retrieving landed space capsules and its cosmonauts) was hunting partridge in this isolated area. He dug a pit close to the water in order to conceal himself and waited for his prey. He was completely alone in this deserted and desolate place.

Scanning the sky hoping to see some birds, the witness suddenly noticed a strange object flying nearby. The object was egg-shaped or an oval craft which was flying at an altitude of about 50-100 meters and was quickly descending. The craft landed at about 500-600 meters from the witness location. According to Karpov's estimation, the object was no more than 10 meters long and about 4 to 4-1/2 meters high and made out of a silver-bluish metal, very smooth and shiny, which reflected the rays of the setting sun. The main egg-shaped body of the craft had 2 big smooth elongated protrusions, positioned on its hull which went straight down into the grass; it did not seem to have any landing gears or props. There was a dome on top of the object which was evidently transparent or had a clearly visible transparent glass-like window encircling the dome.

Vitaliy noticed that when the object landed, a bright light appeared inside the transparent dome. Despite the distance, Vitaliy could see the figures or silhouettes of three black or dark colored humanoid entities inside the transparent dome. Mainly the upper parts of their torsos and heads. Several minutes later a sort of hatch opened on the upper surface of the hull on its left side and extending outwards. Soon one of the humanoid entities came out of the craft while the other two remained inside, apparently watching over their companion.

Karpov was amazed at the appearance of the humanoid, especially when the figure moved close to his position. The witness froze in place and watched the strange creature standing close by. He described the creature as about three meters in height, with a large visibly bald (hairless) head, black in color, he had the impression that the entity was either naked or wore some kind of very tight-fitting dark or black suit on.

162

The most amazing were the upper and lower extremities of the creature; these were disproportional and looked amazingly thin, like match-sticks. The creature was as "thin as a rake." The creature's arms were very short but its thin legs were extremely long. It appeared that the entity had three or four fingers on each hand, but he wasn't completely sure about that.

The strange entity began to quickly move around, evidently collecting soil and other samples. From time to time the figure, occupied by its strange procedure, would bend down to ground, however while walking the creature's legs did not bend at the knees, as if its legs were completely inflexible. All this lasted for about 10-15 minutes. During the whole time Vitaliy felt very afraid, afraid to move or speak.

Finally the entity completed its task and crawled back into the craft, the hatch closed and the silver-bluish egg-shaped object zoomed up and flew away without a sound and with no visible lights. The UFO soon disappeared into the darkness. Afraid of being mocked, the witness kept the story to himself and only told the investigator (source) recently.

HC addendum.
Source: Dr. Anton A. Anfalov PhD.   Type: B

* * * * * * *

Location: Falconara, Italy.
Date: November 19, 1997.
Time: 7:30 p.m.

A woman walking along a deserted road, spotted a bizarre humanoid figure standing still about 3-4 meters from her. She described the figure as about 1.70 meters in height, and very thin. Its head was directly set on the shoulders, completely lacking a neck. The witness could hear that it emitted a strange sound.

Approaching the figure she noticed that the sound emanated from a strange round facial orifice that seemed to be moving in an undulating fashion. It wore some type of dark habit with a type of cape hanging from its left side of the body. The stunned witness reported that the figure appeared to be bi-dimensional, "like a photo."

At one point the figure put one hand on his mouth, extracting a strange tiny object. The witness felt dizzy and briefly turned away from the creature, upon looking back the strange humanoid had vanished.

HC addendum.
Source: Notizieufo, Italy.   Type: E

Location: Ankara, Turkey.
Date: November 27, 1997.
Time: Late evening.

27-year old A.O. a tourism school graduate, was laying down and resting in his bed when suddenly the television set which had been turned off suddenly turned itself on and a green light was spread on the screen and all over the room. He was frozen, unable to move and when the light disappeared, an "alien face" appeared on the television screen (not described).

A.O. then heard a voice inside his head which said that they wanted to impart their technology with earthlings. The voice also said that they hailed from a planet called *"Telbel."* No other information but apparently this contact still goes on today.

HC addendum.
Source: http://www.surfingtheapocalypse.com/ufo.html   Type: F?

* * * * * * *

Location: Marca Huasi, near San Pedro de Costa, Peru.
Date: December, 1997.
Time: Unknown.

During an expedition to the plateau led by guide Jerry Wills, a man saw a woman on the rocks above him and climbed up to join her. As he got closer, he realized she had no legs and was floating in midair. She had long black hair and the face of a cat. The entity snarled at the man and scared him so badly; he had to be immediately evacuated from the area.

HC addendum.
Source: The International Directory of Haunted Places, Dennis William Hauck.   Type: E

Location: Sucice, Czech Republic.
Date: December 2, 1997.
Time: Evening.

A witness reported seeing a tall, 2.2m, very slim figure with a tight-fitting luminous suit walking in a forested area. Footprints were reportedly found in the snow. No other information.

HC addendum.
Source: http://www.ufo.cz/zare/seznamy.htm   Type: E

* * * * * * *

Location: Taos County, New Mexico.
Date: December 10, 1997.
Time: 6:30 a.m.

Ricardo Alfonso was driving to work to the Taos elementary school when he saw a metallic silvery object hovering over a nearby field. He stopped his truck to investigate. When he got closer, he hid behind a bush for a few minutes until the craft disappeared.

As he sat there pondering what had occurred, a bright beam of light illuminated him. Then several "little men" appeared around him, everything then went blank. He awoke later, face down in the field completely naked with bruises on his body.

HC addendum.
Source: UFO Sightings in New Mexico & the World.   Type: G?

Photo of witness.

Location: Cvrljci, near Sibenik, Croatia.
Date: December 12, 1997.
Time: Noon.

On his farm on the outskirts, north of the city of Sibenik, a farmer named Janko Vrancic was herding his cattle when he saw a metallic object shaped like a household flatiron approach from the South-South East accompanied by a low hum and land quietly on a pasture nearby. Four humanoids described only as small and child-like in build, emerged from the object. Vrancic offered them to share his lunch, which was figs and dried ham, but they declined, telling him they were not hungry.

They had no problems in communicating as the occupants spoke a "broken" form of Croatian. After a brief visit that lasted from three to four minutes, the humanoids boarded the craft, which again with a low hum, took off towards the North-Northwest and left. When asked if he was afraid, Vrancic replied that he was not, stating that he had previously seen similar things on television. Vrancic is reported to be well-liked in his village and was described as an honest and down to earth man by his friends.

HC addendum.
Source: UFO Roundup Vol. 3 #3, DUAP Polaris Croatia.   Type: B
Comments: This case was originally and incorrectly reported in UFO Roundup as occurring on January 1998, but the above date is the correct.

Location: Saguache County, Colorado.
Date: December 14, 1997.
Time: 3:00 a.m.

A witness reported seeing a large triangular shaped craft hovering over a field. It moved slowly over the house then over some grain silos. In then came back over the house and shone a beam of white blue light out of its middle and something like a small figure was taken up into the beam. Lights around its edge flashed in rhythm then it left.

HC addendum.
Source: Christopher O'Brien.   Type: B

* * * * * * *

Location: Lakewood, Colorado.
Date: December 24, 1997.
Time: Midnight.

The witness had gotten up to obtain a glass of milk and was sitting in bed looking out the window; the moonlight illuminated the whole area. He then saw the figure of man walking directly to his window from the neighbor's yard. As the man got closer, the witness could see that he was wearing a purple shirt, blue jeans, tennis shoes and had shoulder-length blond hair and carried what appeared to be a red book.
The witness was stunned as the man appeared to walk straight through the fence and he then noticed that the man had large black slanted eyes. Afraid, the witness ran to the living room and did not see the strange figure depart.

HC addendum.
Source: Unsolved Mysteries.com   Type: E

1998

Location: Maldives Islands (exact location not given).
Date: 1998.
Time: Night.

Ibrahim Ismail and several other local youths were out fishing in one of the lagoons when they spotted what they thought was another "man" standing about a hundred feet away from them. The group immediately knew that the "man" was not a human. As it got darker and colder the witnesses stood in frozen stupor as they watched the silhouette of a giant, man-like figure approaching their position. They estimated that the "monster" was at least ten foot tall.

The group was finally able to move and ran towards the shore as fast as they could move. As they looked back, they could see that the eyes of the giant were large, bright and glowing. When the group reached the shore, they saw the giant arrive also but it suddenly disappeared.

A month later, another man was fishing in the area when he saw a similar figure suddenly come out of the water and walk on the water; it also had large glowing eyes.

HC addendum.
Source: World of The Strange.   Type: E
Comments: Attributed to have been a "Jinn" or the equivalent to a "demon" or an elemental.

Location: Houston, Texas.
Date: 1998.
Time: Night.

Pamela Stonebrook, the famous jazz singer, whose first recorded abduction is dated 1994 (but she had earlier abductions, suppressed in her memory since her childhood), reported that she later had sexual contacts with a reptilian entity. The sex was very unlike any sex with any human man.

On that night she was sleeping when suddenly she awoke and found that she was having sex with someone beautiful "like a Greek God." The man was tall, blond, light haired with a beautiful face. At first she thought that it was just a dream. But the sex was so furious that she closed her eyes and enjoyed the all-submerging feelings. And when she opened her eyes next she didn't see the beautiful blond slender man but before her she instead saw a reptilian entity with scaly skin. At that moment she understood that the alien visitor was able to camouflage its appearance. Afraid of the alien's real appearance, she cowered back. But then she heard a telepathic message from her "partner" *"With me you are safe. We have been together forever, we love each other."* Maybe they had been together forever indeed but Pamela only remembered the encounters since 1998.

Pamela described her reptilian lover as very sensitive and very intelligent, his body resembled that of the body of a snake, solid, but smooth, greenish or yellow-green in color. The eyes of the reptilian were larger than human eyes and she noticed different tints in the alien's eyes, golden, red and brown. The alien's eyes reminded her of a cat's eyes, with vertical pupils, but very beautiful. His neck was massive and on the top of his head he had a "crest" and two openings and a small bulge for a nose. Pamela finally was able to talk to her family and friends about her encounters and said, *"Frankly speaking, I don't care a rap if anyone would laugh at my story, because I myself would react the same way, before it happened to me."*

HC addendum.
Source: 'A Personal Experience; The True story of a Jazz Singer and her Extraterrestrial Contact' Pamela Stonebrook, Discovery Channel, 'Most Amazing UFO Stories' Broadcast January 22 2006 quoted by Svetlana Anina in: 'Three years in love with a reptilian' NLO, Saint Petersburg, Russia, February 27, 2006.   Type: E?

Location: Merrill, Wisconsin.
Date: 1998.
Time: Late night.

The witness who lived alone in a two bedroom apartment, was suddenly awoken and found herself looking at three intruders. Two small beings in cloaks that covered their heads that left shadows where the face should have been, and a taller one behind them. The larger one was a little slumped over due to the fact it was taller than the ceiling allowed. What surprised her was that the first thing she said was *"not again!"* From where she was on her right side laying down, she made a fist and proceeded to strike one of the smaller entities. She drew her arm back to hit one of the small ones but it suddenly held up its hands to stop her which it did. She came within an inch of its hand but could move any further, it felt as she was pushing down on an opposing "magnet."

She next remembered being led to a disk shaped object that was leaning against her bedroom wall. She then leaned into the disk shape object and found that the material she was leaning into was very soft. She sank into it. The material was black in color. The disk then lifted her into a laying position and proceeded to float toward the bedroom wall that leads outside. She thought or spoke out loud that there was no way that she could go through the wall. But she apparently went through it, it did not hurt but she could feel going through it. When they were outside, she had the thought that someone in her neighborhood would surely see what was happening. However the disk then floated up and she became very sleepy, she fought it but her eyes closed. The air was blowing on her face and she knew that she was going up.

Her next memory was of waking up in a room that was all white. No straight edges anywhere. The walls, the floor, doors and window were all rounded edges. She got up but does not remember what the bed looked like. She walked towards some curtains that were blowing in the wind and the closer she got to the curtains she realized that it was some kind of balcony. She walked outside and was amazed at the beauty of it all. The sky was pink, a beautiful pink and there were white clouds. The more she looked at the sky, the more she realized that the clouds were not like the ones on earth. It almost appeared that they were "simulated" to look like clouds. She noticed that there were ripples in the pink sky, just like when you drop an object in water and get the ripple effect. She looked down and saw a huge lake also pink in color and rippling. She looked back up and thought, "Oh I see there is a dome over us and is reflecting the water." As soon as she thought this a small being touched her hand and she became sleepy again. Her next memory was of waking up in the morning with a big chunk of her sheet in her mouth.

HC addendum. Source: Direct from the witness.   Type: G

Location: Zaporozhye, Ukraine.
Date: 1998.
Time: Various.

A young Tatar-Muslim woman named Aihsa reported entering into a series of contacts with aliens from an extraterrestrial civilization from the Big Bear constellation (Ursa Major). At one time a man-like humanoid entity entered her bedroom and communicated with the witness via telepathy. The alien was tall, about 1.8m to 1.9m in height, and was dressed in a dark overall, his face was tanned, and he had large slanted eyes, a long straight nose and a slightly protruding chin. He had five long narrow fingers. The alien said that his name was "IMA" and spoke about numerous different subjects: God, evil, and about the 'Five Laws of the Universe.' Sometimes he spoke in Russian and at times bright, living images were transmitted directly into her mind like a cinema. She always saw IMA in front of her as if it were a holographic image, she was told: *"What you see before your eyes, it's not entirely me"* He added, *"Information transmitted to you can be so exact to a degree that you will be able to almost touch it."* At one point they argued as to the nature of the aliens, Aisha stated that they were neither Gods nor demons and she then received the following answer, *"Aisha were are not Gods or demons. We are not from some unnaturally developed civilization. We are the same people as you are, but based on a different genetic base. So that qualitatively makes us people, men, but not in principle. We are not spirits, we belong to the SAINA race."*

The aliens told Aisha that they were inhabitants of a huge star system called "O-NAVAIL." Their star was located in the Great Bear Constellation. They call their star system IR-SHIIR. Their planet is called NIASU which literally means, "The dwelling place." And the center of their entire system (which is a union of five different planetary systems in different constellations) is a spiritual entity called TRON. TRON is the collective mind of all the representatives of the system. Aisha later learned that IMA was subordinated to his alien "boss" which is a female by the name of KILAMANS. IMA was supposed to take her place in this difficult system (Earth?) and have a career here.

Aisha made an astral journey to the alien planet NIASU which she found quite interesting. Everything in the planet was surrounded by stern solemnity, tranquility and as seemed to her, aristocratism. The light there was dim (cloud cover?) but the ultraviolet rays were powerful like in the hottest deserts on Earth. Their cities had many trees and plants, and they build their homes in the immediate vicinity of the water reservoirs, which was cooler than the rest of the planet. At one point Aisha asked IMA if they had created the Earth and IMA answered, *"We didn't create anything, everything is the will of the Universe, but we have kept your planet under control since the moment of its birth."* IMA also added that temporarily they had established a base in the area of the Kerch Peninsula (probably under the Sea of Azov). They are "the fifth unit of a galactic star fleet." IMA is the captain of a flagship named "The Floating Butterfly." They are engaged in guarding and studying the Universe and provide communications within. For some time now they have had responsibility over the human civilization, which was imposed to them as "curators" of Earth. On another occasion Aisha was contacted by an alien named LOESU which she considered to be the ideal of inner beauty and perfection. He was tall, dark skinned, with huge slanted eyes, no hair (his head was covered with something resembling a hood) a long nose, wide mouth and broad lips. He had very long and thin fingers. LOESU also had a very muscular chest, which Aisha saw since he wore something resembling a partially opened shirt.

When asked by local journalists why she had been chosen for contact, Aisha answered that the aliens did not have the right to communicate with any human. They have to follow definite criteria to choose the person they were to contact. The 'Contactee' must have the abilities that can play the role in expanding humanity's mind. The person must have the aptitude for comprehending the existence of other civilizations and to promote others to realize the fact. They told her that they would be transmitting information to her and that she "should write it down or draw it." The aliens told her that they had been preparing her for the final contact and had decided that she met all the requirements they insisted upon. They only asked her to pass the information on to others since they wanted to study their reaction. They also told Aisha that this was needed more by humans than by them, in fact they pointed out that "human souls were the smallest particles of the whole universal soul." That humans had lost their communication with space and must somehow restore it. At one time IMA told Aisha that evil exists only in the mind and that we had the ability to throw it out with our thoughts. That meant that humans must change their attitudes. Only by understanding their role in the Universe, can humans re-establish their connection with the Creator. The Creator will then help humans cleanse themselves from evil. But only the humans had the choice to destroy of save themselves. None of the alien races were able to interfere in this.

According to IMA, the five basic laws of the Universe are:
1. The Priority of Energy.
2. Creation.
3. Non-comparison.
4. Compatibility.
5. Eternity.

HC addendum.
Source: Elena Petriv in: "Mriya" Zaporozhye, August 3-10 2000 and Dr. Anton A. Anfalov PhD.   Type: G & F

Location: Boraceia, Sao Paolo, Brazil.
Date: January, 1998.
Time: 1:00 a.m.

After seeing a strange illuminated object hovering over a field, two of the witnesses armed with a flashlight and a gun went to the field to investigate. On their way there, two pet dogs joined them. The dogs began barking towards the direction of the water and the witness shone the flashlight in that direction. The light illuminated a strange creature about two meters tall. The creature's head was oval shaped. Its arms were curved and reached all the way down to the knees; it had long legs and had a small nose. The witnesses heard a sort of murmur-type sound coming from the creature. Around the tall creature there were several smaller similar looking ones that emitted incomprehensible sounds. At this point the tall creature began moving in the direction of the witness, who terrified, fired a shot at the creature that suddenly vanished in plain sight, along with the other smaller creatures.

HC addendum.
Source: Osmar de Freitas, GEONI.   Type: C?
High Strangeness Index: 8
Reliability of Source: 8

* * * * * * *

Location: Lecce, Italy.
Date: January 2, 1998.
Time: Night.

The witness was sleeping when he was awakened by a "thought" to go out on the balcony. Once outside, he was struck by a ball of light about three cm in size that made him fall to the floor in his room. When he recovered his senses, he noticed that he was now in an oval-shaped room, very dark. Turning around he saw a table with strange instruments on it. On the other side he saw four beings around one meter tall, gray green in color, with large eyes with vertical pupils, and they had high necks, four fingers with equally rounded tips that emitted a sort of squeaking sound. The four beings tried to approach the witness, who took an object from the table and threw it at the beings.

Then a 'door of light' appeared and a different being walked in. This being was different; he was about 1.9 m in height, with shoulder length blond hair, blue eyes and wearing a tight-fitting gray coverall. After being reassured "mentally" and invited to stay calm, the witness was made to lay on a round table of about two meters in size. Soon a triangular shaped instrument with a handle grip was passed over his face; he felt some heat

174

from it. When the being finished he instructed the witness mentally to close his eyes that he would not remember anything that happened. Once he opened his eyes he found himself back in his room, with his pajamas on upside down. Once he removed his pajamas he noticed that his face no longer showed signs of scratches that his dog had made a few days before.

HC addendum.
Source: Center for UFO Taranto.   Type: G

*   *   *   *   *   *   *

Location: Dar es Salaam, Tanzania.
Date: January 3, 1998.
Time: Night.

17-year old student, Zamei, reportedly saw a craft land or about to land, adjacent to his home. It was triangular in shape and large. As he watched, two beings emerged from it and walked past him. He called out to them *"Who are you and where are you from?"* They stopped and made a strange sound, like two glasses being rubbed together, but he could not understand them. They were covered in a flowing cloth like the Arabs wear and Zamei could not see their faces. He received no message telepathically; he just heard the sound from them. After a moment or two they left, but he did see where they went.

Zamei then walked to the craft. It was slightly raised off the ground, as though it was hovering, but the door was open and he decided to go in. The inside of the craft was a large empty room with a very bright white light which seemed to come through the walls. There were no chairs or seats, but at the far end there were buttons and switches. Apparently the witness then exited the craft and it left.

HC addendum.
Source: UFOCAT, quoting Cynthia Hind, UFO Afri News, July, 1998.
Type: B

Location: Maipu, Chile.
Date: January 31, 1998.
Time: Evening.

Several witnesses observed over the roofs of this city, several man-like figures descending from the sky, seemingly without parachutes. Motorists on the motorway saw the figures enveloped in clouds, fly towards the northwest and disappear.

HC addendum.
Source: RR0 France.   Type: E
High Strangeness Index: 7
Reliability of Source: 7
Comments: These flying aliens appeared to have been of the human variety. Similar cases exist in the US, Georgia (former USSR), France, Russia, Italy, etc.

* * * * * * *

Location: Los Cerrillos, Maipu, Chile.
Date: February 14, 1998.
Time: Daytime.

Numerous local witnesses watched seven bizarre human-like figures that glided over the area at an undetermined altitude, all gliding towards the same location and at the same time, separated only by a very short distance. They resembled parachutists and seemed to be operating some unseen apparatus above them. The seven human-like figures quickly disappeared from sight in the distance. A resident of the area supposedly took a video of the group. Apparently no one ever saw them land.

HC addendum.
Source: Revista TOC, Chile.   Type: E
Comments: Same or similar humanoids were seen in the same area in January 31.

Location: Mount Blanca, Colorado.
Date: February, 1998.
Time: Evening.

A recent attack by covert forces with a deadly Saran-like nerve gas on an "alien" spaceport under the Mount Blanca mastiff ended in disaster when the gas overcame the attacking forces and a quarter of the personnel involved had to be medically evacuated. Around thirty people from the CSETI group saw several flying objects nearby. At the same time Greer and Sheri Adamiak went up the trail alone, and remote viewed several entities inside the mountain.

When they came back down the trail to get the rest of the group they all saw Greer disappear in a "gold light" which seemed to be coming from above them. Then a semi-circle of a dozen alien elders of all different sizes, surrounded Greer who seemed to then disappear. The aliens then communicated with Greer. They told him that they were under attack in the mountain by covert military forces. The experience lasted for about twenty minutes.

HC addendum.
Source: Dr. Steven Green, CSETI.   Type: G?

* * * * * * *

Location: Sorocaba, Sao Paolo, Brazil.
Date: February, 1998.
Time: Night.

Celio Lima Batista was on his way home late one night and was walking along a desolate field, when he noticed some lights and figures behind him. Thinking he was going to be robbed, he turned around to face his followers and was confronted by a huge, two-meter tall figure, with large fiery eyes, a huge head, and pincer like hands. He lunged at the creature and took several swings at it, but they all seemed to miss. Tired, he stepped back stunned. Suddenly the huge creature lunged at him, beating him senseless. He was later found unconscious and was taken to a nearby hospital where several large bruises were found on his back and was treated for a wound on one of his fingers.

HC addendum.
Source: Marco Antonio Reynoso, Fundacion COSMOS.   Type: E
High Strangeness Index: 7
Reliability of Source: 7
Comments: I wonder if the creature acted in self-defense or did it mean to injure the unfortunate witness?

177

Location: Las Palmas, Fajardo, Puerto Rico.
Date: March, 1998.
Time: 5:00 a.m.

Felix Polanco had gone to work in a field at a construction site and had boarded the excavating equipment when as he turned the engine on, he saw a short gray thin figure run from behind the machine and quickly disappear into a nearby wooded area. The figure was described as about 3-feet tall, with long thin arms & fingers with a large pear shaped head that ended in a pointy chin. The being did not appear to be wearing any clothing and was totally gray in color & smooth.

HC addendum.
Source: Jorge Martin Evidencia OVNI #17.   Type: E

* * * * * * *

Location: Limay Mahuida, La Pampa, Argentina.
Date: March, 1998.
Time: 6:00 p.m.

The witness, who requested anonymity, was working for an Italian mining/minerals firm in the area, observed an enormous elliptical-shaped and luminous object on the ground, about a 100 meters away from his location. He was also able to see several very tall and thin entities that were moving around the object at great speed. They seemed to have been able to jump from place to another as if completely weightless. Eventually the entities returned back into the object and it left.

HC addendum.
Source: RAO Argentina Casuistica 98, quoting Group "Hemisferios."
Type: B

Location: Near Voronezh, Russia.
Date: March 4, 1998.
Time: Night.

According to local communication and media, local inhabitants observed the fall of an unknown object trailing a plume of smoke. It apparently crashed in the area of Arkchangelsk and Bershev. A large-scale search and rescue operation was launched involving several police and government units. A crashed UFO and dead humanoids were reportedly found and transported to a secure area. No other information.

HC addendum.
Source: Anton Anfalov quoting media sources.   Type: H
Comments: Recent information received by the source indicates that what crashed there could had been most likely a cruise missile or other type of missile accidentally launched from a military aircraft that had inexplicably changed its flight path. Obviously the military did not want to assume responsibility for such an irresponsible act. There is a military proving range in the region.

*   *   *   *   *   *   *

Location: Rho, Lombardy, Italy.
Date: March 8, 1998.
Time: Afternoon.

A farmer saw a white object in the shape of an upside down pear hovering above a field. He called his wife and both watched the object for about half an hour. During the episode, a hatch slid open and an occupant emerged. He was described as only about 40 inches tall, with two huge black eyes. The being floated in the air close to the object for about ten minutes, then re-entered the object which suddenly rose vertically and left at high speed.

HC addendum.
Source: UFO Roundup Vol. 3 #13.   Type: B

Location: Thuringen, Germany.
Date: March 28, 1998.
Time: Night.

The witness, not knowing how, suddenly found himself sitting on a comfortable chair or couch. The room was extremely illuminated and as he looked up, he saw six strange figures looking down on him. He could only see the facial features of one of the creatures, which appeared "dwarf-like." It appeared to have normal eyes, ears, nose and neck. The back of its head appeared to have a large curved bump-like protrusion. The couch appeared to be free-floating on the floor in front of a large screen display. It showed what appeared to be a space scene with the highest quality colors he had ever seen.

Linguistic communication with the humanoids was made with a kind of "language computer" the voice was clearly understandable, slow and in flowing German. The figures left the room and the witness was left alone to ask questions. On the screen there appeared a view of the solar system. He was shown what appeared to be a huge floating space station around the moon and numerous small flying objects. He was instructed to push several buttons, which enable him to hear detailed technical explanations.

The aliens told the witness that they came from a planet (name not understood), which could be possibly be detected by humans with today's radio telescopes, however it was thousands of light years away. They pointed out however that distance was insignificant for them since they use "nine dimensions" to travel. They also mentioned that there were countless of inhabited planets with intelligent life in the universe.

He was told that many of the alien's races were genetically mixed with humans. The whole time there he saw free floating images of what appeared to be sites in ancient temples in South America during festive periods in the past. He also saw old locomotive engines, circa 1890. However he was not shown future images. Soon he was submitted to different physical examinations. Soon he was suffering from a terrific headache and at that point a figure wearing a tight-fitting dark green coverall approached him. It had extremely thin legs, large lash-less staring eyes; it was totally silent and emotionless. The witness was given a type of pill; within minutes the headache was gone.

Soon after that he was apparently shown what appeared to have been a hologram, which displayed three-dimensional images of the human body. A round black hole appeared in which the witness inserted his hand, as he did the image of the hand seemed to divide itself into nine separate images. After that, still in front of the white wall, an image of larger dark hole was shown, in which the light appeared to be absorbed. Then three-dimensional images of what appeared to be a computer screen with instructions in English appeared in front of the white wall.

Feeling very exhausted the witness was given additional pills. Many of the formulas displayed on the white wall were unintelligible and he could not understand many of it. He was apparently shown formulas and images having to do with gravity and anti-gravity devices. He was eventually released by the aliens back to his home.

HC addendum.
Source: Greyhunter UFO site, Germany.   Type: G

* * * * * * *

Location: Orkelljunga, Skane, Sweden.
Date: April 4, 1998.
Time: Early morning.

The witness, Jan Olsson, was on his way to deliver a load of fish to the central market and was traveling south on the E4 Road that leads straight to Orkelljunga. At this point, Olsson suddenly noticed a strange craft approaching over the road. He immediately thought it was a normal aircraft experiencing engine trouble, but noticed that it was shaped like a long narrow fuselage, white as snow, approaching in a very steep approach. He came close in dialing the emergency phone number but stopped himself, making sure he did not call in a "false alarm." The strange craft was moving slowly, just under 30 kilometers per hour, it then disappeared behind an embankment to the left of the road. There was hardly any other traffic on the road so he stopped his truck, expecting to see smoke and a ball of fire rising from behind the embankment.

However as he approached the area, he saw the strange object again, this time flying a few meters above the embankment and it glided over

181

the road, moving very slowly. This time he did see the object very clearly. It was long and narrow, with narrow swept back curved wings located on the front center of the object, curving back towards the rear of the object. He now saw several large windows along the side of the object, everything was completely white.

On the front of the object he saw a sort of large clear cockpit and inside were two creatures with large heads and large dark eyes, apparently sitting behind a command console, one of the creatures is looking directly at Olsson! He noticed that the creatures were hairless and had round faces. The black eyes could had been dark-colored goggles (Olsson thought that was appropriate since it was very sunny).

At this point Olsson was afraid and fumbled with the pedal and was unable to leave the area, his legs shaking. He noticed that the object was headed towards some factory buildings on the right side of the road apparently on a collision course. Olsson lost sight of the object behind the embankment on the right side of the road, and he immediately drove away from the area, completely convinced that he had seen "creatures from an alien world."

HC addendum.
Source: Clas Svahn citing Anders Berglund UFO-Aktuellt, #2, 2015.
Type: A

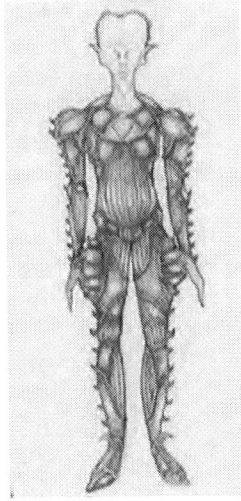

Location: Bustuchin, Romania.
Date: April 7, 1998.
Time: Evening.

Hearing noises outside his house, 60-year old farmer Gheorghe Cucaila stepped out and saw a tall man-like figure resembling a "manikin" standing on a nearby field. It stood still for a moment and then it rose up into the air without any means of propulsion. It quickly disappeared from sight into the distance.

HC addendum.
Source: Romanian UFO Network.   Type: E

* * * * * * *

Location: Near Netanya, Israel.
Date: April 10, 1998.
Time: Evening.

At the same time that several saw a flashing yellow light above a wheat field, residents reported seeing tall glowing human-like figures that seemed to be watching the farm animals which were acting very nervous. No other information.

HC addendum.
Source: Gil Bar, Timeline of UFOs in Israel.   Type: D

Location: Las Candelarias ranch, Sancti Spiritus, Las Villas, Cuba.
Date: April 17, 1998.
Time: 3:10 a.m.

51-year old Damaso Rosales (involved in other encounters), was awakened by lights which approach his location from the southeast. As they got closer he could see that it was an object with multicolored flashing lights and silent which began to descend near his house which was located on a hill located about 1km from town. As he approached to within five meters from the object he could see that it was egg-shaped, silvery in color. Immediately he began to hear a very "soft and sweet melody" as the object began to cover itself in a sort of thick mist, covering the lower section of the object completely, thus Rosales was unable to see if the object was resting on the ground. Suddenly a bright beam of light from the object illuminated Rosales and paralyzed him. Everything then became dark and Rosales felt "people" around him that touched him and apparently measured his body and arms.

Later the light turned on again, while he could still hear the soft melody. Slowly the object then began to rise from the ground and then at high speed disappeared towards the north. While he was close to the object he also heard a humming sound, like that of a "sophisticated engine." He also felt a warm air apparently also emanating from the craft. He estimated the object's diameter as that of 25-30 meters. It was found that the grass at the scene of the landing "was different" than from other places.

HC addendum.
Source: Gabriel Mesa & Marcos Rodriguez in Revista Signos #45, Cuba pages 154-155, from Orestes Collado Girbau orestes100350@yahoo.es
Type: G?
Comments: The witness was to have further contacts.

* * * * * * *

Location: Gamboa da Bica, Bahia, Brazil.
Date: April 20, 1998.
Time: 7:30 p.m.

At least twenty witnesses watched a UFO on the ground less than fifty meters from the River Jacuruna. At first it was nothing but a weak light, it began to grow in size and then when about 60 cm in diameter it began shooting out colored beams of light in different directions.

A few minutes later, a second light appeared, much larger and more fluorescent than the first one, there appeared to be small colored images floating around its vicinity. Seconds later, some of the witnesses noticed a humanoid figure about 1.8m in height standing close to the lights on the riverside. One of the witnesses attempted to approach the location and ran away terrified as additional figures now appeared next to the first one by the river's edge.

The figures approached the witness followed by the hovering colored balls of light. The lights then flew to the other side of the river and shone circular beams of light on the surface of the river as if searching for something. Moments later, the larger light dimmed, taking the form of a luminous tube, it then disappeared, and the other light also disappeared at this point.

HC addendum.
Source: Alberto Romero, Portal UFO-Genesis.   Type: C

* * * * * * *

Location: Bridlington, Yorkshire, England.
Date: May, 1998.
Time: 3:00 a.m.

The main witness and his partner had a day out in Bridlington and stopped off to visit the Rudston Monolith on the way home. He remembers touching the Monolith and getting a kind of electric shock from it. He laughed about it at the time and during the drive home. Afterwards he felt a bit 'strange,' kind of giddy and not quite with it.

They went to bed that night and around 3 a.m. he woke to a very bright light beaming down on him. The next thing he knew he was in a strange room without windows with a tall human-looking being who (without speaking words, but he understood) told him to follow him and not to be afraid, which he did. He led him to another room with a window and told him to change into some clothes (like white surgeons clothes) which were laid out, and that he would come for him. He changed into the clothes and while he was waiting, he had a look out of the window, through which he could see the Earth, which he remembers looked quite far away. As he was looking at the earth, the being came back and again asked him to follow him, which he did, to another room which was very large and had a large open space in which were placed sofas and chairs. He was told to sit down on a sofa which he did, next to two other humans. Then another being spoke to them (again he heard it in his head) and asked them to talk about (amongst themselves) what they thought about the leaders of our planet, and did we think they were leading us and the planet in the 'right direction.'

He remembers that the woman sitting next to him was from Sheffield, because he asked her where she was from and if she knew why they were there. She told him she went to bed just like him and the next

185

thing she knew she was here. After they had talked for a while about earth the being who he had met initially, came and took him back to the room where he had changed clothes and told him to change back into his pajamas which he did, The being then came back (he looked very human except he was taller than most humans and fairer) and took him to another room where there was another being who had a device in his hand. He again was told not to be afraid, and the being with the device approached and put it on his earlobe. His "guide" being told him that the device was to put a chip in him so they would know where he was and would be able to communicate with him. He then took him to a kind of chamber, again telling him not to be afraid, and that it would send him home.

He told him not to talk about his experience, he said for his own benefit, as people on earth would not believe him if he did. The next thing he knew he was awaking in his bed. In the morning his girlfriend, before he had a chance to say anything, said *"I had the strangest feeling in the night that you were gone, you just weren't here."*

HC addendum.
Source:http://alienabductionhelp.com/phpBB3/viewtopic.php??f=5&t =387   Type: G

* * * * * * *

Location: Trans-Danubian region, Hungary.
Date: May 2, 1998.
Time: Night.

A couple, Stephen and Suzan, were driving home late at night. Stephen who was driving, noticed that the trees alongside the road were unusually bathed in a strong light. Curious he slowed the car down. Suzan's next memory of the event is of sitting in the middle of the road inside the vehicle, and looking at a blinding light over the roadway ahead. A tall human-shaped figure was walking towards them from the bright light. The tall figure approached the passenger side window were Suzan is sitting and told her, *"Do not be afraid, it's ok, but you should come with me."* Out of instinct, Suzan turned and looked at Stephen thinking it might have been an accident and looked inquiringly at Stephen, who seemed frozen and unable to react. The tall man then says to Suzan, *"He stays, don't worry, everything will be alright."* Her next memory is of entering a metallic slightly rising corridor, bathed in strong light, the light was so bright that she was unable to see details on the walls. The tall man walked in front of her and from somewhere behind her a shorter thin figure appeared.

186

Her next memory is being in a small room, accompanied by a man who apparently "interviewed" her, asking several questions which she responded, what she was asked, Suzan is unable to remember. Later she found herself in another room where several small figures no taller than 1 or 1.5 m, stood around looking up at her, they had large bluish skull-shaped heads. She saw another taller figure, sitting on a couch-like setting. According to Suzan, this creature's face was hideous, its eyes were frightening, greenish in color which emitted an eerie glow. Its lower eyelids were made of a jelly-like substance. The room was well-lit and when the shorter figures went out the room it became translucent. She could see outside from behind the translucent wall and realized that the object was moving up at incredible speed. She could see the trees, road and the car with her husband below, she then saw the city in the distance and then the horizon, and she was not able to recall anything further.

Her next memory is of standing next to the car feeling a cool breeze. She then heard Stephen's voice, *"What the hell was that?"* She frankly answered that she had no idea. Stephen could only recall a bright light floating above the road and his wife jumping out of the car watching the light, which quickly disappeared above the trees at an incredible speed.

HC addendum.
Source: Kriston Endre RYUFOR Foundation Hungary.   Type: G

* * * * * * *

Location: Fort Walton Beach, Florida.
Date: May 13, 1998.
Time: Daytime.

A day after several witnesses reported seeing a triangular shaped craft hovering over the Gulf of Mexico, just offshore, south of town, the same witnesses reported seeing men in frogmen suits in the water, in the same area where the lights from the object had been shining down. There was also unusual military aircraft activity in the area.

HC addendum.
Source: CAUS (Citizens against UFO secrecy).   Type: D
Comments: Military operation?

Location: North Conway Lake, New Hampshire.
Date: May 13, 1998.
Time: Around noon.

Dr. Gary Lincoff and his wife were boating on the lake near the North Conway mines. They had paddled into a deep hidden canyon, entering between huge boulders, which formed a narrow gateway. Later they pulled the boat up onto the narrow beach and sat down for lunch. Soon they felt the air vibrate strongly like an explosion's aftershock. Dr Lincoff climbed up the boulder in order to check the area. After reaching the top, which was, split and he could look out through a sharp cleft in the rock.

Two large, shiny round craft floated on the water just beyond the narrow entrance to the cove. Stunned he scrambled down and got his wife. Both climbed to the well-hidden perspective. Both craft were 50 - 60 ft wide and about 20 ft thick. Round, black-edged ports covered the rim at a distance of very four feet. On the topsides, hatch covers were open and moving slowly around its surface were spindly creatures that moved in unison like robots. On both ships over their heads from a central position was a slowly rotating hoop-shaped object. When the hoop reached a point directly opposite the husband and wife it stopped. So did the creatures, they stared toward the couple's hiding place and remained motionless. Sure that the creatures had spotted them they ducked down.

They hid until a deer approached the edge of the lake to drink. They then went up for another look and noticed that the hoop was rotating once more, operated by a creature standing below it, which wore a small, scarlet head covering. All were small and wore close fitting dark suits and blue helmets. One creature placed a shiny green hose in the water, drawing in water and at the same time discharging something from another hose. Again the hoop stopped and all the figures froze. They stared toward the couple on the rock. Husband and wife ducked down, moments later they inched up for another look.

Two hours later, dazed, and confused the couple ambled back to their boat unable to account for those two hours.

HC addendum.
Source: IRAAP Encounters.   Type: C or G?

Location: Hod Hasharon, Israel.
Date: May 14, 1998.
Time: Night.

A large plate shaped object with balls of light around its perimeter hovered over the area and projected a beam of light toward the ground as if searching for something. That same night a local resident was confronted by a short creature, almost transparent in nature and with a huge head with fine lines running through it, above the creature's head was a shimmering cloud and something like the old Hebrew alphabet letter 'Zhbim.'

HC addendum.
Source: Gil Bar UFOs in Israel Timeline.　　　　　　　Type: D

* * * * * * *

Location: Near Petrozavodsk, Russia.
Date: Summer, 1998.
Time: Morning.

Farmer Igor Nikolayevich Petukhov was working on the fields when suddenly his attention was drawn to a gradually increasing metallic sound. Looking around him he saw at about forty meters away a bluish luminous "strip" hovering in the air. The object then slowly moved behind the nearby storage shed causing a degree of uneasiness on Igor. The witness then put down his tools and walked towards a nearby barn in order to hide from the strange object. However several seconds later, something flew towards Igor from behind the storage shed. To Igor's surprise it was a very small humanoid figure about 25-30cm in height.

At first Igor attempted to run away but he could not move his body as it felt as it was being held down. The small entity hovered at about three meters from Igor. The figure was proportional in nature and was dressed in tight-fitting coveralls. It wore a black cap on its head. Its head was small, about five cm in diameter, black eyes, and a slit-like mouth and a hardly distinguishable nose. During the entire speechless encounter, the small figure hovered in front of Igor, using up and down motions.

According to Igor, as soon as the small figure flew over his head, his fear vanished completely, replaced now by curiosity. After about fifteen minutes, the small figure unexpectedly flew away. Next day as he worked in the garden, Igor Nikolayevich saw two small figures, similar to the one he had seen the day before. The same taciturn mutual observation was repeated. On the third day Igor again saw hovering above the porch a small figure that appeared to be looking around, giving Igor the impression that "the little fellow" was looking for him. As soon as the small humanoid saw Igor, it flew up near his head and minutes later, disappeared.

After the described events Igor Nikolayevich began to notice changes in his body, which were officially confirmed by relatives and his doctor. After his contacts, he no longer suffered from chronic heart disease.

HC addendum.
Source: Aleksey Popov, 'Strange Visitors in Karelia.'   Type: C?

* * * * * * *

Location: Austin, Texas.
Date: June 18, 1998.
Time: Night.

After a powerful storm and twister passed over the area, the two witnesses were out surveying the damage. As they drove along an isolated road they came upon a hovering saucer shaped object. As they approached the object on foot, two humanoids (undescribed) suddenly confronted them. The humanoids asked them what had just happened. They wanted to know what the twisting funnel was. The witnesses explained the nature of tornados to the aliens and their next memory was of lying on the ground and seeing the object shoot away at high speed.

HC addendum.
Source: EBE On-line.   Type: C or G?

* * * * * * *

Location: Ulldemolins, Terragona, Spain.
Date: June 21, 1998.
Time: Midnight.

A man named Augustin was walking his dogs along an isolated field when he noticed a bright light to his left. The bright white rotating light approached and disappeared towards the nearby road, apparently landing. The witness could hear a moderate humming. Suddenly the light went dark and two humanoids became visible both walking on the road in the direction of the witness.

The beings wore fluorescent helmets and boots and tight fitting silvery outfits, no other details were visible. The dogs were barking in a panicked state.

Terrified, the witness and his dogs ran towards the opposite direction, not looking back at the humanoids. The night before another local had seen a potent white light hovering over the house.

HC addendum. Source: Josep Guijarro, Karma-7 #295.   Type: C

* * * * * * *

Location: Between Petro-Svistunovo and Orlovskoye, Ukraine.
Date: Early July, 1998.
Time: Night.

A group of fishermen and their families including Sergey Kalinichenko were camped out on the banks of the River Dnepr. One late night, Sergey and his oldest daughter, Tatyana spotted a pulsating light between the trees. The pulsating light was located somewhere on the right side of the wooded area; it seemed to pulsate at intervals of about 5-10 seconds. They observed the light for quite a long time and others in the camp also woke up to see the light.

30-40 minutes later the witnesses noticed several humanoid figures moving in between the trees. The humanoids were dressed in white overalls and were moving in a strange manner, apparently floating just above the ground. In total the witnesses counted four humanoids. The witnesses debated as to what the figures were, some thought they were hunters and went back to sleep. However about an hour later Sergey was awakened by his daughter Tatyana and younger daughter Irina. The witnesses again saw the strange pulsating light in the trees. The male campers were awakened, and armed themselves with axes and sticks and rushed towards the pulsating light. As they approached, the light grew dimmer until it was totally dark.

When the men reached the clearing where the light was emanating from, they saw a strange triangular shape craft flying from east to west at an altitude of a five story building. The triangular craft was sharply positioned downward, and multicolored lights flashed on the top section. The craft was moving slowly and disappeared behind some trees. The men then returned to the camp. The same or similar object was seen again on July 10, 1998 at 11:30 p.m.

HC addendum.
Source: Zaporozhye UFO Research group.   Type: D
Comments: This area is considered an anomalous zone called "The Varvarovka anomalous area."

Location: Near Ponta Grossa, Parana, Brazil.
Date: July, 1998.
Time: Afternoon.

Two explorers reported entering a tunnel in an isolated area and spending five days in a subterranean city of more or less fifty inhabitants. During the tour, the men were provided with fruits grown hydroponically underground. The men also claimed to have entered another tunnel in Rincano and discovered a staircase underground leading to four different levels.

In another case, a mountain guide in nearby Joinville, said that many times luminous flying discs have been seen around the opening of the tunnel and that he had heard a chorus of men and women singing underground near the tunnel entrance. Then he encountered a group of subterraneans who were standing near the tunnel. They were white with red beards and long hair, very muscular. As he approached them they fled.

Another explorer claims he encountered a beautiful young woman in a tunnel who did not appear more than 20-years old. She spoke to him Portuguese and said she was more than 2,500 years old. Another man encountered a similar tunnel in the Serra do Mar mountains, and sampled a mysterious fruit from an orchid. He also saw several "subterraneans" talking to each other in high-pitched voices in an unknown language.

HC addendum.
Source: SOCEX Brazil.   Type: E?

* * * * * * *

Location: Aguas de Pau, San Miguel, Azores Islands.
Date: July 8, 1998.
Time: Morning.

During a peregrination to the shrine of Aguas de Pau a nun, announced that she had been contacted by a 'beautiful maiden' dressed in a beautiful flowing white dress. The maiden spoke of the chaotic situation facing the planet.

Immediately after the encounter, dozens saw a bizarre luminous oval-shaped phenomenon that seemed to cover the sun, it occurred repeatedly giving the strange effect of the sun appearing to blink intermittently, however with virtually no luminosity, somehow eclipsing the rays of the sun.

This phenomenon lasted for about six minutes; one of the witnesses included the local parish priest and was filmed by a local resident.

HC addendum.
Source: Apovni, Portugal.
Comments: Shades of Fatima.

Type: E or F?

* * * * * * *

Location: Puerto Rico (exact location not given).
Date: July 11, 1998.
Time: After midnight.

The witness was sleeping when she suddenly heard a masculine voice that woke her up. She then began to float towards the ceiling. A tall human like figure with black hair (previously encountered) accompanied her, holding her by the hand. Somehow they went through the ceiling and she saw something resembling a "cloud" floating overhead. They entered this "cloud" and she found herself in a large room with windows and bench-like seats all around it. The room was dull silver in color and there wasn't anybody else present. The man then took into a semi-dark room and told her to wait there. The room suddenly became hot and then cold in a matter of seconds. The man then returned and they exited the room. She was able to look out one of the windows and saw a view resembling that of "Alaska" (snow covered mountains). She also saw a sea that had something like a waterspout in the middle and within the waterspout she could see, trees, rivers, vegetation, etc.

She was then taken to a wall and a door suddenly appeared, she entered the door and found herself in a metallic room with a metallic "table" floating in the mid-air. In the room where three of the short gray creatures, this time wearing the white coveralls with a red star-like insignia on their chests. Another tall human was present; he wore a tight-fitting light blue metallic coverall, with a silvery belt with a buckle with what appeared to be glistening quartz like stone. He wore gloves, but his shoes seemed to be part of the one-piece metallic uniform. Only his face was visible on his body. She remembered encountering this man before. He told her that they were going to remove a cyst from her body, and promised not to leave any scars. She then apparently fell asleep and woke up later on her bed.

HC addendum.
Source: Lucy Guzman.

Type: G

193

Location: Juruaia, Minas Gerais Brazil.
Date: July 14, 1998.
Time: 10:45 p.m.

Local rancher, J. S. C. had been noticing that some of his hogs were turning up missing. One night as he stood watch he heard sounds coming from behind the bush and a bright yellow light came shining through. Thinking that it was a tractor he went to investigate. There a disc shaped object on the ground confronted him.

Next to the craft he saw a small humanoid that appeared to be collecting vegetation from the ground and putting it inside a luminous blue sphere. The witness hid behind a tree and observed the scene. The small humanoid had a huge head in comparison to the rest of its body, a dark thin body, and long thin arms with three fingered hands.

The craft was disc shaped and emitted a strong heat wave. Suddenly a bright beam of blue light shone on the witness temporarily blinding him. After about six minutes he was able to see again but the figure and the object were now gone.

HC addendum.
Source: Revista Brasileira de Ufologia.   Type: C

Location: Vieste, Puglia, Italy.
Date: August, 1998.
Time: 2:00 a.m.

Six friends were walking along the waterfront after attending a party watched a luminous object in a descending trajectory. It continued on a horizontal flight and then descended vertically over a small nearby islet. The object hovered changing colors from blue to yellow and then red.

Thirty minutes later, one of the witnesses confronted a strange figure standing behind the automobile. He described it as a black humanoid, lacking eyes, nose, or mouth. It had long arms ending in a point. He did not see hands or feet. The figure suddenly ran away in the opposite direction of the witness at very high speed.

HC addendum.
Source: CISU Puglia.   Type: C?

Location: Lake Stensjomala, Blekinge, Sweden.
Date: August, 1998.
Time: Afternoon.

Ingvar Andersson was picking wild mushrooms in a wooded area near the lake, and had followed a trail into a pristine forest full of emerald green moss, crumbling twisted trees and shapeless boulders.

As he followed a narrow dirt road through the pine forest in the direction of the lake, he suddenly saw a strange figure cross the path from the right at about thirty meters ahead. Not understanding what he was seeing, he stared at it. The figure was barely one meter in height with a pointy head, and quite evenly gray from top to bottom. Both Ingvar and the strange creature stood and stared at each other for maybe half a minute, but it may have been much longer as Ingvar felt almost paralyzed, to Ingvar it felt almost as 'if time had stood still,' it was difficult to explain. The creature then walked into the woods on the left side of the trail. It resembled a tiny "shrunken" man, but still not human.

He really does not remember any details of the face except that it was gray in color like the rest of the body. Ingvar was now determined to catch up with the small figure and rushed quickly to the trees. He followed a trail where he had last seen the creature disappear into the trees. He went right up to a small lake, and then turned back, the whole time looking in all directions, but the elusive gray figure was nowhere in sight. After the event Ingvar returned to the location on several occasions but never again saw the figure again.

However on February 1999, he had gone out for a walk, the sky was dark and the snow was white between the trees. As he walked near the forest the dark sky suddenly and inexplicably began to brighten. Ingvar felt confused, as the pale light turned into an attractive blue glow and lit up the forest in front of him. Thinking that the forest was burning he ran to his car and drove quickly away but as he looked back he realized that there was no fire, but the strange light in the forest was now almost silver metallic in nature filling the whole forest.

HC addendum.
Source: http://www.hemmetsjournal.se/Manniskor/Den-Lilla-varelsen-stannade-framfor-mig/

Type: D?

*   *   *   *   *   *   *

Location: Szyelkino, Kazantip peninsula, Sea of Azov, Crimea, Ukraine.
Date: August, 1998.
Time: Evening.

Traffic police captain, Vasiliy had been fishing for bullhead at a small bay near Tatarskaya bay on a Sunday evening and satisfied with his catch, he began collecting his fishing gear, intending to prepare some fish soup. At that same moment, he saw a strange creature at a distance of 30-40 meters away, straight across from him, coming out of the waters of the Sea of Azov.

The creature was humanoid in appearance, looking evidently like a woman. Her body was completely white and he estimated her age to be around thirty years old. She had huge inhuman blue eyes on an incredibly beautiful face. She stared intently at the witness. The strange woman was not walking but rather floating over the surface of the water and her arms were stretched forward. Vasiliy crossed himself, but the female figure did not vanish. She had long black hair falling down below her waist. The woman raised her arms and said in a tender voice, *"Vasya, come to me, I have everything in here"*

The witness felt paralyzed, unable to move any part of his body. Like hypnotized and under total control, his body began slowly approaching the strange woman. When the distance from her was only several meters,

197

Vasiliy finally snapped out of his stupor and reacted fiercely, screaming obscenities at the woman, who slowly turned around and disappeared under the surface of the water, Vasiliy then regained control of his body and he was able to move on his own accord. Terribly frightened he ran home not remembering how he got there. Upon arriving home he realized that he had left his fishing rod and catch behind. He never told anybody about what occurred until 2004.

HC addendum.
Source: Vladimir Zheleznyak, 'Secrets & Mysteries of the Crimea,' 2004.
Type: E

* * * * * * *

Location: Peldehue, Colina, Chile.
Date: August, 1998.
Time: Various.

Five young people, Hector Contreras Fuentes, 19, Nestor Berrocal Diaz, 29, Maritza de la Cerda, 16, and the brothers Manuel & Claudio Silva Baeza were camping in this picturesque area and had set up a tent to stay for the night. While several of them collected twigs and branches near the tent one of them noticed a "person" looking down at them from a rocky cliff above. Together they watched the stranger for a good while. They described him as tall, approximately 1.9 m in height, all dressed in a tight-fitting white diving suit, however they could not see his feet or any facial features.

At first the group did not think it was anything anomalous and continued their work. Soon they noticed that the stranger was now crouched down and still staring at them. One of the witnesses became somewhat irate and began yelling at the stranger, but this one apparently ignored him. Once it stood up again the group noticed that the figure was very slim and athletic in built. A strange nervous calm now overcame the group and they realized that there was something definitely strange about the figure. Suddenly the figure seemed too vanished in plain sight of the group. They immediately searched the area but found no trace of the strange entity.

Later around 6:00 p.m., the strange figure was again spotted on top of the rocks, this time its clothing seemed whiter and shinier and difficult to look at directly. At the group stared at the figure it suddenly outstretched its arms and rose up from the rocks disappearing from sight as the stunned witnesses watched. The group now really became nervous and some of them proposed to leave the area and return to Santiago, however calmer heads prevailed and the group stayed.

Around midnight, as the group was chatting around the campfire, the figure again appeared on top of the rocks. This time he was totally fluorescent in appearance, this time it seemed to perform several incomprehensible movements or maneuvers with his arms and hands. The group remained sitting around the campfire staring in disbelief. Still staring at the group the stranger again spread his arms and rose slightly over the rocks floating slowly back & forth. At the same time the figure appeared to "contort" its body in a way that it resembled that of a "ballet dancer." Suddenly the figure pointed its hands towards the ground and at the same time there was a loud booming sound apparently from the nearby military training range, this apparently caused the figure to vanish instantly.

Later that morning, several of the group who had not been able to sleep decided to explore their surroundings, only Maritza remained behind in the tent. As the group climbed the rocky slopes the luminous man-like figure again appeared ahead of them on top of the rocks, still staring at them. The figure again began to float in mid-air and to contort its body and move its arms around. Suddenly the figure began to slowly float towards the four men and approached to within 30 meters from their location. After what seemed like an eternity to the witnesses the figure suddenly began to float back to the rock. At this point the four men ran down the slope to the tent.

Around 5 a.m., the group heard loud and heavy footsteps outside their tent. Terrified, none of them dared to look outside. After a few moments the heavy footsteps left the campsite. The group then finally went to sleep and awoke around noon the next day. They soon packed their belongings and left the area. For some reason the lone female witness insists that they had seen the apparition of the "Virgin Mary" but the others do not agree and think that it was some other type of anomalous entity.

HC addendum.
Source: Osvaldo Murray in: Revista Revelacion Año 3 #32.   Type: E
Comments: Translated by Albert S. Rosales.

Location: Garrucha, Almeria, Spain.
Date: Early August, 1998.
Time: 1:15 a.m.

The witness, Albert Jean de Vilez, had not been able to sleep due to the oppressive heat, tired of tossing and turning on his bed, he decided to take a stroll around his chalet, located on the outskirts of town on the way to Mojacar. He decided to head towards some abandoned ruins located about 300 meters from his home. There was a wide field and a very large rock next to the ruins; he sat on top of the rock.

As he sat on the rock he observed a brilliant bluish light above some nearby crumbling stone walls, at first he thought it was some type of motion detection alarm until he realized that no one would install such a safety device on a ruined structure. Then he heard footsteps around him, he couldn't see anybody but he continued to hear the footsteps. There were no large trees or shrubs around him and there was a bright full moon so there was perfect visibility, but he still wasn't able to see anybody.

Suddenly he felt cold, and he had been out of the house for about 15 minutes and decided to return, since the temperature had strangely dropped very quickly. As he walked back to the house he remembered the bluish light that he had previously seen, he looked towards the ruined structure and verified that the light was no longer there, and he could no longer hear the footsteps. Even though concerned he ignored the events and he continued on his way home, however on his way there he felt a strange abrasive sensation on the left side of his tongue.

The next morning de Vilez went to purchase some lottery tickets at a local business but was told that as to the rules, that they could not process all tickets purchased after noon. Very surprised and confused he looked at his watched which only displayed 10:15 a.m. Now convinced that something very strange had indeed occurred that night and contacted some local investigators which attempted to hypnotically regress him using a local professional on two occasions but to no avail. They decided to postpone the third section for May.

On the third try he was able to recall that he had suddenly found himself inside a light or a 'machine.' He was very confused and didn't know how he got there. He felt somebody or something next to him but could not see anything. He was sitting down and could not get up. He was sitting on what resembled a sort of plastic chair, very comfortable, but he was still unable to move. He was only able to move his head. Suddenly he was able to see something moving in the room, and noticed what he described as extremely bizarre creatures, not animals or machines, something that he had never seen before. They somehow resembled "giant bipedal squids," but not really squids, they are something totally different. Suddenly he was unable to see the creatures

200

seen a strange fog had now enveloped the 'room.' He felt as he were being examined but was unable to see who was examining him. He felt unseen 'hands' touching him and examining his eyes. He was very scared, and felt the creatures lift his hands. They keep probing and poking him and he was still unable to move.

Suddenly he heard a very soft humming sound and saw a blinking light in front of him. At this point the unseen entities grabbed him and then they were suddenly gone and he was back on the field, walking home. No additional information was obtained.

HC addendum.
Source: Vicente Vaquero Lorca in: MAS ALLA. Type: G?

* * * * * * *

Location: Claut, Pordenone, Italy.
Date: August 8, 1998.
Time: 5:30 a.m.

Five witnesses spotted a UFO and a flying humanoid over a soccer field. Two farmers, the groundskeeper, and a pair of tourists watched the flying humanoid overhead and rejoin the hovering object. The craft then shot straight up into the sky.

One of the farmers, Angelo F, was having breakfast when he saw an object of many colors. Angelo the groundskeeper saw the object as it flew overhead and hovered over the field.

The witnesses described the humanoid as having a large head and a small body "like a puppet." It was about 4-feet tall, wearing what appeared to be V-shaped body armor equipped with a luminous backpack.

HC addendum.
Source: Antonio Chiumento Type: B

Location: Near Massape, Ceara, Brazil.
Date: August 12, 1998.
Time: Evening.

Five local youths reported seeing a huge object land near the Mondubim lagoon. Three humanoids resembling robots exited the object and proceeded to collect shrubs and rocks. The youths fled the area and notified some nearby military units, however they failed to locate anything.

Later on, one of the witnesses Joao Lira decided to return to the scene and saw the same object on the ground. As he approached it, he suddenly felt dizzy and passed out.

He was found three hours later next to the lagoon, shirtless, sweating and with partial amnesia.

HC addendum.
Source: Revista Brasileira de Ufologia.　　　　　Type: B & G?
Comments: A possible unexplored abduction event.

* * * * * * *

Location: Citta Di Castello, Italy.
Date: August 21, 1998.
Time: Afternoon.

In the outskirts of the city, witnesses spotted a small humanoid in a field. It was crouched down like an old woman gathering weeds. When it failed to respond to shouts from the witnesses they approached to about 200 meters from it. Suddenly a silvery cylinder shaped object appeared and hovered about two meters above the small figure. The small humanoid then levitated into the craft, which then quickly accelerated out of sight.

HC addendum.
Source: UFO Roundup September 16, 1998.　　　　　Type: B

Location: Praia do Frances, Alagoas, Brazil.
Date: September, 1998.
Time: Evening.

Several locals observed a strange being that was coming in from the sea. As the witnesses approached, the entity ran towards a nearby wood 400 meters away, taking tremendous strides, similar to a kangaroo. The creature was described as human in shape but luminous and semi-transparent in nature. Soon after, from the same wood, a sphere of light ascended to the sky at high speed and disappeared.

HC addendum.
Source: Arnaldo Augusto de F. Rebelo Revista Brasileira de Ufologia, #66 August, 1999.   Type: E or C?

* * * * * * *

Location: Cipolletti, Rio Negro, Argentina.
Date: September, 1998.
Time: 9:30 p.m.

A young woman named Alicia was traveling in a bus on the 131 route, listening to music from an FM station on her Walkman. There were only a few other passengers on the bus. At one point the station's musical programming changed suddenly, rather than a soft instrumental music, a sort of choral music performed in a foreign language made itself heard. Alicia tried changing stations, but could not. Her fingers were paralyzed, as well as the rest of her body; a light or white fog began to encase her body. Her bus surroundings vanished. She was then transported toward a luminous point in space, which gradually turned into a glowing spaceship.

Inside the vessel, Alicia reportedly saw a large headed dwarfish creature that took her hands and began touching certain points of her body. The creature softly felt her abdomen. Soon after, still enveloped in the strange fog and listening to the same music, she felt herself transported back to the bus and was able to see the familiar surroundings again.

Upon arriving home the strange music still issued from the Walkman and later from the home stereo. She and her mother listened to the strange music, which was accompanied by an unpleasant sound. A few seconds later the original frequency was suddenly restored. The witness suffered from nightmares after this bizarre incident.

HC addendum.
Source: Guillermo Aldunati ORTK.   Type: G or F?

203

Location: Santo Domingo area, Dominican Republic.
Date: September, 1998.
Time: Night.

Security personnel at a local motel reported encountering a five feet tall and three feet wide and bipedal reptile type creature, lurking around the woods of the motel (it was described by source as similar to the "Loveland Frog").

HC addendum.
Source: http://www.blackvault.com/wiki/index.php/Loveland_Frog
Type: E

* * * * * * *

Location: Metz neighborhood, Athens, Greece.
Date: September 14, 1998.
Time: Just before sunset.

Two women were sitting on the balcony of the house of one of them, at Markou Mousourou Street, opposite to Ardittos hill. They saw a small blackish object in the sky, about 1 km away. At first they thought it was a helicopter but there was no sound. When the object approached, they saw it was a humanoid figure in a standing position. Getting closer, the flying humanoid turned its body once to nearby Zappeio park and then in the opposite direction, without changing speed or posture. It started to coming down and seemed to land somewhere inside the forest on Ardittos hill. They thought that the flying creature was wearing something like an "astronaut suit" because from time to time the sunset light gleamed on it. After the landing, the figure made some small mechanical "hops" ascending the hill until it reached a point just before the top, when it stopped. When hopping, it was not bending its arms or legs. Ten minutes later the creature transformed itself into a "bright spot" and then vanished. During the incident, there was a strong wind blowing but the movement of the creature's flight was steady.

HC addendum.
Source: Thanassis Vembos   Type: E
High Strangeness Index: 7
Reliability of Source: 9
Comments: Modern day report of an apparent flying humanoid, the creature appeared to have been able morph itself into a bright "sphere" or spot in order to leave the area.

Location: Torriglia, Italy.
Date: September 18, 1998.
Time: 9:00 p.m.

Several witnesses watched a luminous blue oval shaped light apparently on the ground on Mt. Prela for about an hour. In front of the light, a small child-like figure was seen walking back and forth as if inspecting the area.

HC addendum.
Source: CUN Genova.   Type: C

* * * * * * *

Location: Extension Forest Hills, Bayamon, Puerto Rico.
Date: September 21, 1998.
Time: 8:00 p.m.

The night that Hurricane Georges struck this island, the witness, Iris Rodriguez was outside her home doing some wash when the winds began to pick up strength. She went back inside her house and soon as she looked outside her window she noticed a bright sphere of light making triangular movements in the sky. Suddenly the sphere descended lower and hovered above a neighbor's home. Moments later in the center of the red light, a bright white oval shaped hole appeared. Then a figure became visible inside the white light. The figure seemed to move back and forth apparently looking out. The witness described the figure as tall, thin, and man-like. It wore a tight-fitting gray colored outfit and his skin appeared to be also gray or pale. As the wind became stronger, the witness lost interest in the object and its occupant and eventually lost sight of it. That same night others saw speeding red balls of light over different areas of the island.

HC addendum.
Source: Jorge Martin, Evidencia OVNI #18.   Type: A

Location: Mariano Escobedo, Veracruz, Mexico.
Date: October, 1998.
Time: Evening.

45-year old Lina Lozano Villa was alone at home after her husband and children had gone out when suddenly she felt extremely tired and fell into a stupor. In a state of lethargy she climbed into bed. Moments later she heard somebody enter the bedroom, locked the door and sit at the foot of her bed. She opened her eyes and noticed a figure extending a hand out to her, automatically she extended her hand also, but she wasn't able to touch the hand since her hand stopped 3 or 4 centimeters from the figure's hand.

Her next memory was of standing outside a landed domed disc-shaped UFO. A hatch opened on the left side of the dome and the enigmatic figure invited her onboard. Inside there was another alien who communicated telepathically with Lina and told her he was going to show her "their city." At this point the witness realized that the alien's mouth did not move when she heard the words and it became obvious that all the communication was mental. Surprised she asked the alien how was he able to talk without moving his mouth and was told that they did not need their mouths to speak.

He then motioned to her to follow him; she sat on the lone armchair located at the end of an empty hall. The room was illuminated by an unseen source of light and as she sat down, she had the sensation of riding up in an elevator at high speed. She did not where the two aliens had gone. After an unknown amount of time, the tall alien appeared out of nowhere and motioned her to follow him. The hatchway opened and at that point she noticed the other alien standing next to her.

Walking outside she came to an area completely illuminated by white light. The alien asked her to go on, but she refused, afraid that she might fall. He assured her that would not, and took her by her hand, she felt as she was walking in mid-air. Soon she was at a location standing on a rock, not on a normal rock but on what appeared to be a metallic rock formation, metallic-gray in color. Pointing with his hand he told Lina, *"Here is my city."*

She then saw an incredible sight, what appeared to have been a huge city within a "crater" encased in a transparent dome. She could not see sky, clouds, or a sun, only a white light. As she contemplated the scene she asked the alien why they have brought her to see their city. The alien answered but she could not remember what he told her. And then the alien said, *"You will remember some things and others you will not."* At this point using two fingers, the alien touched Lina's forehead and her next memory was of waking up in the morning on her bed, which was neatly made up. She described the aliens as very tall, light skinned, small slanted eyes, very small mouths, lacking eyebrows or eyelashes, their eyes were of an undefined color. She felt at peace with the aliens, and felt that the aliens were friendly and wanted to make contact but were afraid of how humans would react. They seemed fragile in nature. She noticed that the humanoids wore tight-fitting gloves that somehow seemed to adjust and opened up to the movement of the fingers. She could not understand how it was possible.

HC addendum.
Source: http://www.eldurmientedeorizaba.com   Type: G
Translation by Albert S Rosales.

* * * * * * *

Location: Vernal, Utah.
Date: October 19, 1998.
Time: 12:30 a.m.

Several men were out elk hunting in an isolated area when they saw what appeared to be a plane crashing. They exited the truck and proceeded over the ridge to investigate. As they neared the area they saw two more craft apparently hovering over the area. On the ground they saw what appeared to be some "people" gathering around. No other information.

HC addendum.
Source: NUFORC   Type: C?
Comments: Close to the location of the infamous 'Skinwalker Ranch.'

* * * * * * *

Location: Near Asuncion, Paraguay.
Date: October 22, 1998.
Time: Late night.

Closing his rural store a man named Jesus was about ready to walk home when suddenly all around him is illuminated by a vivid white light; frightened he runs to the back of the store and attempts to open the door. He is not successful and runs towards a nearby shed about 50 meters away. After a few steps he feels something descend from above and looking up he is terrified to see an enormous object, from which hung three huge hook-like protrusions on ropes. On a fourth rope descended a bluish humanoid figure that moved quickly towards him. It grabbed the witness, which quickly fought back.

Jesus was able to grab the strange bluish creature by its neck and began to squeeze. Suddenly the creature began to shake violently. Seeing this unexpected reaction, Jesus loosened his grip and the figure instantly slipped up and with an elusive motion hangs one of the hooks on Jesus belt. The hook rose up and the witness hung helplessly in mid-air. The UFO began moving away gently pulling the rope with the witness hanging at the end.

When Jesus arrived next to an opened hatchway he pushed himself away with his feet from the object and slid down the rope fortunately landing on some bushes and suffering only minor injuries. His sister Rosalita witnessed the whole event from nearby.

HC addendum.
Source: UFO 2000 LM Moscow Corp. Type: B & G

* * * * * * *

Location: Soldini, near Rosario, Argentina.
Date: December, 1998.
Time: 9:30 p.m.

Laborer Maximiliano Poire was working in his field, on his tractor, when he noticed standing ten meters away, two strange figures, with disproportionately large heads, about 1.30 cm in height with very thin torsos and long dangling thin arms that reached to their knees. They also had long thin fingers. The eyes were round and appeared to be green in color. Their skin tone was dark green in color and they seemed to be nude. The creatures then moved into a nearby wooded area and disappeared.

HC addendum.
Source: Nuevos Tiempos, Argentina. Type: E

* * * * * * *

Location: Cartago, Costa Rica.
Date: Late 1998.
Time: Various.

A man reported being contacted by a race of intelligent beings for a period of six months. He reported that they were very similar to humans with the exception some had only one nostril opening. He also mentioned four races of beings. Some that were pigmy like, others were tall etheric looking giants (seven feet or more). They all had their ancestral specialty, working symbiotically to support the whole community. He was also told that they resided in four specific regions in the Hollow Earth.

Near the inner equator, he was shown that gravity was at its lowest there. They could jump as high as twenty feet or more, floating gently back to the inner Earth. He noted that none ate the flesh of animals, eating was a minimal occurrence. They apparently did not require the level of food sustenance as humans do. Partly because of their efficiency of how they think. He was also led to believe that their inner sun also provided nutrients through the absorption through the retinas. Hollow Earth inhabitants have that spectrum of light available all the time. On the surface we must wait for the sunrise or the sunset to gaze and obtain nutrients, which explains why over millennia beings become etheric (transparent) their whole body absorbs raw full spectrum light energy; eating "food" is no longer necessary. Food is nothing more than a dense form of light at specific wavelengths. The Sun is full spectrum light.

They also revealed that their means of propulsion was through what we call "magnetism" with the exception they utilized it in a way that redefined gravity as we know it. There were other forms of travel ranging in different spectrums of light. Light is far more complex that we could possibly understand at this time in our evolution of science. Our Sun communicates with the Inner Sun and all the Suns in the Universe instantaneously in every moment. Music is a rich part of their culture. The witness described what looked like a guitar with strings, but it wasn't plucked with a pick or finger, instead it was a shiny sphere when brought into close proximity to the strings, the sound was like that of a hundred crystal bowls playing in unison. The witness passed away in October 2003, at the age of 64.

HC addendum.
Source: Jack Barakitis in: http://ufoexperiences.blogspot.com
Type: G?

1999

Location: Grand Teton, Wyoming.
Date: 1999.
Time: Afternoon.

While on a hiking trip, the witness fell off a steep edge of a trail and broke both legs, the left one just above the ankle and the right femur which was a compound fracture. He was alone at the time. He awoke in some brush well off the trail just after dark. As soon as he tried to move the pain was unbearable. He laid there with a water bottle and three energy bars.

Two days later the water and the energy bars were gone. His right thigh had swelled to the point he had to cut his pants open from the crotch to the knee. He was also passing in and out of conscience. Suddenly a "being" came along and picked him up and he awoke in its arms and it carried the witness down to safety. The being looked human, but when they reached the trail head, the being closed its eyes and a red glow seemed to appear around both of them, in a moment it was gone. The witness thought he was hallucinating.

About ten minutes later another person or being came along. He was either in a costume or the witness was again hallucinating, for he was completely covered in light blue feathers. He was not wearing anything else. The other being was still holding the witness as the feathered one examined his thigh and ankle. He then laid his hands on the witness chest, closed his eyes and the red glow once again appeared. A few seconds passed and the first being stood him up, both legs were now completely healed and he felt as if nothing had happened at all. (!) He felt great. The being that was holding him was now standing beside him. He, in his natural form was also covered with blue feathers. The witness was to learn that these beings were members of an alien race known as "the Feathered Peoples."

According to them, there are nine alien races currently on earth. All are dangerous to humans. Only the feathered ones are potentially friendly. And according to them, they are here to protect us and allow our natural progression to continue unabated. He also learned that the one that had carried him was a male and the other had been a female.

HC addendum.
Source: http://www.alien-ufos.com/forum   Type: E
Comments: Clear beneficial intervention by positive forces, but why this specific witness, why not others in similar or worse situations? 'Blue avian' description. Healing claim.

* * * * * * *

Location: Camp Garcia, Vieques Island, Puerto Rico.
Date: 1999.
Time: Various.

Local sea cadets in the eastern part of the island around 'El Tapon' lagoon, reported encountering strange "little dark men" that were very fast and ran speedily from one place to the other, sometimes in zigzagging motions and at other times in jumps. They were described as three to four-feet tall, skinny with long arms with large egg shaped heads.

At times the cadets would see the little dark men jump into the lagoon, disappearing underwater. Around the same time they also observed shiny blue-white spheres that varied in size four to eight inches in diameter that also entered the waters of the lagoon.

HC addendum.
Source: Jorge Martin, UFO Magazine Vol. 16 #1.   Type: E
High Strangeness Index: 7
Reliability of Source: 8
Comments: This Island has for a long time being a flashing point of controversy, both politically and in the Ufological standpoint. UFOs and anomalous entities have been seen there for years according to the source and his recent book.

Location: "A mountain village" (no further information), Turkey.
Date: 1999.
Time: Various.

Several school students reported that while playing near a wooded area they all observed strange beings resembling modern day "astronauts." Apparently this event repeated itself. According to the eyewitnesses the beings seemed to be "faceless" and wore some type of helmet.

The beings seemed to ignored the young witnesses and were always silent. They seemed to glide silently over the fields in what appeared to be "skateboard" or hover-board type objects or apparatuses. After gliding over the fields for a while the beings would then disappear back into the jungle.

HC addendum.
Source: Murat Aksoy, UFO Turkey quoting, 'Turk Halk Kulturunde Memoratlar Veh Halk Inanclari,' (book).   Type: E

* * * * * * *

Location: Samara, Russia.
Date: 1999.
Time: 12:00 p.m.

Mrs. M. G. Korshunova was standing in her kitchen talking to her son about common mundane matters, when suddenly she physically felt two impulses go through her brain, like two waves originating in the cerebellum and ending in the area of the forehead.

When this was over, she found herself not in her kitchen, but on the surface of some alien planet. Everywhere, from horizon to horizon, she saw a sandy colored surface. The sky above was yellow. She saw three buildings nearby, pyramid-shaped, resembling dwellings, but their doors and openings were hollow and dark.

She found herself walking towards those buildings, but not alone, she saw around her several humanoid entities wearing grayish overalls, approximately 140cm in height. They appeared tanned with Mongoloid features. When they approached the building, she felt suddenly as if a "curtain" in her brain had been suddenly pulled down.

Mrs. Korshunova then appeared back in her kitchen. Her son was still talking to her; apparently he never noticed her brief visit to another planet.

213

HC addendum.
Source: "NLO" Magazine, Saint Petersburg #7, February 9, 2004.
Comments: Obviously some type of mental or astral journey, triggered
by unknown means.   Type: F?

* * * * * * *

Location: St. Catharine's Ontario, Canada.
Date: 1999.
Time: 3:00 p.m.

A couple stopped at a traffic light on Welland Ave. in front of the A &
P store, noticed something just above them. After sticking her head out
the window and yelling at her husband to do the same, both spotted a
long ship hovering about 500 yards away and she could also see people
looking their way from inside what appeared to be an observation deck.
They too seemed to be in a bit of a shock, and then in an instant it
vanished (the sky was clear, not a cloud in sight). The shaped of the craft
was like a silver bullet trailer but a lot longer and larger. There appeared
to be an observation deck and they could see people inside. Underneath
this platform were many small shaped windows like those on a ship. It
was white/silver in color. No blue, red or orange lights that they could
see, no haze was seen either.
    The "people" on the craft noticed the witness looking at them and for
a brief moment the wife made eye contact with one of them. This being
looked very much like a human female, neither she nor the others
appeared to have large heads and big eyes. The craft then vanished in an
instant. There was no sound that they could hear.

HC addendum.
Source: Brian Vike, HBCC UFO.   Type: A

* * * * * * *

Location: Opolskie Wojewodztwo, Poland.
Date: 1999.
Time: Afternoon.

A woman picking berries in the forest noticed a strange small man
wearing an outfit that appeared to be made out of tin foil standing several
meters away. He wore a helmet also aluminum in color with a black visor.
No other information.

HC addendum.
Source: Ayman Cielebia woe_vp@pl.com   Type: E

214

Location: Near Mirto, Messina, Italy.
Date: 1999.
Time: 2:30 a.m.

Four men were out in the countryside hunting boar, and had set up camp in some woods in order to wait for their prey. Suddenly at around 2:30 a.m. they all saw in a nearby clearing, a very bright object that had apparently landed behind some trees. However they couldn't see any details because of the foliage and decided to approach it.

After about 150 meters the men were able to see within the light two short thin figures with long arms which appeared to be coming towards them very rapidly.

Frightened, the men fired several shots at the beings, which seemed to fall down in a strange 'bouncing' manner as if unaffected by the bullets. Suddenly a very strong white light appeared, emitting an unbearable heat and blinding the men. There was also a strong whistling sound, the whistling intensified. The men were terrified by this point. After 3-4 minutes, the light disappeared and everything became silent.

After this point the four men claim to experience a memory lapse; they believe they had lost consciousness. They have a strong memory of vomiting and nausea and then it was suddenly broad daylight. They realized that they had empty cartridges and all their guns have discharged.

They phoned their families and were told they had been gone for fifteen hours. Once at home, the men suffer from fever and vomiting for three days in a row. They never went hunting again.

HC addendum.
Source: UFO Research Center-Messina, Italy.   Type: G?
Comments: Sadly this is the Universal human "greeting" to something which we don't understand and fear it. This is an unexplored abduction event.

Location: Vancouver, British Columbia, Canada.
Date: January, 1999.
Time: Late night.

Eva Trent who lived in a small apartment at the time, had retired to her bed at the usual hour. Having fallen asleep, she awoke to a "buzzing sound." Opening her eyes, she was horrified to find two strange creatures standing on either side of her bed. The "entity" to her right was about seven to eight feet tall, weighed around 300 pounds, had apparently no clothes on and seemed to have either a crocodile or snake type skin covering. The creature to her left was identical in appearance but smaller in height and weight. They seemed to be communicating in a chirping manner. Each of the visitor's eyes glowed.

Eva quickly discovered that she was unable to move. As she stared in terror at the two intruders, she found that they were giving her instructions telepathically. The nature of this was seemingly for her to create mentally visual scenes of various kinds and then "they" proceeded to distort that particular pleasant scene in a perverse manner. (i.e.) a romantic interlude. Much later she concluded that the intent was to not only observe her emotional reaction, but also possibly feed off the energy that was produced.

After an unknown period of time she became so upset with this ongoing deliberate mind manipulation that she began to mentally resist. Not only did she pray in an earnest fashion, but began to mentally cover herself from head to toe in white light. At this point she detected that the two "visitors" were confused by this reaction (or action). A short time later she fell back to sleep.

When she awoke the following day it was in a state of physical exhaustion and a confused mind that was not only attempting to put the night events in some sort of order, but alternately accepting and rejecting what she believed to have been a "real" event.

However, the clincher was yet to come. Located about six feet from her bed was an audio cassette storage rack. It stands about three feet high, is four-sided and felt lined. Eva's surprise when later that day she went to extract a music tape to play, she discovered five of her precious tapes (inside the plastic cases) were grossly distorted.

Of the five, three were badly buckled, as if extreme heat had been applied. On closer examination, some interesting contradictions emerge. None of the cassette tapes display any type of unusual odor that one would reasonably expect under such circumstances. Stranger still, despite the intense heat required to create this warping effect, the actual tape (sound) filament showed no sign of having been melted. The felt storage unit had no apparent evidence of heat being applied in close proximity.

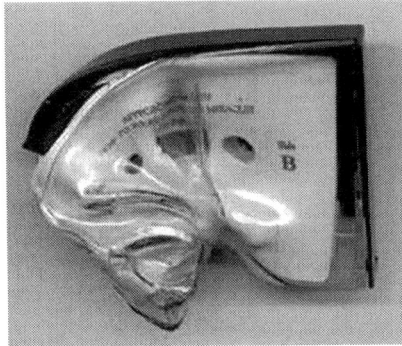

HC addendum.
Source: Graham Conway
http://www.ufobc.ca/Experiencer/buckled_v2.htm   Type: E
High Strangeness Index: 8
Reliability of Source: 9
Comments: This is a highly disturbing bedroom visitation by supposed "reptilians." The source is a longtime and respected Ufologist.

* * * * * * *

Location: Campo Grande, Mato do Rio Grande Sul, Brazil.
Date: January, 1999.
Time: 5:00 p.m.

A total six people, including the main witness, Felipe Castelo Branco, (involved in other encounters) were strolling down a little path in the valley when all of a sudden they saw a strange light, about 20 to 30 meters away, like a glow. They all stopped. The light was all different colors, orange, yellow, blue, etc. The glowing lights were going around in a circle, then the lights turned off and they could see a perfect shape, a metallic shape, about 30-meters in diameter. They could see it perfectly well because there was still some light. It was disc-shaped, silver in color and it was it had now turned its lights off. The main witness turned to his friend and told him to run to the compound and get Urandir. So he ran to the compound and brought Urandir.

When he came, three beings came out of the ship, one woman and two men. The witness had binoculars and he could see them clearly. They were about 20 to 30 meters away from the craft. He described the beings as human-like, but having very thin hair in a "Channel" cut, the color was blond, very light blond. The eyes were transparent green, and slanted, Japanese like. The beings wore light colored glowing jumpsuits, and their skin was very white just like porcelain.

217

Then one of the tallest beings came closer to the group of witnesses and his forehead lit up and began flashing lights. At the same time Felipe felt his stomach get nauseated and very dizzy. Also Mr. Urandir Oliviera's forehead began flashing just like the tall being. Felipe then turned to Urandir and asked him if they could approach the beings, but Urandir said, *"Do not approach them because the energetic field of the ship would harm us."* So the group remained stunned watching the scene, looking at Urandir flashing his forehead back at the being. Then they stopped, and the beings returned to their ship.

The ship lit up again with the same flashing lights and disappeared completely in a flash. Later Urandir told the witness that he had received telepathic information from the beings, which explained to him that there were going to be Earth changes, ocean tides are going to go up and certain cities are going to be effected and there is going to be an economic collapse and there is going to be problems from bacteria coming as a result of biological warfare.

HC addendum.
Source: Earthfiles.com   Type: B

* * * * * * *

Location: Punta del Hidalgo, Tenerife Island, Canary Islands, Spain.
Date: January, 1999.
Time: Night.

A married couple, who had parked their car near the beach, claimed that they witnessed a semi-spherical craft land in front of where they were. The couple said that a number of tall long-haired alien beings came out of the craft, which had been glowing, and that the entities walked about on the seafront before getting back in their flying saucer and leaving.

HC addendum.
Source: http://tenerifeislander.hubpages.com/hub/UFO-sightings-and-Tenerife   Type: B

Location: Cerro De Las Chacarillas, Chile
Date: January 1, 1999.
Time: 3:00 a.m.

Approximately 25 witnesses watched a large bright white light that began to grow in size in the middle of the mountain. It turned red and then orange in color and then it transformed itself into two huge figures; that of a man & a woman that were holding hands and appeared to be at least 25 meters in height (a record for humanoid encounters.) They moved down the mountain using movements resembling those of someone walking down a flight of steps.

The area has been the site of numerous bizarre light phenomena in the past and present.

HC addendum.
Source: Osvaldo Murray, Año Cero   Type: E?
High Strangeness Index: 7
Reliability of Source: 7
Comments: Very unique case, although it appears to be in the psychic realm as far as encounters go. The height of the figures is troubling, I can think of similar cases in Greece and the former Soviet Union.

*   *   *   *   *   *   *

Location: Crawley, West Sussex England.
Date: January 7, 1999.
Time: 6:00 a.m.

Lindsey Knott reported seeing flash like bursts of lights in her room then finding herself onboard a round object with low continuous windows. She saw control panels located at the center of the craft that were manned by two gray metallic robot-like creatures and two dark hooded beings.

She also met the apparent leader, described as human-like, tall, blond shoulder length hair, pale eyes, very pale skin, and wearing a dark blue jump suit.

The night after the incident she awoke to find her room very warm and cloying. The air appeared distorted and fuzzy; she also saw more flashes of light. She suffered from headaches and toothaches after the incident.

HC addendum.
Source: UFO Abduction Raw Data Page, UFO Watch.   Type: G
High Strangeness Index: 7
Reliability of Source: 5

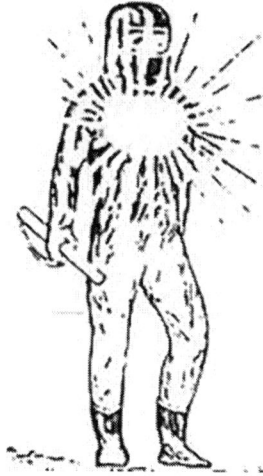

Location: Near Mohedas, Caceres, Spain.
Date: January 14, 1999.
Time: Late night.

Construction worker Jose Luis Garcia was approaching the Gabriel and Galan swamp when he noticed a strange luminosity moving very slowly alongside the road. Thinking it was some kind of road crew he slowed down. As he did he was stunned to see that it was really the figure of a "man" at least three meters in height, which emitted a tenuous luminosity and apparently was wearing some type of tight-fitting suit. Terrified the witness grabbed a knife that he usually carried with him and accelerated the vehicle. At the same time he noticed that the creature seemed to be taking slow, measured steps. He could not see any facial features and its head was shaped like an egg. He also did not see any arms or hands. He further realized that the humanoid was not touching the ground but floated just above it. It took the humanoid two quick "steps" to cross the road and disappear from sight.

That same night, dozens of residents in the towns of Las Mestas, Riomalo, Ladrillar and Caminomorisco and other smaller communities watched a strange reddish object which was very large and remained static over the area emitting different colored flashes of light.

HC addendum.
Source: Iker Jimenez, "El Paraiso Maldito" (Cursed Paradise)   Type: E
Translated by Albert S. Rosales.

Location: Near Pavlovskiy area, Altay region, south Siberia, Russia.
Date: January 21, 1999.
Time: Unknown.

Victor S. a long range truck driver who drove constantly through the Altay region, reported to the local newspaper a weird encounter he had. He and his partner had departed in a large truck on January 20 and on the second day they were approaching the outskirts of the Pavlovskiy area. As Victor reported, the engine suddenly coughed and stopped working. He did not wake his partner, relying upon his own abilities.

Casually glancing out the truck's window he saw something gray-bluish in color on a meadow covered with white snow. At first Victor thought that it must have been a stump, but it looked strange. Then the "stump" smoothly rose up into the air and landed about ten meters from the asphalt road. And then Victor distinctly saw that it was not a stump, and not an animal and not a man. He especially remembered a pair of huge eyes, which he described as "looking from outer space."

Moments later, a greenish twinkling beam of light appeared from behind the nearby forest, shining directly on the gray-bluish figure. The beam appeared to suck the figure into it (probably some type of transporter device). Victor remembered getting a strong ache between his temples as if his head was being squeezed by a pair of pliers. His partner awoke only when the truck engine started again and saw nothing.

Remarkably the date of the encounter, January 21, coincides with the day when a spectacular UFO was seen over Barnaul airport in the capital city of Altay which caused a stir in the region.

HC addendum.
Source: 'Altayskaya Pravda' newspaper #53-54 quoted in, Ufological Digest #10, March 2001.   Type: C?

Location: Oakland, California.
Date: January 23, 1999.
Time: 9:30 p.m.

The main witness, a woman and a third passenger were southbound on I-80, the woman was driving and the witness was in the front passenger seat. As they began the large curve past the Oakland Post Office, they noticed what appeared to be several miles away, a large yellow light over a white light. It appeared to be between the Oakland hills and them. After making the curve at the point where the freeway begins, they spotted the unusual light again.

At this point it began to turn and changed to a cylindrical shape viewed broadside. It was emitting yellow light from its entire length. It was cylindrical in shape but slightly tapered. There were no wings, rotors, no thrust port and it was clearly not a blimp. On its underside, at each end were two very large white lights. It was traveling end forward and perpendicular to their direction of travel. On the front of the cylinder, above was a small, irregularly fluttering green light, on the front underside a small red irregularly fluttering light.

As the witnesses continued southbound the object arrived at a point between them and the Oakland Federal buildings. At this time they began to make out details including four equally spaced vertical separations and a horizontal deck. Towards the leading end they could barely make out shapes. The craft possibly passed within 100 yards of the buildings as it continued to approach.

Suddenly, in a moment faster than the witness "could blink," the object leaped from the location near the Federal buildings and stopped about sixty feet from their windshield. It covered perhaps two miles in a manner that should have killed anything living that might be inside. The entire side of the craft that was facing the witnesses was transparent. It was as if one half of the object became transparent and the side facing away from them was opaque. It was emitting a very yellow light from its interior. Inside it had a deck evenly dividing it in half, lengthwise. There seemed to be five evenly spaced vertical ribs against the opposite wall from the one the witnesses were looking through. The entire interior of the craft appeared to be visible. It seemed to be completely hollow, with no "engine compartment" or any other furnishings. It had similar dimensions to a cardboard toilet paper tube.

The main witness became aware of three shapes that were visible at the front end of it. The first was somewhat obscured by the large, white external light directly underneath. The other two were evenly spaced from the first. The stunned witnesses now realized they were looking at aliens. At the front-end of it with their hands resting on a thin bar or table were three people. They seemed so similar that they looked like paper dolls. They were standing, and were backlit by the yellow light and it was reflecting off the flat sides of their heads. They were staring straight at the witnesses. Their heads were oversized; their foreheads were about a third larger than that of a human being. The eyes were very large and dark and they had an occipital ridge, eyebrow, oriented like humans. They seemed to have narrow shoulders and hips and they had longer upper arms and upper leg bones than human beings. They appeared to be the same size as humans. Their faces were small, but because of the backlight, the witnesses could not see any other details. The witnesses went below an overpass, and the craft intercepted them on the other side, it seemed to be flying sideways from its original end-on-orientation about 75 to 100 ft from the car and about 50 ft in the air. It was very difficult to see the structure behind the craft's lights as it hovered briefly in front of the witnesses before it slowly passed in front of them.

At this point, a third witness in the backseat of the car saw the object, which was completely soundless. Then the main witness had the internal mental impression, *"Stop the car,"* the other witnesses had the same sensation. They did not stop the car. The craft then passed to their right, continuing to fly next to the car and in their direction of travel. Then it passed behind them, crossing back over the freeway and returning toward the east. As they drove away from it they could make out the very rectangular silhouette of a cylinder viewed side on. The craft finally was lost from sight above the Oakland Hills.

HC addendum.
Source: NUFORC   Type: A

*   *   *   *   *   *   *

Location: Near Warrington, New South Wales, Australia.
Date: February, 1999.
Time: 9:30 p.m.

Mr. Robert Carlo was followed by a blue glowing "flying saucer," while driving along Mulgoa Road. He was on his way to visit friends at Warragamba, when this bright blue-glowing craft suddenly descended above him and kept pace with his car. He was worried at what was going to happen next. He could see people along the road pointing and yelling, so he knew he wasn't imagining things.

Then this big bubble-shaped craft appeared in front of him, keeping pace with his car and about 30ft ahead. It was pinkish-colored, and there was a large round window, through which he could see two humanoid creatures momentarily before it suddenly sped away to the west over the Blue Mountains. All he can recall of the beings were their longish heads, human-like faces, and bare chests, long arms and their skins being of an orangey color.

HC addendum.

Source: The Temple of Nim Newsletter, November 2009.   Type: A

*   *   *   *   *   *   *

Location: McMinnville, Oregon.
Date: February 2, 1999.
Time: Night.

    Several campers at an isolated ranch were sitting around a campfire when they heard some noises in the brush. They went to look and found some weird footprints and followed them. They went through the woods and into a meadow and saw a huge bizarre creature resembling a walking tree, except for the head. The creature was walking through the meadow at a very fast pace. It scurried away as they shone a flashlight at it. Later that night the campers saw a bright light shoot over the area at high speed.

HC addendum.
Source: Filer's Files #6   Type: D?
High Strangeness Index: 6
Reliability of Source: 7
Comments: The location is indeed the scene of the famous 1950 photographs of farmer Paul Trent.

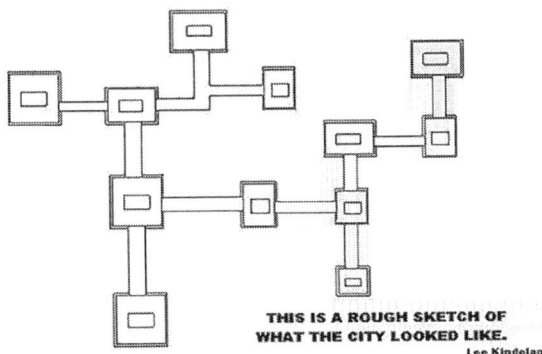

THIS IS A ROUGH SKETCH OF
WHAT THE CITY LOOKED LIKE.
Lee Kindelan

Location: Maryborough, Queensland, Australia.
Date: March, 1999.
Time: Late night.

Lee Neville Kindelan suddenly found himself in his backyard. It seemed like normal and he seemed to be awake. Something made him look up and he could see a bright beam of light, through thick mist that wasn't there before. Then from out of nowhere, three "people" appeared, an older man with gray hair and a gray beard, a woman and another younger man. They were wearing red and gray suits with some sort of symbol, but unfortunately he couldn't remember what it looked like. The older man walked up to Lee and said, *"We have come for you Lee."*

The next thing he remembers was waking up looking out of a window and seeing this huge city made up of buildings and walkways, brightly lit up as far into the distance as the eye could see. He seemed to be in space and the city just kept going into the depths of space with no end. There was not one patch that wasn't city, and even at his altitude could not see the edge of the planet. Also whatever it was he was looking out of was going at extremely fast speeds, and seemed to move unlike any known aircraft, it felt like he wasn't moving at all, no G forces.

Then he "woke up" and it was daylight. After that he had ringing sounds in his ears and a sore nose for a week after.

HC addendum.
Source: Brian Vike, Director HBCC UFO Research Home. Type: G or F?
Comments: As a child the witness had another experience but it wasn't an abduction.

Location: Lucignagno, Arezzo, Italy.
Date: March 8, 1999.
Time: 4:00 p.m.

A married couple was taking a walk along the Calcione Forest when they noticed a luminous triangular-shaped object hovering still in the sky. Moments later, further ahead on the path, they spotted a human like figure of normal height that was wearing coveralls with a helmet and visor. Inside the visor they could see a pair of blue eyes, eyebrows, pale skin, a human like nose and a barely noticeable mouth.

In a metallic sounding voice the figure said *"Peace."* Then a loud whistling sound coming from the hovering luminous object distracted the witnesses. They saw the object move slightly then gradually disappear from sight. When they looked back on the path, the strange figure had also vanished.

HC addendum.
Source: CUN Florence.   Type: C
High Strangeness Index: 7
Reliability of Source: 7

* * * * * * *

Location: Near Altoona, Pennsylvania.
Date: March 10, 1999.
Time: 2:00 a.m.

The witness had gone out for a walk early one morning, when he heard a strange hum that was not coming from any farm machine known to him. Intrigued he followed the noise.

In a baseball field near where he lived, he found a cigar-shaped object with two 7-ft tall men with blond hair that was braided down their backs and wearing tight-fitting glittery silvery suits, that appeared to be working on a square section of the object that was opened up like a car door would open. For about an hour he watched them and saw many multicolored blinking lights that appeared to be connected to whatever they were doing since they were only in the section of the craft they were working on.

According to the witness, the men were using what appeared to be glue-guns that had a strange steady light emanating from them. After about an hour, they closed the square section of the craft and walked towards the rear of the object and got inside. They both moved in a steady smooth gait.

Shortly after the hum became louder and the ground around seemed to vibrate, kicking up rocks and other debris into the air. The hum built up into a loud booming sound and the craft lifted up into the clouds, disappearing from sight, lifting and then knocking the witness down to the ground. For the next week or so he reported seeing helicopters flying through the area, which was also a very unusual sight.

HC addendum.
Source: Mufon CMS   Type: B

* * * * * * *

Location: Almirante Tamandare, Parana, Brazil.
Date: March 10, 1999.
Time: 3:00 p.m.

Pedro da Rosa was working in his vegetable garden, when he heard a loud buzzing sound. Turning around, he saw at about 500 meters away a strange silvery metallic oval-shaped object. At first he saw it was near a neighbor's brand new tractor. Five minutes later he noticed two short humanoids walking around and under the object. The short figures re-entered the object, which then emitted a loud whistling sound and shot up towards the sky at high speed.

HC addendum.
Source: Thiago Luiz Ticchetti, EBE-ET.   Type: B

* * * * * * *

Location: Altonia, Parana, Brazil.
Date: March 15, 1999.
Time: 11:15 p.m.

18-year old Rodrigo Friedrich was returning to his home from a party, when he noticed what appeared to be numerous shiny "stars" in the sky. Suddenly one of the "stars" began to descend at high speed. He thought it was a shooting star and completely ignored it. Forty minutes later as he was arriving home, a bright glow attracted his attention about 1km away from his location. Curious he approached the light and encountered a huge 30-meter sized disc-shaped object completely illuminated. Near the object were six short humanoids running back and forth as if looking for something.

At this point Rodrigo, began to experience a headache, and attempted to yell out to obtain additional witnesses. As he walked away he looked back and saw the object climbing up into the sky at high speed. Several days after the encounter Rodrigo began experiencing nightmares in which he saw short gray colored humanoids.

HC addendum.
Source: Thiago Luiz Ticchetti, EBE-ET.   Type: C

* * * * * * *

Location: Vale Do Jatoba, Minas Gerais, Brazil.
Date: March 22, 1999.
Time: Night.

Grasiele Guedes was taking a short cut through a valley when she came upon a short creature with large yellow eyes, emitting a blue beam of light.

She tried to get closer to the creature to obtain a better look, but then the figure suddenly approached her. Afraid, she ran home. Later the witness returned to the area with her mother but the creature was nowhere to be seen.

HC addendum.
Source: Revista Brasileira de Ufologia.   Type: E

* * * * * * *

Location: Hellin, Albacete, Spain.
Date: April, 1999.
Time: Night.

During local festivities (Jornadas de la luz del Pardal), a local man was standing by a window smoking a cigarette and saw over the monument to the Virgin a bright light that projected a solid beam of light towards the ground, the solid beam appear to act as a 'ramp' for about twenty small oval-shaped lights. Once they hit the ground, they transformed into human-like figures and disappeared into town.

HC addendum.
Source: Jose Antonio Iniesta in Lo Occulto, 'Ovnis en España.' Type: B?

Location: Santana do Ipanema, Alagoas, Brazil.
Date: April 1, 1999.
Time: 4:00 a.m.

Two men, Jose Trajano & Milton Leite were preparing their boat in order to go fishing and were exiting the boat storage garage area when they spotted a cylinder-shaped object, hovering just above them. The object was 15 meters in length and was reddish in color. The craft then shone a beam of white light towards the ground and a short figure suddenly appeared within the light on the ground. The witnesses watched from about 600 meters away as the short figure moved back and forth within the lighted area then floated back up into the object and disappear. At this point the object became brighter and rose up quickly, disappearing from sight.

HC addendum.
Source: Thiago Luiz Ticchetti, EBE-ET.   Type: B

* * * * * * *

Location: (Undisclosed location in the south of the state) New Mexico.
Date: April 18, 1999.
Time: 7:00 p.m.

The witness was riding his horse in an isolated area when his horse became uneasy; he then noticed a strange smell in the air. He then saw at about 1000 yards away near mile marker 6, a hovering bright object and under it several glowing, red-colored humanoid figures.

Frightened he rode away from the area. He contacted the border patrol and the next day he saw several black unmarked helicopters flying over the area.

HC addendum.
Source: NUFORC   Type: C

Location: Near Amsersfoort, The Netherlands.
Date: April 22, 1999.
Time: 2:15 a.m.

The witness was alone on a highway when suddenly the front windshield became dark. He was not able to see and he hit a car in front of him. He then skidded off the highway and crashed into a tree. He looked at the car but it was not damaged. A police officer then came by and asked him if there had been an accident. Confused, he said no. After the officer left, a man appeared who told the witness to follow him.

Soon they came upon a landed disc shaped object with a dome on top, shiny silvery in color. He took the witness inside and explained to him that he was not from another planet that he was from planet Earth but from a different "frequency" or dimension. He told the witness that the car he hit was one of them and the driver was one of them. They had repaired his vehicle. The man then showed him around the object, and explained to him how the object operated. He was eventually allowed to return to his vehicle and went home.

HC addendum.
Source: NUFORC   Type: G

*   *   *   *   *   *   *

Location: Barre, Vermont.
Date: April 24, 1999.
Time: 1:30 a.m.

Police officer Alan George was patrolling an isolated wooded area when he noticed something strange about the night sky; it would seem to open up and show an eerie glowing light and then just disappear back into the darkness. As he drove through a rather large patch of woods on the outskirts of town, he noticed a faint light in the distance that soon covered the entire night sky. The lights and colors were so bright at one point that he had to shield his eyes from the glare; it had red, green, blue and orange glows.

He stopped the car and got out, staring in amazement at the spectacle. The colors just seemed to dance across the sky in a circular motion. Mesmerized, he began to see a picture emerge. He began to see the face of a longhaired man with a beard, thunder then erupted and flashes of light covered the night sky. These flashes where not normal as they seemed to be colored also and the tremendous roar from the thunder was like nothing he'd ever heard before. Suddenly everything disappeared and returned to normal.

HC addendum.
Source: Weird Science.   Type: E or F?
Comments: 2000 years ago it would have been interpreted as a vision of
God. But what was it?

*   *   *   *   *   *   *

Location: Quebrada Culebritas, Colombia.
Date: May, 1999.
Time: Early morning.

    In this mountainous area, locals reported seeing strange oval shaped
metallic crafts landing. Short occupants were seen coming out of them.
A Mr. Augarita encountered two short beings with shiny red eyes. The
two humanoids wore shiny metallic outfits and scampered quickly up a
hill and entered a landed metallic craft. A red light and a yellow light
came on, and then the craft ascended at high speed, disappearing from
sight. Another farmer reported seeing several short, large-headed
humanoids that walked very quickly without emitting any noise.

HC addendum.
Source: Virgilio Sanchez Ocejo, Quoting El Especial newspaper. Type: B

*   *   *   *   *   *   *

Location: Teorama, Colombia.
Date: May, 1999.
Time: 2:00 a.m.

    A farmer woke up one morning and went outside to see two short
humanoids standing in the patio. Startled, he asked what they were
doing there and both walked away silently, entering a nearby landed craft
that then left at high speed. The humanoids wore silvery metallic outfits.
Another farmer in nearby San Calixto encountered a short humanoid
that spoke to him in a deep grave voice, telling him that his crops were
going to be plentiful this year. He felt that the small man had brought
good luck to him.

HC addendum.
Source: Virgilio Sanchez Ocejo, Quoting El Especial.   Type: B & E

Location: Ghana (exact location not given).
Date: May, 1999.
Time: Late afternoon.

After a hard day's fruit picking in the fields, 13-year old Kwane Afram started back to his house on foot. As he went around a bend in the road, the boy was surprised to see three giant beings ahead of him. Frightened by the sight, Kwane thought it best to hide in the long grass and take a different route home. However, as the boy would later tell his friends and family, he didn't manage to duck down in time.

After an unfruitful search which involved police and neighbors, Kwane's parents sought help from a group of witchdoctors, who promised to do what they could. At once they performed a number of magical rituals and then announced that the boy would come back four days later. And so it was. On the fourth day after their intervention Kwane appeared in one of the witchdoctor's bedrooms. Kwane told the wizard, Kofi Sarfo, that he had been captured by a giant who had carried him off to a place where little goblins lived. There he had been helping them with domestic chores for a few days. The child, who accompanied his parents to the local constabulary to call off the search, explained his adventure to the police, who remained skeptical of the whole matter. (There is an old myth from West Ghana concerning little creatures that would come into the villages at night, and take away people, and then return them much later).

HC addendum.
Source: Roy Hale UFO Updates, Toronto.   Type: G?

* * * * * * *

Location: New Fairfield, Connecticut.
Date: May, 1999.
Time: 11:00 p.m.

Henry Miller (involved in other encounters) was driving home from work along Route 37, listening to the radio. It was a very foggy night and the roads were dark. He came upon a roadblock in the road, and a man walked up to the car and told him to turn left because there is an accident up ahead and he had to take a detour. He turned left, he couldn't remember the street and then all of a sudden he heard a voice say, *"Hello Henry."*

He looked to the passenger seat and there was 'Auriel' sitting there, smiling. Auriel was a tall man-like figure with long white hair, green eyes and very white skin. He said, *"I told you I would be back."* Henry replied, *"But it has been over thirty years!"* He replied by saying something like, that time has no meaning and although the passage of time seemed long to Henry, from his perspective the last time they met was only a short time ago. He told Henry that he was going to take him to a ship in space and there he would meet other people and have a procedure done that will allow his people to send information through him.

All of a sudden, the car was lifted off the ground, and the next thing Henry knew he was inside what looked like a big hangar. Auriel was standing next to him and told him to follow him. It was strange; as he walked, his body felt so light he thought he could fly. Auriel seemed to be reading his thoughts because every time he thought of a question, he answered.

They came to a short flight of stairs and walked into a room, which was full of people. They walked by the entrance to another room and he could see five beautiful women sitting there, smiling. They were dressed in glowing gowns of the most vivid red, blue and green that he had ever seen. He wanted to go into the room and talk to them, but Auriel looked at him and said, *"You can't talk to them yet. Since they are on a higher level and your quantum vibrational signature is not matched to theirs, it would cause problems."*

He then led Henry to a room where he introduced him to a man that looked like it could be his brother. Auriel said, *"This is Aerial and he is a doctor. He is going to help you with you work."* The 'doctor' took him by the arm into a room as Auriel said goodbye. The doctor then asked him to lie on a table. The room was bare except for the table, which was the color of gold and was glowing with a red light. He lay on the table and the doctor waived his right arm, and a device that looked like a gold DVD appeared and hovered above his forehead. Then the disk began to vibrate and he could feel energy of some sort going into his head. Then the doctor opened up his hands, and there were three ruby-like crystals. He placed them one by one on Henry's head and he could feel them being sucked into his brain.

He said, *"We are finished. You can go home."* He got up and heard a buzzing in his head and before he could say anything, the doctor said, *"Not to worry, the sound will go away before you are back in your world."* Then a man came to the entrance of the doctor's room. He was human and had dark hair. He put his hand on Henry's shoulder and told him to follow him. As he did, he said, *"We are going to take you back to your car."* He asked him if he was from another planet. He said that he was from Earth and that he was taken three hundred years ago to work with this group of 'angels.' They went back to the hangar and his car was there. He got in and then there was a flash of light, and he was back on the road again, driving home.

The next morning he got up and started writing; in about ten hours he had a manuscript that was five hundred pages long. The strange thing is, he couldn't remember writing the manuscript nor did he feel the passage of time. He thought he was only writing for a half hour and did one page. He was shocked to see what he had done, but it was in his handwriting and about three-quarters through it he changed pens and he doesn't recall doing this.

HC addendum.
Source: Philip Imbrogno, 'Interdimensional Universe' pp. 224-226.
Type: G

* * * * * * *

Location: Near Varginha, Brazil.
Date: May 2, 1999.
Time: Midnight.

A bright light coming from outside awakened Geraldo Galdino, a resident near the local exposition park. His wife also woke up. They both saw a large object on the ground on a nearby field. Three short humanoids exited the object and walked around the area for a while apparently collecting items from the ground.

HC addendum.
Source: Revista Brasileira de Ufologia.   Type: B

* * * * * * *

Location: Bariloche, Rio Negro, Argentina.
Date: May 4, 1999.
Time: Night.

A 45-year old man was leaving his parent's house when he went missing. He was found eight days later by bloodhounds in an isolated canyon, dehydrated and suffering from hypothermia. He claimed he had been picked up by "extraterrestrials." Two men dressed in white and an attractive woman that apparently wanted to operate on him. He has no other memories as to what happened to him.

HC addendum.
Source: CE UFO Argentina.   Type: G

Location: Batu Lintang, Malaysia.
Date: Middle of May, 1999.
Time: Various.

Independent witnesses saw several small greenish beings in the village road. The beings were described as around 1-2 feet tall, with large baldheads, greenish skin and apparently not wearing any clothing. They were seen sometimes alone and at other times there were three of them.

One of the witnesses Jamsari Mohamad, 24, claimed that early one morning around 3:00 a.m. he and four other friends had spotted three strange beings, greenish in color which appeared out of some bushes and crossed the road. The beings appeared human-like under the street lamp, but very small. As the witnesses attempted to approach, the beings they suddenly vanished.

HC addendum.
Source: Ahmad Jamaludin, FSR Vol. 46 #1.   Type: E

*   *   *   *   *   *   *

Location: Vila do Principe, Caico, Rio Grande Norte, Brazil.
Date: May 20, 1999.
Time: 10:00 p.m.

A young woman by the name of 'Aninha' was returning home from a party at a nearby suburb, when she noticed something "parked" on the soccer field located just across the street from her residence. When she noticed that it did not appear to be a conventional object, she called her Mother, Maria, and both were able to observe the strange craft.

They described the object as resembling an oval-shaped bus, with two rows of multicolored lights and between the rows of light what appeared to be "iron bars" which covered the side of object completely. They noticed that the appeared to be suspended a few inches above the ground; the light from the object did not illuminate its surroundings. They stood about fifty meters from the craft.

At this point they both observed from ten to fifteen heavyset small creatures, wearing tight-fitting coveralls moving slowly around the object. The creature's heads were a bit larger than normal. The witnesses could hear a sound similar to the buzzing of bees, but could not tell if it came from the creatures or the object. The creatures always stayed closed to the object and close to each other. They moved slowly over the sand as if it were quicksand.

HC addendum.
Source: Equipe IPURN Brazil.   Type: C

Comments: The source does not provide details on how the creatures and the object departed.

* * * * * * *

Location: Mambau, Malaysia.
Date: May 23, 1999.
Time: 4:30 a.m.

17-year old Fahmi Mohd was awakened by the sound of wind blowing. He noticed some bright lights outside the house. He looked out the back door and was surprised to see an object hovering low over some bushes near the house. The object was about 20-30 feet from the house and gave off a very bright blue light. He could not tell its shape due to the brilliance of the light. He continued to watch in amazement, forgetting to wake up his parents. He then saw a small being, about half a meter tall, come out from the bottom of the hovering object. Again because of the bright blue light, he could not distinguish any features, but he could see that it had drooping ears, and a slightly pointed head with very long arms. Scared, he reentered his house. He looked out again to see the object shoot up at an angle into the sky and disappear from sight. He did not see the being re-board the object. But he did hear a mechanical sound right before the object shot up. Several small footprints were found at the site.

HC addendum.
Source: Ahmad Jamaludin   Type: B

* * * * * * *

Location: Corner Brook, Newfoundland, Canada.
Date: Late May, 1999.
Time: 3:00 p.m.

While walking in a logged out valley outside of Corner Brook, and having made his way up the side of a long low mountain, the witness for some reason decided to cut his walk short after a feeling of uneasiness. He took a short cut and slogged his way through a marshy area and was about five minutes away from where he had parked, when he suddenly felt more relaxed and decided to dash over to a nearby pond and enjoy the scenery. He walked up the path and as he was nearing the pond, something caught his attention.

He was shocked to see a tall white humanoid figure hovering just over the surface of the water. This thing was about twenty meters in front of him and seemed to be in a trance like state, just floating in the air. The figure was solid and big and dressed in a white suit from head to toe and had what looked like a gray shield over where the eyes would be. The witness was so terrified that he was paralyzed for a moment and could not move. Soon he was able to turn slowly and started to walk along the side of the pond. By this time, the being had sort of "awakened" out of its trance and without so much as a splash of water, it was on the other side of the pond (opposite to the witness), who could clearly hear branches and twigs breaking. The witness then ran to his car and immediately drove back to Corner Brook and did not tell anybody what he had seen.

HC addendum.
Source: Brian Vike, Director HBCC UFO Research.   Type: E

* * * * * * *

Location: Sarasota, Florida.
Date: Summer, 1999.
Time: Unknown.

The main witness, Christine, who lived on a two acre lot outside Sarasota, reported that one day her teenage son Ryan and his sister had been playing in the lot when they discovered a bright orange rock jutting out from the soil in a brushy area where they had been playing. It was so unusual looking and so bright that they decided to dig it up. The rock turned out to be entirely orange and about as big as a large watermelon.

They put it on a wheelbarrow, brought it into the house and managed to get in onto the screened porch, and the minute it was there all the power in the house shut off. No other house experienced this in the area, so it was not a general blackout. Also the phone went dead almost immediately. As it got darker, they saw that the orange rock glowed, but it was a dim glow. Christine was more worried about the power than anything else, and for some reason she knew to blame the rock on the porch and asked the kids to put it in the yard away from the house. They did and instantly the power and phone came back. They covered it with a tarp which hid it. The next day was Saturday and as Christine was doing the dishes a large white van pulled up and two rather muscular young women got out, walked straight to the tarp, pulled it off the rock, picked up the rock, threw it in the van and drove away without saying a word.

The rock had been completely hidden, and there was no way that they could have seen it in the yard from the driveway. The same day, someone from the office of the development company called and said that their lease on the house and property was cancelled effective in two weeks. They were supposed to have the property for another two years. They were warned that "evidence of improper usage" had been gathered on them and not to fight the eviction. Their rent was paid up, but the person

237

on the phone said they would receive a refund check for the current month, and they sent it, no further explanation was given.

HC addendum.
Source: Your True Tales, November 2007.   Type: X?
Comments: What was the strange orange rock? An alien artifact? Who were the young women who came to retrieve it? Hybrids?

* * * * * * *

Location: Bulls, North Island, New Zealand.
Date: Summer, 1999.
Time: 5:00 a.m.

A female farm worker was up early about to bring in the cows for milking. It was still very dark. She went out to the shed to start up a small tractor and heard a bump in the shed which she assumed was a possum. She was not normally scared by such things, but on this occasion she recalls that her hair "stood on end" and something did not feel right. About fifteen minutes later she was rounding up the cows. For some reason she felt a great sense of relief to be with them.

As she was bringing them up the track, the left hand headlight (the only one working) picked up some sort of creature lying against the roof of the hayrack, which had been turned over on its side next to the fence. The witness noted that the creature appeared very black in the headlight. The closer and brighter the light became, the denser the blackness of the creature appeared to be, she noted that it was almost as if its body absorbed the light as there was no visible sheen. The outline of the creature appeared to be rough, not smooth. The witness's immediate impression was that it was definitely not a dog, cat or possum. The eyes were huge and round like large English teacups, and they reflected a bright almost lime green color. The size of the eyes was disproportionate to the entire size of the creature, which was about three feet long. They looked far too big for its head. They looked at each other as she moved past seated on the tractor. It never moved, just watched. The witness was stuck behind the herd, and was certainly not keen to approach the creature.

She reassured herself with the fact that the cows continued moving at a brisk pace. However she thought it was unusual that none of the cows stopped to sniff and investigate whether this 'animal' was a potential danger, as they would do with a farm dog or cat, but nor did they become spooked and set off at a gallop. She wondered if they had seen it before. She moved the herd onwards up the track, dawn was just breaking. Above her the sky was black, but towards the horizon it lighted to dark gray, continuously lightening.

238

As they neared the next paddock, she noticed something in the center of it. She could make out a solid, black cylindrical object. It was taller than it was wide, but in the gloom however she could not clearly see the top or bottom of the object. It was to the right of the tractor where the headlight was not working. She was astonished to see such an object in the paddock. Her instant thought was that it must be a landed craft of some sort, but she stated that she would never have believed a craft could be shaped like this. Then she noticed movement in the area around this object. She could make out supple "gliding figures" tall and skinny. As they moved, their spine appeared to undulate in an out, whereas a human spine is more straight and rigid. Because their shape was soft and indistinct, when they stopped moving they became more indistinct and seemed to blend in with the background. The one closest to her seemed to do just that, blend in with subtle movement. She counted five or six of them in the area. They didn't appear to move in a hurry and they looked very black against the shades of dawn gray. She was not able to see any details like heads, limbs or features. Again the cows did not panic.

The witness realized the high strangeness of the scene but felt no fear at this point. However she admits that if the cows had reacted differently to the presence of these figures, she would have been very scared. She continued herding the cows up the farm to the 'safety' of a line of pine trees. Upon returning to the paddock later, she found nothing out of the ordinary.

HC addendum.
Source: Suzanne Hansen, 2007, www.ufocusnz.org.nz   Type: C

* * * * * * *

Location: Don Torcuato, Buenos Aires, Argentina.
Date: Summer, 1999.
Time: Night.

The witness claims that on repeated occasions she has seen a huge winged creature, resembling a gargoyle descend and land on the roof of her house. She described the creature as very muscular, green in color, with human-reptile combine facial features. It had two large horn-like protrusions on its head.

It stared briefly at the witness with a malevolent look, and then it rose up and quickly flew away into the darkness. The stunned witness was unable to move for a few minutes after the creature left.

Another time her and other family members had heard footsteps on the roof of the house.

HC addendum. Source: Contacto #13.   Type: E

Location: Moscow, Russia.
Date: Summer, 1999.
Time: Night.

Right before a mysterious explosion rocked a Moscow apartment complex, killing over a hundred people, two elderly pensioners at a nearby complex reported seeing several flying creatures that had human outlines with legs, arms and head, apparently flying over the area.
HC addendum.
Source: Pravda   Type: E
High Strangeness Index: 6
Reliability of Source: 7
Comments: Modern day Mothman report? Source seems to imply a connection between the winged humanoids and the ensuing tragedy. A gas leak or terrorist activity cannot be ruled out.

* * * * * * *

Location: Khavarovsk, Russia.
Date: Summer, 1999.
Time: Evening.

The main witness and a friend were sitting on the balcony of his apartment located on the fifth floor of the building right in the city center. Suddenly his friend yelled out, *"look!"* the witness then looked in the direction where his friend pointed. What he saw was a flying figure gray/silver in color. It moved in the sky from left to right and it was rather difficult to estimate its size at first. It did not fly as birds or bats did, its movement was very similar to that of squids in the water, spastic in nature. Its silhouette was similar to a sea manta. Around its perimeter or its fringe was an area that flashed every time it moved. The creature moved in the sky very smoothly and in complete silence, emitting a dim light.

Both witnesses observed the creature for about a minute and were still unable to estimate its size, it then flew over the roof of a house directly opposite where the witnesses stood, and both realized that it was huge in size. The creature then disappeared behind a façade of a nearby tower and it was not seen again. Later the frightened witnesses learned that hunters on the nearby taiga (forest) have reported seeing similar creatures which emit strange shrill-like screams resembling that of a woman in distress.

HC addendum.
Source: http://www.mothmanonline.com/sightngs/archive   Type: E

Location: Rural area, Quebec, Canada.
Date: Summer, 1999.
Time: Night.

The main witness and several friends were camping overnight in an isolated camping ground that had cabins and such. One night he was walking with a friend outside of the circle of cabins, it was a very clear and bright night and there was a campfire going and in one of the cabins there was a party with music. As they walked, both of them suddenly felt a weird "sensation" as if they were being watched.

They both turned and saw a blue figure, very tall, about 7ft, walking through the trees. It was completely silent. It was bright blue and glowing, walking through the forest. It was emitting a shimmering aura and both witnesses became very frightened.

They shouted at whatever the figure was and asked it what it was. They received no reply. They stared at it as it walked away and out of their field of vision. They ran back to the group of people at the campfire, screaming and describing what they saw. Another youth reported watching the figure from a distance and was just as frightened as the two main witnesses.

HC addendum.
Source: Your True Tales, April, 2004.   Type: E

* * * * * * *

Location: Peski, near Samodurovka, Voronezh region, Russia.
Date: June, 1999.
Time: 10:00 p.m.

Irina Zaharova, 13, was walking in a park located behind the local fire station and near the bus stop. At this late hour she was alone in the park and she had somehow felt compelled to go to the playground area without any apparent reason. Coming close to the playground she saw a strange object on the ground. She was at about 50-meters from the object. The object resembled a "space rocket" but standing on a horizontal position. The object was basically triangular in shape, quite large and it appeared to be somewhat camouflaged with its surroundings, therefore difficult to spot. The object was black in color and only when she came closer did several lighted portholes appeared on the craft, illuminated by a weird bluish white light. Becoming extremely curious she decided to investigate what the object was.

Now closer to the object Irina noticed an entity standing near the craft. At first she thought the entity was just a man, and approached even closer to the figure. She soon realized that the figure was not totally

241

human in nature. The humanoid seemed quite tall, about three meters in height, without a neck, a bulge just above the shoulders and three eyes in the bulge. Two eyes positioned on each side were yellow in color and the third eye positioned in the center was red. Somehow she felt no fear as she saw the alien figure. The humanoid entity was dressed in black overalls and she didn't notice any gadgets or instruments on the uniform. Suddenly the alien spoke to her in perfect Russian without any accents, however the voice seemed kind of gruff and computer like. The entity asked the girl who she was. In turn Irina answered by asking the entity who he was. The alien answered, *"I am Kirhiton."* Irina then asked, *"and what is Kirhiton?"* The humanoid said, *"That is my name"* The girl then said, *"My name is Irina let's get acquainted."* The alien then asked her if she would agree to "fly with them." She then asked, *"To where?"* the alien then answered that they would take her to the place where they live. Irina asked why and the alien answered that he thought that it would be very interesting for her to visit his world. Irina then asked who the other aliens were. The alien then spoke in an unfamiliar language and four other identical aliens appeared out of the object. Their language was similar to Japanese or Chinese according to Irina. Kirhiton told Irina that his home planet was called Daraal and was located somewhere in the Cassiopeia Constellation.

The aliens then invited Irina inside their spacecraft. Kirhiton asked Irina to sit down and to begin "counting." She began counting the seconds and when she reached to 15, Kirhiton told her that they had already arrived to their planet. (!) Amazed, she asked how they had arrived so quickly to their planet which was obviously many light years away from Earth. The aliens explained to her that they used a "gravitational engine." In short, it was explained, that there were some particles that exist in space and due to these particles gravity exists. These particles are called "gravitons" Apparently the speed of these gravitons exceed of that of photons, in other words the speed of gravitons is faster than light (300,000 km per second). The aliens explained that their propulsion system used gravitons and when their engine was activated, the speed of the gravitons became even faster, allowing their spacecraft to travel from one place to another in an instant. The aliens then pointed out that what was science fiction for humans is reality to advanced alien races. Moments later the girl and the aliens went out to the surface of the alien planet. However according to Irina the view was disappointing at best, there was no flora visible at all and the animals were very few in numbers. She was eventually returned back to earth after a brief stay. Irina was of course not taken seriously after she spoke of her experience and refused to speak about it anymore.

HC addendum.
Source: Archives of Mikhail Gershtein, Saint Petersburg, Russia. Type: G

Location: Near Penco, Chile.
Date: June 19, 1999.
Time: 4:00 a.m.

A cab driver was driving back from a fare along a lonely road when he saw something standing on the side of the road near a hill. It seemed to be a dark figure, with two brilliant reddish points of light where the eyes should have been. The strange figure began to move towards the vehicle and the driver began to accelerate away from the area.

Suddenly the figure seemed to rise up in the air and he briefly lost sight of the figure. Then it apparently landed on the roof of his vehicle. The driver saw the figure hanging to the rear of the cab, through the rearview mirror. He could see the outline of a face and forehead. He briefly looked away, and then looked back and the figure was gone.

Later while checking his vehicle he was stunned to see that the odometer reading had nearly triple from where it was the night of the incident. He could find no explanation as to why that happened.

HC addendum.
Source: UFOPR
Type: E

* * * * * * *

Location: Near Albany New York.
Date: June 22, 1999.
Time: 9:30 p.m.

Three women walking around a forested area in a small town were about a quarter of a mile from the house when they saw a pair of huge glowing red eyes they were about 50 yards away. When they got to about twenty yards away they got a better look at the creature.

It walked on two legs, looked like about six or seven feet tall, and had wings that resembled those of a bat. When they got to about ten yards away from the creature, it spread its wings (which stretched to about ten feet) and silently started to rise into the air without even flapping them and disappeared at very high speed. There was an apparent time lapse involved.

HC addendum.
Source: David Icke.
Type: E

Location: Vitoria, Espirito Santo, Brazil.
Date: June 22, 1999.
Time: 9:00 p.m.

Valdir Espinosa was fishing in a beach near Vitoria when looking up to the sky he noticed a "star" descend down to the beach shore about 100 meters away. From the star-like object five short figures emerged and approached the witness who panicked and ran away from the area, not looking back. Two hours later he returned to the area with two friends and the object and humanoids were gone, so was his catch of two fish that he had left behind.

HC addendum.
Source: Thiago Luiz Ticchetti, EBE-ET.   Type: B

* * * * * * *

Location: Fauquier County, Virginia.
Date: June 27, 1999.
Time: 2:00 a.m.

A 44-year old woman was attending a camp-out with her daughter, when she felt compelled to leave the camp-out and told one of the other adults she was going home. She drove her van to a now closed military base. She parked in a parking lot next to a picnic area just outside the fence. She got out of the van to look at the full moon. She then noticed a bright blue light approaching the area. The light approached from her right side and as it got closer she noticed it was egg shaped. The object hovered over a clump of trees in the field 200 yards away. Then the egg shaped object hovered inside the nearby fence.

She then saw three humanoid figures suddenly appear under the object. They were about three to four feet tall, green in color, with only four fingers in each hand that appeared to be gathering soil samples. The beings then noticed her. They then started moving toward her.

Her next memory was of waking up inside her van with the doors locked. Later she was able to remember that the beings came through the fence and stood on each side of her with one behind her. The three beings then took her back through the fence to the still hovering object. She was floated up in a very bright light beam that was shining down from the bottom of the hovering craft. She was then led into a room, and was put on an examination table and was apparently examined.

HC addendum.
Source: Richard Lang, Mufon.   Type: G

Location: Prague, Czech Republic.
Date: July, 1999.
Time: Night.

Blanka Slemendova saw three glowing golden man-like figures hovering in the sky near her apartment complex. She apparently received telepathic communication from the figures. The witness was involved in other encounters.

HC addendum.
Source: Direct from witness.   Type: E

* * * * * * *

Location: Near Moscow, Russia.
Date: July, 1999.
Time: Night.

Retired Air Force Colonel Alexander Smirnov (involved in a previous encounter) and three friends were fishing in a remote forest outside of Moscow. At night they had parked their car under a large oak tree. The weather was excellent and the sky was cloudless. Smirnov friends went to sleep but he remained awake looking at the clear and beautiful night sky filled with stars. He briefly felt asleep but was suddenly awakened and noticed an unusual dead silence in the area. Suddenly he noticed a star move side to side and stop in one place, it then descended to the ground sharply.

Filled with curiosity he walked towards the landed object. About 15 meters from the craft he felt paralyzed and a dense of air hindered his movement. The alien craft appeared to be inside some sort of force field. Suddenly a hatch opened on the lower part of the craft and a platform descended to the ground. Several strange entities stood on the platform, they remotely resembled humans and had on "space suits" but very different from terrestrial spacesuits, they resembled the suits wore by deep-sea divers. Their faces were not visible, and the suits were dark. He had a sudden feeling of being watched or scanned and then heard a voice that told him that, "They were not going to do anything wrong" that they were just collecting water and soil samples. Smirnov told the aliens that he was a former pilot and his great curiosity made him approach their craft. All conversation was via thought or telepathically. The protective wall of dense air remained. Smirnov told the aliens that he had contacted them back in 1990 and they said, *We know.* The wall of air suddenly dissolved and he heard the command to come in. He approached the circular craft with a tripod landing gear, resembling the time he had seen back in 1990.

The craft consisted of two sections with its lower half rotating. The aliens told Smirnov that they had "modified their technique" and told him to climb in. He obeyed and the platform ascended. The aliens were still wearing their suits and their faces were not visible, and Smirnov wanted to see them. He then heard a response, *"It is early, your air is not yet acceptable to us, and in time you will see us, come to the control post."* He approached the console, the instruments were giving light in the semi-darkness and he could see three chairs in the middle of the room. He was told to sit on the control console and was told how to operate the instruments. He was told to start testing the engines and not to "mix up the sequence." Smirnov began following the instructions but nothing occurred, the craft did not take off.

He then heard that everything was Ok that he was not ready yet that it had only been a test to probe his reaction. They said that they would teach him how to control the craft the next time; they recommended not telling anyone about their encounter. They added, *"We establish contacts gradually, we do not need a panic among the earthlings."* The witness then stood on the platform and descended to the ground. He then heard a slight humming sound and the UFO ascended over the ground, the tripod landing gear retracted into the object. The lower section of the craft began to rotate, first slow and then at very high speed. The craft then sharply zoomed up and disappeared from sight.

HC addendum.
Source: Anomalous News Saint Petersburg #30, 2000. Anton Anfalov.
Type: G

* * * * * * *

Location: Fleetwood, England.
Date: July 5, 1999.
Time: 6:00 a.m.

Paul Norton remembered seeing bright lights in his room. Soon he found himself at a brightly lit location where he encountered a seven-foot tall figure, with large almond shaped eyes. The creature had no hair and was wearing a red band around its shoulder and waist. It had a small mouth and gray-white skin color. The witness reported finding a peculiar scar around his genitalia.

HC addendum.
Source: UFO Abduction Raw Data Page, UFO Watch.   Type: G

Location: Near Moron de la Frontera, Sevilla, Spain.
Date: July 10, 1999.
Time: 1:30 a.m.

About 20 members of the "Adenex" association were performing a UFO alert with international connections in an area known as "Los Llanos del Arahal" about 10 kilometers from the joint Spanish-American base of Moron de la Frontera. For those assisting the watch or alert in particular to one Juana Barragan, the night was not uneventful like it usually was during these occasions. On this date a very large bluish light was seen flying over the military base while it was followed from the ground by several potent beams of light. Minutes later other smaller lights were seeing following the same trajectory of the larger bluish light, but this time flying in a zigzag pattern.

Excited by such spectacular display those attending decided to form 'an energy wheel or ring' holding hands and asking for peace on Earth. Minutes later Juana Barragan suddenly felt dizzy, it was a sensation that forced her to look at a certain point, there in the darkness she saw the silhouettes of two 2 meter tall humanoid figures. One of them wore a luminous reddish belt very bright in nature, the dizzy spell became stronger, and as the others present became aware of the situation and were notified by Juana the two figures had already vanished. Around the same time another member of the group Carmen Paredes, while resting in a vehicle, was able to see the silhouette of a very tall man wearing a sort of hooded outfit. The humanoid, realizing it had been seen, crouched down and disappeared seemingly into the ground. Later as Carmen Paredes inspected the ground where she had seen the humanoid figure she found a scorched reddish and square stone which she kept.

HC addendum.
Source: Jose Manuel Garcia Bautista.   Type: E

* * * * * * *

Location: Mt Adams, Washington.
Date: July 14, 1999.
Time: Night.

James Gilliland was outside when he was hit by three balls of light within a stream of energy after which a woman appeared to him wearing a strange headdress apparently used for communication and other higher consciousness and energy works.

Then a ship came in as a golden light from the north. It dropped down real low and hovered.

Gilliland had been in telepathic contact with "aliens" for 12 years after an NDE. Later he went to bed and woke up with a bright red circular burn on his chest right over his heart.

HC addendum.
Source: UFO Resource Center.   Type: C or F?

* * * * * * *

Location: Khabarovsk, Russia.
Date: July 14, 1999.
Time: 12:20 a.m.

In order to relieve the extreme heat, Gritsuk I. stepped out into his balcony and saw on a nearby football field a hovering disc-shaped object, which then landed silently. He briefly saw two glowing green figures exit the object. The figures then immediately re-boarded the craft, which then rocketed off at high speed.

HC addendum.
Source: UFO Kiev.   Type: B

* * * * * * *

Location: Virgilio, Sicily, Italy.
Date: July 14, 1999.
Time: 11:45 p.m.

Three men were walking back home from a local pizza parlor when they spotted a sphere shaped object, bright red in color descending slowly at a 60-degree angle. It had a weak yellow light on its upper section. It was about 200 meters away above a nearby rooftop when first seen.

Before reaching the ground, the object stopped at about six meters from it and hovered. Through an opening on the top of the craft the witnesses saw a vaguely human shaped figure. Immediately after that, the craft shot up and disappeared over the rooftops in a horizontal position.

Five days later, around 2:30 p.m. the main witness was returning home when he saw a white vehicle occupied by two men, parked in front of his house. Soon after he went in, the two men knocked on the door. He described them as very tall, about 40 years of age, wearing white shirts, and gray pants. They appeared to have nametags on the shirts, which they quickly covered.

They basically asked the witness several questions about what he saw and harassed him.

HC addendum.
Source: CUN Italy.   Type: A & E?

* * * * * * *

Location: Caicara, Venezuela.
Date: July 25, 1999.
Time: 8:00 p.m.

In a rural remote area of eastern Venezuela in a clear and moonless night the witness was having dinner with some friends when he stepped outside to retrieve something out of his truck. It was very dark and he had to use a flashlight. While he walked towards the truck he noticed a light coming from above, looking up he saw a round object about 200 ft wide hovering right over the house. The object had a reddish light in the middle. Immediately he called his friends and they all came out to look at the object. One a girl in the group flashed a light towards the UFO while some others panicked and ran to the house.

Ten minutes later, the light on the middle of the object became a beam of light that landed right on the roof of the house. Soon a human shaped figure floated up and down within the beam of light, apparently looking down at the witnesses. It was impossible to see any facial details because of the light, and the figure looked dark gray in color. After a few minutes it slowly left. The next day a circle of flattened dead grass was found in the area.

HC addendum.
Source: NUFORC

Type: B

* * * * * * *

Location: Poggio, Umbricchio, Italy.
Date: July 28, 1999.
Time: 6:30 a.m.

Two young brothers, Giacomo and Alfio were collecting mushrooms in a pine grove near this city when a loud rustling sound attracted their attention to some nearby trees. They stood looking at the spot where the noise had originated from and waited in total silence for about 15 minutes. Suddenly they heard loud grunting sounds coming from the brush. Curious, both boys walked toward the brush to see what was making the strange sounds.

Suddenly out of the brush stepped out a bizarre humanoid covered in dark black hair, about 1.50 meters in height, with an oblong shaped face with four eyes, two on top and two closer to a snout-like nose. It had normal hairless ears and what appeared to be five clawed legs. The creature stared at the boys with a malevolent gaze full of hate, as both watched in horror four other similar creatures walked out of the woods. Both witnesses fled the area in a panic. Later they debated whether to notify local authorities, but they decided against it.

HC addendum.
Source: Gianfranco Degli Esposito, CUN Bologna.

Type: E

Location: Cagepa, Paraiba, Brazil.
Date: July 26, 1999.
Time: 1:30 a.m.

42-year old Antonio Gadelha was parked in his vehicle in the outskirts of the city when a brilliant light suddenly surrounded it. Soon several short shiny silvery humanoid figures approached the vehicle, completely surrounding it. At the same time he heard the humanoids apparently communicating with each other, in loud beep like sounds. After about 10 minutes a strong beam of light originating from a hovering oval shaped craft illuminated the group and the humanoids rose up one by one quickly disappearing from sight. The object then departed.

HC addendum.
Source: Centro Paraibano de Ufologia.   Type: C

* * * * * * *

Location: San Nicolas de los Ranchos, near Popocatepetl, Mexico.
Date: Late July, 1999.
Time: 2:00 p.m.

A group of friends who had just graduated were invited by another friend (Celso) to visit the region and camp near the small village of Nealtican. At the time there was a great festival in the village and all the men participated in the festivities and were cleansed in age old rituals and given amulets to "ward off evil spirits and monsters." They spent the night in San Nicolas de los Ranchos and in the morning they left to hike near the famous Popocatepetl Volcano.

The men and women joked about the amulets given to them by the local natives and one of them guessed that it was for protection against the many local and supposedly mythological deities and beings. After a certain point their truck could not go on due to the rough terrain and they all disembarked to begin the foot hike.

Soon the group began to hear strange noises as the landscape became even harder to traverse and isolated. After about 20 to 30 minutes the group saw a figure on the path in the distance. They didn't think nothing of it since usually there were numerous tourists and alpinists in the area that would go on and climb up to Popocatepetl or Iztacihuatl.

It was around 2pm and the sun was beating down on them, it was very hot. Their guide, Celso who was a native of the area was in front, followed by the main witness, Gerardo Z. behind him two women, Evelyn and Patricia who were busy chatting, and at the end three men, Saul G. Omar C. and Manuel S. There was a total of seven witnesses.

Gerardo walked on, not looking ahead, looking down since he was worried about injuring himself as a result of a misstep, as he was carrying a heavy load. On one side they had thick woods and forest and on the other side a steep embankment of about 15 meters.

Suddenly Gerardo looked up and saw a strange figure ahead which immediately he could tell it was not human or animal. He noticed that the figure was very tall, at least 2 meters and a half. The figure was also wearing clothing which was inappropriate to the climate and area. It wore tight fitting suit pants and a shiny shirt. The figure was also very thin, however its chest or thorax area was very wide, which did not seem to match its extremely thin body.

When he came up to the figure Gerardo looked up and only thought to say *"Hello"* as locals normally saluted strangers and tourists. As he did he was stunned to see the face of the figure which seemed reptilian and vicious in nature. Its face was brightly lit by the bright sun and according to the witness he was looking directly at a bipedal dragon or dinosaur. Apparently the others had also noticed the strange creature and were staring at it, not believing what they were seeing.

As Gerardo watched, he saw something strange taking place in the creature's face. The creature's face seemed to be getting distorted, something similar to an old television screen when it overheated, but it was only the face of the creature that seemed to be going through some kind of metamorphosis. It had a large crest on its neck and back similar to that of a triceratops. Its skin was a gray-green color, scaly, definitely reptilian in nature. But the strangest part of its face was the eyes. It had large black deep-set staring eyes that seemed to know your thoughts as it stared at you, it was a cold, inhuman stare.

Gerardo immediately averted his glance and walked quickly ahead, leaving the strange creature behind, and also passing by his startled companions. He looked back to see that the creature had moved an incredible distance already. Terrified, Gerardo began to tremble and experienced some vertigo.

He ran for about 200 meters and stopped, quickly followed by his terrified friends, the two women were in hysterics. Celso thought that the creature briefly followed them and then stopped, apparently searching for something, it then entered the forest at very high speed and vanished.

The terrified group discarded the idea of camping in the area and returned to the vehicle using the same path. At first the group commented on the experience frequently, but soon they all seemed to stop talking about it and refused to bring up the subject.

Later Gerardo was to learn from the local inhabitants that the area was known locally as "the mountain of the lizards."

HC addendum.
Source: http://contraperiodismomatrix.com/un-cirujano-mexicano-ve-
un-reptiliano-metamorfico-en-san-nicolas-de-los-ranchos-cerca-del-
popocatepetl/   Type: E

* * * * * * *

Location: Santiago Del Estero, Argentina.
Date: August, 1999.
Time: Late evening.

Walking through a wooded area, Sebastian Jarre kept hearing a noise
resembling labored breathing approaching him from the woods. It drew
nearer and louder. Suddenly from out of the darkness something ran
across the path. Jarre dropped his lantern, but was able to see a huge
hairy figure, two meters in height, with strongly built hairy legs, and a
face and head resembling that of a wolf. The figure quickly approached
the witness making loud groaning noises. At this point the witness
panicked and stumbled into his bicycle quickly peddling away from the
area.

HC addendum. Source: El Dragon Invisible.   Type: E

* * * * * * *

Location: Chicago, Illinois.
Date: August, 1999.
Time: Late night.

A man who was visiting a friend's house and sleeping on the sofa in
the bedroom, suddenly woke up feeling very panicky and totally unable
to move. Looking towards the front door he saw a huge humanoid figure
over 7 ft tall standing by the door. The figure resembled a large "praying
mantis" and was wearing something resembling a black and purple
cloak. Its skin was dark gray in color. It slowly approached the witness
and reached out to him with a large hand with long thin fingers and
grabbed his shoulder. At this point the witness lost consciousness and
does not recall anything else of the incident. He remembered also feeling
very cold during the encounter.

HC addendum.
Source: Direct from witness.   Type: E

Location: Near Buckhead, Morgan County, Georgia.
Date: August 1, 1999.
Time: 6:30 p.m.

Two boys were riding four wheelers near Buckhead when they "heard growling and looked and saw a big black figure running" toward them. They said the creature, which had intelligent-looking eyes, was seven feet tall, ran hunched over like a chimpanzee, and smelled like a wet dog. Area residents had also noted cracked trees, unusual footprints and strange sounds.

HC addendum.
Source: Jim Miles, "Weird Georgia" pp. 64-65   Type: E

* * * * * * *

Location: Battle Mountain, Nevada.
Date: August 6, 1999.
Time: Daytime.

On the above date, Battle Mountain exploded into several simultaneous range fires in what would be known as 'the Battle Mountain Complex Fire.' A *Bigfoot* was supposedly injured in the fire according to an anonymous government employee, who alerted the Bigfoot Research Organization (BFRO). In a letter to BFRO dated 7th of August 1999, from Battle Mountain, Nevada, the anonymous government employee, states:

"I observed an animal wounded by fire moving on all fours not like a bear. More like an ape. Fire fighters captured animal, contacted local vet and medical doctor. U.S. Department of Fish and Wildlife, Department of Interior, and Bureau of Land Management on the scene.

Animal tranquilized and moved to unknown location. Those at the scene told not to talk about what they saw. Animal approximately 7.5 feet long/tall, human-like arms and legs, face not like man or ape but mixed between. Genitalia: male, uncircumcised and human-like. Hair covering most of body except chest, chest has hair but sparse, hands with sparse hair, palms bare, with five digits with human opposition of thumb and 5th digit.

Speech: Attempted to communicate with care-givers once it realized they were attempting to care for it. Multiple burns on hands, feet, legs and body; some 2nd and 3rd degree burns, using "rule of nines" approximately 45 per cent of body with burns. Doctor and Vet working together providing care and moved it to unknown location locally. This notice given in violation of orders given by BLM, DOI and DF&W.

254

Witnesses numbered in the area of 30-25. Word is out in the government and among the firefighters, since an M.D. was called out. Many thought a firefighter was injured. Please note that I am a government employee of one of the listed agencies fighting brush fires in wilderness area of Nevada (large scale fire approximately 70,000 acres burned) and under orders not to disclose information. I believe a cover up is in the making, people need to know, the animal needs to be kept alive and studied and released in protected area."

The incident happened in the early afternoon. About twenty firefighters were directly involved. The injured patient apparently wandered within sight of the fire crew, and was then surrounded. The patient "seemed to know that he was captured," because he soon gave up. The patient sat down on his buttocks, giving no evidence of a will to resist. The patient was laid out on the ground at first. His injuries were rather serious, including burns to the hands, feet, legs, and trunk, as well as much singed hair. It didn't take long for medical services to get to the scene. The attending medical team included the regular M.D. for the fire crews, a vet and one or more paramedics. The Vet was taken aback at working on a creature so human-like, and he is reported to have allowed the physician to do most of the work. At some point Demerol and morphine were administered. The patient was placed on a spine board, which was too small. He was then placed on a regular ambulance stretcher. The sides were left down because part of the body hung over too far. The feet hung off the end.

A cut-down was performed to obtain an intravenous line, and fluids were administered. During the treatment of his wounds and the efforts at life support, the patient communicated with moans, groans and grumbling. Bowel sounds were heard by several who were standing close to the creature. No language-like vocalizations were heard. The patient responded to touch, specifically patting and stroking to calm him. Two or three times the patient was observed to have been especially responsive to a young Native American woman who started ministering to him right from the very beginning. The patient was removed from the scene in the back of a utility truck, not in an ambulance. The total time from the initial sighting to extraction was estimated at three hours.

There was no urination, defecation or vomit at the scene. The patient (being) did not eat anything during that time. Serum and blood were leaking from the burned areas of the body. The area of the arm on which the cut-down was performed was shaved. The hair probably fell to the ground. There was significant blood from the cut-down site and from the subsequent insertion of a venous line, and some of that blood dripped to the ground. No one knows where the patient was taken. No video cameras were on the scene to film any aspect of the incident. The fire commander was present. He had a camera and he did not record what he saw.

The being was described as about seven feet tall with most of its body covered by brownish hair about two inches in length; no gray hairs were evident. There were no mats noted on the coat. There was an odor about the patient, very hard to describe only that it was 'natural.' The head was not sloped, the forehead was 'heavy boned,' the lips large, but human-like and tight to the head, with the ear lobe attached, not dangling. The head was about two times the size of a human head. There was hair on the face, but not on the palms or soles of the feet.

HC addendum.
Source: Phantoms and Monsters blog quoting BigfootEvidence.com
Type: H

* * * * * * *

Location: Bassano del Grappa, Italy.
Date: August 14, 1999.
Time: 11:30 p.m.

Attilio B. had briefly gone out to a field next to his house in order to satisfy a physiological need. Soon he noticed some shiny multicolored lights coming from a nearby field behind him.

Investigating closer, he saw a huge circular object hovering about 2 meters from the floor. The craft was somewhat turtle shaped and was about 30 meters in diameter. The top part of the object was so completely transparent that it appeared "invisible." The lower part consisted of a green platform that presented a central hollow section. He could not see any instruments inside.

Inside a well-lit whitish dome the witness was able to see five occupants. These were described as short in stature (about 80 cm) with large heads as respect to their bodies. According to the witness, the humanoids heads resembled somewhat that of a donkey. They had extremely long faces and their heads were covered with short black curly hair. They had large round black eyes about 5cm in diameter, lacking pupils and very close to each other. Their noses were large and "potato" like. Their mouths were large and wide, resembling those of a monkey with large meaty lips. On each side of their heads were two large pointy ears, resembling those of a wolf. Their skin was light brown in color and they had six digit hands.

As the witness watched, one of the humanoids, made a gesture, which he interpreted as a salute. The humanoids wore tight fitting yellow outfits that went up to their short necks. Their footgear resembled pointy sandals, similar to those worn by "Gondoliers." He continued his observation feeling a sense of "joy and tranquility." He felt that the humanoids were gentle and kind. One of the humanoids seemed to be counting some yellow paper like objects resembling "banknotes." The whole episode was completely silent. After about a minute and a half the object lifted up vertically disappearing from the area at very high speed.

HC addendum.
Source: Antonio Chiumiento.   Type: A

* * * * * * *

Location: Unknown island in the White Sea, Karelia, Russia.
Date: August 23, 1999.
Time: Evening.

A research group from St Petersburg was studying the many ancient labyrinths and other monuments and artifacts scattered throughout the region when they were able to observe a very interesting phenomenon.

They had already finished their work for the day when suddenly from the center of one of the stone spirals floated a strange opaque cloud, it then transformed itself into a pillar of light.

No sooner had the observers seen the pole, then it transformed itself into 'a human figure.' The outline of this human shaped figure was seen quite clearly and it had a brilliant green color while the center part of the body emitted an orange foggy glow. The body was transparent and was observed by the stunned group for about fifteen minutes.

The strange shape remained in one place and grew in size to about 200 meters in height. (!) Soon the body began to slowly shrink until it disappeared into the center of the spiral stone. That same evening the researchers moved their camp from the area and in the morning went back to St Petersburg.

HC addendum.
Source: http://www.tainoe.ru/anomalia/zoni   Type: X?

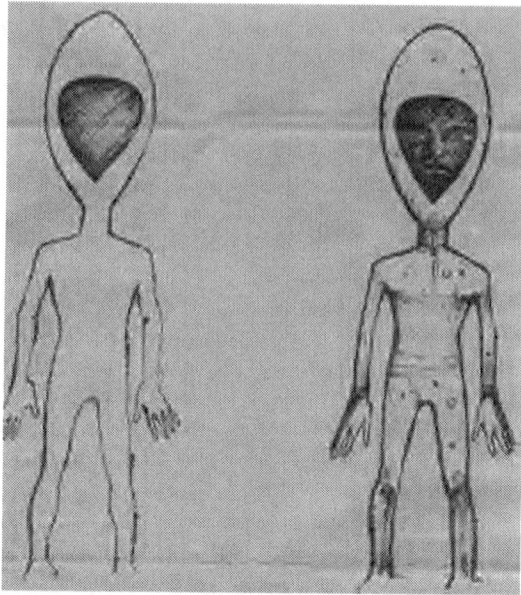

Location: Trenque Lauquen, Buenos Aires, Argentina.
Date: August 25, 1999.
Time: 4:30 p.m.

Carlos Colon was returning to town when as he neared some cross roads, he began hearing a loud humming sound that seemed to be getting more intense. He decided to stop the car. He began checking the radio thinking it was the origin of the strange sound, when suddenly out of the corner of his eye he noticed five figures walking on the nearby embankment.

The figures were described as man-like very tall; with large tear drop shaped heads, and a long neck. The facial area was covered by a dark upside down teardrop shaped area; no facial features could be seen. They all wore tight fitting dull white coveralls. They approached the witness to within twenty meters. Colon noticed that the figures seemed to be behind some type of "viewing" screen like a projection of some kind. He stared at the figures for some time, then looked back at his vehicle and noticed that it was now facing the opposite direction. He walked away, entered his vehicle, and drove away. Afterwards he felt a strange malaise and felt very apprehensive for some time.

HC addendum.
Source: Francisco Fazio, Centro Internacional Reportes OVNI.   Type: E

Location: California (exact location not given).
Date: August 25, 1999.
Time: Evening.

The witness was working in the yard of a rental property when he suddenly looked up to see a huge craft, gray, seamless, that took up the whole yard plus portion of the other house. An opening became visible and he could see a wood-like wall inside plus blinking red lights, switches and two pilots that wore gray uniforms with hats with black bills and an insignia on their arms. He was eye to eye with the one closest to him, in his mind he saw images of his childhood, and the alien closest to him said telepathically, *"Yes, we have watched you since you were a child."* He could not move, but was not frightened. He noticed hair on the alien's ears. They were very dark, neat and he could feel the 'superiority of them.' He wanted to ask questions, but he only thought of one other incident of hearing and feeling something. They said they would be back.

In his peripheral vision he could see portholes and indentations on the craft's hull which was smooth, rounded on its sides. He could not take his eyes off the entity closest to him; he had on dark large 'sunglasses.' At one point he turned to the other pilot and they communicated, then he looked back at the witness. He didn't know what was said but was sure it had been about him. They both watched him but the one closest to him did the communicating. Suddenly he was able to move again, he tried to look around and the craft had disappeared, he heard no noise, and all he could think of was that nothing that big could leave so fast.

HC addendum.
Source: Mufon case reports, http://mufon.com/   Type: A

*   *   *   *   *   *   *

Location: Osasco, Sao Paulo, Brazil.
Date: August 30, 1999.
Time: Night.

Valdineia Oliveira had gone to check her chicken coop as the animals seemed to be in an extremely agitated state. She looked inside the coop and saw nothing amiss then walked outside and was stunned to see a short figure, perched on top of a wall that was observing her. The humanoid was apparently also startled and ran away. Minutes later a bright ball of light rose from the ground and then disappeared in plain sight.

HC addendum.
Source: Thiago Luiz Ticchetti, EBE-ET.   Type: C

Location: Roslindale, Massachusetts.
Date: Fall, 1999.
Time: Evening.

The witness was walking in a wooded area in the Arnold Arboretum along a paved path, when he became aware of a figure moving at great speed coming from his left. He was surprised to see the figure was moving much too fast to have been walking, so he assumed it must have been a biker. He noticed that there was no noise at all and the figure seemed to be wearing a long black cloak. Looking up at the figure he was stunned that it was at least eight feet in height and skimmed along over the ground while hovering without any evidence of a bike or propulsion.

The figure stared fixedly ahead and since its path was perpendicular to the witness, he was never able to see the figure's face clearly. It had a hood covering it. Strangely he found it difficult to focus on the cloak, his eyes could stay in focus when he looked at it and became watery and blurry. The figure struck him as frightening and out of place but not menacing or malevolent. The figure passed in front of the witness then suddenly vanished in plain sight.

HC addendum.
Source: Fortean Times http://www.forteantimes.com/   Type: E

* * * * * * *

Location: Satellite Beach, Florida.
Date: September, 1999.
Time: Daytime.

On a beautiful clear blue day without a cloud in the sky the witness was standing at the foot of her driveway when she looked up to the sky and saw what she could only term as an "angel." It a very tall male figure with huge wings which floated above the treetops over a field across from the witness house. The figure was huge, she estimated it to have been about 15 ft tall, and the witness doesn't recall seeing any feet just a tan or white robe. His hair was light brown styled into a pageboy, shoulder length, and it didn't move even though it was slightly breezy. The floating figure appeared to be looking down but not directly at the witness. The most astonishing part of the incident was the figure's wings, they were very large and started above his shoulders and came down to the bottom of his robe, and the feathers were blowing gently, very detailed. She remembered everything being white and tan in color. The total length of the sighting was 10-15 seconds before the angelic figure vanished.

HC addendum. Source: direct from mitoys1@webtv.net   Type: E

Location: Near Mount Blanc, France.
Date: September, 1999.
Time: Late afternoon.

Sylviane Dubois, her husband Jacques and some friends, had gone on an excursion to the mountain when they suffered a flat tire on one of the peripheral roads. Under a slight drizzle, the witness husband and the other man left them behind while the two witnesses remained, exploring the area.

Suddenly the women were stunned to see, seemingly detaching itself from a block of ice, a small humanoid creature about 1.2 m in height and translucent in nature almost resembling an animated piece of ice. Its body was rather athletic, with a very strong appearing chest. The two witnesses stared at the creature almost in a trance-like state. A strong chill filled their bodies and both were paralyzed with fear. Sylviane could only pronounce the name of her husband, Jacques. It seemed that the creature was able to sense their panic, as it approached the pair slowly, at this point one of the women, Suzanne lost consciousness falling to the ground, this apparently startled the being, which scurried away and disappeared within a crevasse in the ice. Soon after, both men reappeared but refused to believe the women about what they had seen.

HC addendum.
Source: Oculte Net, France, http://www.occulte.net/accueil.html
Type: E

* * * * * * *

Location: Villa San Rafael de Calama Chile.
Date: September 15, 1999.
Time: 11:00 p.m.

Enrique Fowler and his grandson, 13-year old Jean Fowler were just arriving at a location on Yerbas Buenas street. Enrique was parking his truck when they both suddenly noticed a strange figure standing only four meters in front of them. Terrified, both saw the creature clearly illuminated by the truck headlights. The creature was described as bipedal and only 1 meter in height, ape like in appearance, dirty gray in color, and very hairy. It had a short neck, with a long rounded torso.

When first seen, the creature was standing with its back to the witnesses. Then the creature suddenly "twisted around" making an incredible 180 degree turn with the top of its body, in order to look directly at the witnesses. The terrified witnesses could now see that the creature's face was gray in color, with large glowing almond shaped eyes, and a small mouth that kept opening and closing as if very exhausted. It appeared to have a long scraggly beard and several tufts of unruly hair hung from its head. It had very short arms, resembling that of kangaroos that it kept close to its body. Its hands had three fingers with long sharp gray colored nails. A curious feature was that the creature's toe nails seemed to protrude and then go in again, in some type of rhythmic sequence. Suddenly the creature turned again, and made a three meter leap, quickly disappearing from sight in the nearby trees. Enrique Fowler was so stunned that he waited nearly fifteen minutes before he exited the truck. Both were soon struck by a severe skin allergy after the encounter. On October 31, 2000 Enrique Fowler, only 60-years old, died of a massive heart attack.

HC addendum.
Source: Calama UFO Center.   Type: E

*   *   *   *   *   *   *

Location: Peppertown, Indiana.
Date: September 27, 1999.
Time: 6:30 p.m.

A hunter was walking through a wooded area when he smelled something resembling burned ozone and heard a strange noise like a low electrical hum. He then walked down the hill into the valley and saw three silver clad humanoid figures around a deer carcass about 150 yards away. Behind the beings was a round metallic object, sharply defined with a 12-foot radius and ten feet high. After about 15 minutes another being came out of the stainless steel like craft and pointed in the witness direction. The beings then began moving towards the witness, who panicked and fired five shots into the air and ran up the hill. He later heard a strange sound 90 seconds later, apparently caused by the craft leaving.

HC addendum.
Source: Filer's Files, 1999 #44.   Type: B

Location: North Baltimore, Ohio.
Date: Late September, 1999.
Time: Evening.

Rosie Baney and her daughter watched a large round silver ball-shaped craft descend slowly between trees growing around a bean field about three quarters of a mile from their house. It looked like it was real close to the top of the trees and it went down into the field. It did not land, but it hovered silently in one spot. Soon it shot back up and disappeared. A few days later Rosie and her husband were jogging near the area where she had seen the silvery ball, when they saw what appeared to be a tall, hairy man cross the road in front of them and disappear into the woods. The ape-like creature walked upright. It had extremely black hair about three inches long, or more. It had a big, cone-shaped head that extended down to a big hump on its back. Its legs were much longer that an ape's. And the arms were shorter than an ape's and seemed to swing as it walked by.

HC addendum.
Source: Linda Moulton Howe, Earthfiles.   Type: D?

* * * * * * *

Location: Melbourne, Victoria, Australia.
Date: October 17, 1999.
Time: 8:25 p.m.

Two cylinder shaped craft were seen maneuvering over a road near the city. Two vehicles reportedly stalled as the objects approached and several of the witnesses felt dizzy at the presence of the objects. The objects were silver in color and highly polished. Each object had a row of about thirteen yellow-orange lights. There was also a blue haze around one of the objects. Also at least two silhouettes of beings with large heads were seen in each of the crafts. The eyes of the beings were red and fiery and were like slits. The crafts did not land but came close to the ground. Suddenly there was a thunder like sound and the objects disappeared. Scorch marks were reportedly found on the ground near where the objects hovered.

HC addendum.
Source: NUFORC   Type: A
High Strange Index: 7
Reliability of Source: 7
Comments: Interesting report, fiery slanted eyes reported before in different types of UFO related entities.

Location: Anna area, Voronezh region, Russia.
Date: Early November, 1999.
Time: Daytime.

A man from the city of Lipetsk, who called himself Vladimir Tormyshov, wrote at the end of 1999 or early 2000, to the Oryel based magazine *The Improbable World* about his recent extraordinary experience. According to him one of his family members from Moscow, a doctor of science, a physicist, had telephone him asking for his help. Vladimir was in need of money, and was skilled as a professional photographer, and his Moscow family member was aware of this. The doctor from Moscow told him, *"We shall be with you tomorrow. Take all the equipment. It will be interesting to you, I think,"* he explained.

They drove from Moscow to Lipetsk early in the morning, and soon were driving all night, a very long distance. They were accompanied by two other PhD's which Vladimir didn't know. In the car they brought many boxes filled with sophisticated equipment. Curious Vladimir asked, *"Where are we going?"* The answer from his family member was, *"Near the city of Voronezh, a UFO has crashed, that's where we are going."*

From further inquiries, Vladimir found out that his relative had been hunting not far from Voronezh near the town of Anna, and had observed the crash of a UFO. As he asserted, this UFO was brought down by some new weapon which, most probably "plasma based" and could bring down a target from thousands of km's away. All this sounded very incredible to Vladimir. When they arrived at Voronezh they were then driven to the location of the crash. Driving through an isolated road among impenetrable marshes, the vehicle soon arrived at a military checkpoint, a cordon of soldiers all armed with AK-47 assault rifles. The driver apparently attempted to by-pass the checkpoint but the vehicle was soon blocked by an armored troop carrier. As it appeared they were very close to the impact area since they could see several heaps of extraordinary, shiny brilliant fragments lying ahead. Several men dressed in civilian clothing were hurrying about the debris.

The men in the vehicle gave Vladimir the order to start filming the event. This seemed to anger the military officers present and these ordered the soldiers to beat up the two men accompanying Vladimir and to rush the car. While this occurred Vladimir noticed that from the depths of the pile of rubble two men carrying a stretcher walked out, the stretcher was covered with a white sheet. Unexpectedly something moved under the sheet and Vladimir saw an arm covered in gray-brown overalls. Whoever was under the white sheet then pulled the sheet off and Vladimir saw a humanoid entity similar to a human being, only with an unusually large head, large eyes and disproportionately long arms, the entity was dressed in overalls without seams, buttons or zippers. It

264

seemed to be attempting to rise from the stretcher. But several soldiers then ran up to the stretcher and blocked Vladimir's view, but before this occurred Vladimir swore that he had seen "tears" on the entity's eyes. The very next moment the door of the car swung open and something heavy struck Vladimir on the head, he then lost consciousness.

He woke up some hours later. His camera was empty of film, and his other film was missing also. The men responsible for the cover up (evidently FSB 'former KGB' officers) threatened Vladimir to keep quiet about the event, but this did not deter Vladimir from writing the letter to the newspaper.

HC addendum.
Source: 'Paranormal meetings' by Vladimir Tormyshov, 'The Improbable World' Oryel Russia # 102, & http://www.incredible.spb.ru
Type: H
Comments: Such plasma weapons described in Vladimir's letter indeed exist and were developed in Russia (even before the collapse of the USSR). The crash (if it really took place) apparently happened during nighttime more than 100 kms southeast of the city of Voronezh and about 10-15 kilometers south of the regional center of Anna. The hunter allegedly saw how the UFO 'stumbled' upon some kind of 'wave' and rapidly lost altitude and fell to the earth, but not before breaking into several fragments. The stunned hunter apparently immediately telephoned (using his cell phone) several Moscow friends and told them what he had seen. The shiny pieces of the UFO were scattered all over the forest near the river Bitug.

The Russian military has apparently studied the use and theory of plasma weapons for years and had also studied the vulnerability of some UFOs while back-engineering several seized crafts at their top-secret subsurface research base in the tundra northeast of the Arkhangelsk region (outside the town of Naryan-Mar) where is reported that no less than five captured and downed UFOs have been kept. The plasma impulse is aimed to destabilize the plasma envelope surrounding the alien spacecraft, causing termination of normal flight mode and collapse, and then eventually a rapid descent to earth and crash.

Nikolay Subbotin, Director of RUFORS has confirmed that the Russian military has acquired the ability to shoot down UFOs for a long time now. Apparently in the Anna crash a living extraterrestrial was captured and placed in an extremely secured facility in a sterile environment to study and communicate with, in an attempt to extract technological data from the humanoid. Apparently the reason the UFO was shot down in this area, is because the Voronezh region near the Hoperskiy nature reserve is one of the most active UFO zones in Russia.

The military had apparently organized a secret operation in an attempt to shoot down a UFO in the region using a secret military installation capable of generating plasma impulses apparently located in the forest near the Novovoronezh nuclear power station (located about 40km south of the city of Voronezh). The place where the weapon is located is apparently 90-100km west of the UFO crash. This powerful high tech weapon needs a lot of electrical power, so it was strategically placed not far from the nuclear plant.

* * * * * * *

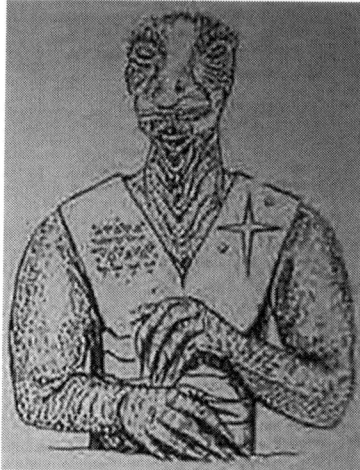

Location: Grove Hill, Alabama.
Date: November, 1999.
Time: Morning.

After local police received calls about a strange entity seen at a local field, assistant deputy Gene Sheffield responded to the site. At the field Sheffield and another man saw a bizarre humanoid described as very tall, muscular and reptilian in nature with its body covered in what appeared to be scales.

Sheffield gave chase on foot but was unable to capture the elusive being. Footprints were reportedly found.

HC addendum.
Source: Año Cero XII

Type: E

Location: Chilla Well, Northern Territory, Australia.
Date: November, 1999.
Time: Daytime.

A craft resembling two plates put together and about four foot between, with a silvery blue light in the middle, came down in this aboriginal settlement and hovered just above the ground. Several human like figures exited the craft; these had only three fingers on each hand and spoke the aboriginal language. As they walked towards the aborigine witnesses, they ran away in fear. The humanoids told the aborigines not to be afraid and the aborigines asked them if they needed diesel fuel. They said no, that they were looking for "blue crystal" for their craft. They were then told to go to a nearby location. The humanoids re-entered the craft and this one went away. It never touched the ground while there.

HC addendum.
Source: Douglass from UFO Research Northern Territory.   Type: B

*   *   *   *   *   *   *

Location: Lujamanu, Northern Territory, Australia.
Date: November, 1999.
Time: 4:00 p.m.

Phil and some other aboriginals saw a 4-wheel vehicle drive pass thru town, there was a woman and some men in it, the car was all dirty. Later that day, Phil and two aboriginal men set up camp outside of town. While sitting around the fire they noticed the car again, this time it was all clean and shiny, then they saw a huge UFO in the sky, greenish in color, long and flat with a round belly underneath. As they watched, the bottom of the craft opened up, and the car was gently taken up inside of the UFO, and then the UFO went up and disappeared.

HC addendum.
Source: Douglass, from UFO Research Northern Territory.   Type: B?

*   *   *   *   *   *   *

Location: Minion Falls, NSW, Australia.
Date: November, 1999.
Time: Afternoon.

The main witness, who lived in a fairly large property near the lava flows of nearby Mount Warning and a very thick rain forest area, had ventured near the mouth of the forest with his brother in order to explore and play in the area. His brother was then called away by other friends and the witness remained alone behind. He had been sitting there for about 15 minutes when all of the sudden he felt a chilling presence down his spine and the very strong feeling that he was being watched by something with not a "nice intent." Slowly he turned to where he felt the presence and right near the mouth of the forest he saw something terrifying standing on the next hill watching him. The figure was over 7-8ft tall and almost as wide as it was tall, he recalled that the figure had deformations on its back which may have been wings folded against it. He also remembered that the eyes seemed to glow red. He couldn't recall how long he stood there staring at the creature, and he felt like he was paralyzed and unable to move. It felt as if the creature was not only looking at him but was "probing" his mind as well. As soon as his eyes unlocked from the creature the witness was able to move and fled down the hill to his house and noticed that the creature was loping away in huge leaps and bounds back into the forest, using both hind legs and one forearm to support itself.

HC addendum.
Source: http://www.unexplained-mysteries.com/forum   Type: E

* * * * * * *

Location: Gansu Province, China.
Date: November, 1999.
Time: Evening.

The driver of a bus with about sixty-two local residents, saw a kind of "whirlwind" approaching the bus which immediately enveloped it. At the same time several bus passengers became sleepy and felt as if the bus was "rising into the air." Soon the passengers of the bus found themselves in what appeared to be large well-lit hangar. Some of the passengers exited the bus and were confronted by a figure about 250cm in height with a tight fitting overalls with "red buttons."

The humanoid apparently communicated telepathically with the group and advised them to re-enter the bus. Once onboard, the passengers again experienced the feeling of flight, flying through a sort of fog, which gradually dissipated. Soon they landed on the outskirts of a city which they soon found out was Urumqi, which was located at a distance of more than 1500 km from their original location. (!) Their watches showed that six hours had passed even though it had not seemed to be more than thirty minutes.

HC addendum.
Source: Herman K. Kolchin, Moscow, 2009.   Type: G

Location: Manaus, Amazonas, Brazil.
Date: November 23, 1999.
Time: 5:40 a.m.

After hearing a kind of telepathic command in his mind, Maciel Bezerra de Amorim was compelled to step outside. He stood outside looking towards the horizon and immediately spotted a very bright light that began approaching in his direction. He was then surprised as in seconds the bright light was hovering above him at an altitude of 25 m. He was now able to see that it was a large metallic spacecraft. Maciel heard a sound like air decompressing as the craft descended emitting a white vaporous mist which was very cold. Soon a hatch on the front of the craft opened and a bright beam of light levitated the witness onboard the craft.

Once inside he was confronted by a tall woman dressed in an elegant white suit and matching white boots. Upon seeing the witness, the woman smiled and placed the palm of her hand over her heart at the same time inclining her head slightly forward, understand this as a form of greeting the witness did exactly the same. She then asked that he follow her since she was going to give him a tour of the spacecraft. Inside the object everything was white and luminous however the witness could not see the source of the lighting, the atmosphere inside also felt very comfortable. He saw numerous other crewmembers walking by in different directions, they were all human in appearance but different from each other. His escort was very beautiful in appearance, about 1.60m in height, with long black straight hair. She wore a white belt on her waist from which hung what appeared to be a communications device.

While passing by an adjacent corridor the witness noticed a small robot-like object or figure. When he asked his escort what it was, he was told that it was a type of monitoring device which watched over the crewmembers aboard what he was told was an "education vessel." Indeed the spacecraft possessed several laboratories and research facilities. He was then led into a hall where a woman sat behind a console-like device, and introduced to the woman who immediately asked if he wanted to conduct a "knowledge test." He agreed and was handed over several papers which contained numerous questions most of which were personal in nature.

After answering the questions he handed the papers back and was told that now they could go the exit bay of the ship. His escort then bade goodbye with a small hug and Maciel was then lowered to the ground within the same beam of light which initially took him onboard.

HC addendum.
Source: Portal UFO Genesis, Relatos de los visitantes.   Type: G

Location: Coari, Amazonas, Brazil.
Date: November 25, 1999.
Time: 4:30 p.m.

Maria de Jesus was outside washing some clothing in her yard when she felt something moving near her, to one side. Turning around she was confronted by a short creature about 1.2 meters in height, with large black eyes, wearing metallic clothing and holding a cane-like instrument in his left hand.

The humanoid gesticulated towards the witness, who screamed in fear. This startled the humanoid who then seemed to levitate and disappear behind a nearby stonewall.

Seconds later from behind the stone wall, a large ball of fire appeared and shot up into the sky at very high speed. The encounter lasted for about three minutes.

HC addendum.
Source: Thiago Luiz Ticchetti, EBE-ET.   Type: C

* * * * * * *

Location: Pusalu, China.
Date: December, 1999.
Time: Night. `

A luminous golden shimmering figure, human in shape, was seen by dozens of villagers, *"It was beautiful"* remarked a witness, Wang Cunquio. It ascended slowly from the barren hills behind the town into the dark skies above. *"It looked like someone flying up to heaven,"* remarked witnesses.

HC addendum.
Source: The International Directory of Haunted Places.   Type: E

Location: South Windsor, Connecticut.
Date: December, 1999.
Time: Various.

Debbie Summer reported seeing a tall scaly humanoid with spikes on his head and glowing red eyes and wearing a black cape. She reportedly saw this creature on several occasions. Around the same time her youngest daughter reported seeing an unknown object hovering outside their window. No other information.

HC addendum.
Source: Direct from witness & I was abducted.com   Type: C?

* * * * * * *

Location: Near Murgon, Queensland, Australia
Date: December, 1999.
Time: Night.

In scrub country north of Chinchilla, a 4-wheel drive vehicle was being driven by two men along a dirt road late one night. At one point on that dark night their headlights caught a tall image in the distance, which as they got closer was seen to be a silvery-glowing 3.5 meter tall featureless human-like shape. It then quickly strode off the road and stood there as they drove past, fearful of what might happen if they tried to approach the 'out-of-this-world' being. In another incident earlier that year, one night a carload of people afterwards claimed they drove right through a "huge glowing man" that suddenly appeared from out of nowhere on the highway directly in front of them, at a sport north of Childers, they hurriedly got out thinking they had hit someone, but there was nothing there. Over the years, along the same road and also near Dalby and Kingaroy truck drivers have reported on and off of seeing either the same being, or one or more smaller ones, all white glowing beings.

HC addendum.
Source: The Blue Mountains UFO Research Club Newsletter March, 2009.   Type: E

Location: Pato Branco, Parana, Brazil.
Date: December 5, 1999.
Time: 10:00 p.m.

Maria Alice Medina was sitting at her verandah drinking some coffee when she observed a short 1.2 meter tall humanoid approach her. The humanoid wore a silvery coverall, and blue boots. His head was bald and he had large black eyes. The humanoid attempted to communicate emitting strange sounds, which Maria was not able to understand. The humanoid then turned around and walked into some nearby woods. Soon she saw a bright light rise from the woods and shot up into the space.

HC addendum.
Source: Thiago Luiz Ticchetti, EBE-ET.   Type: C

* * * * * * *

Location: Fangshan district, Beijing-Qinhuangdao, China.
Date: December 11, 1999.
Time: Midnight.

School Headmaster Cao Gong went to bed about 2200 and was sleeping separately from his wife and children in another bedroom. Cao Gong reports that at approximately midnight he suddenly heard a whirring noise moving towards him from the aluminum alloy glass windows at the north side of his bed. He sat up and saw a man and a woman dressed in strange attire standing by the side of his bed. His first response was that they were thieves, and he became extremely frightened. The male visitor was approximately 5 ½ feet tall, and the female was slightly shorter. Their eyes were in the shape of circles, and their mouths were empty round holes. Their heads were relatively large, and their bodies were fairly frail. Their stomachs were comparatively thin, and their faces were fair-skinned without any color. The pair was wearing silvery white tight-fitting clothes, similar to tinfoil, and they had their heads bound so that it was difficult to see clearly whether or not they had hair or ears.

As he was studying them up and down, Cao Gong heard the woman say to her companion, *"He is the one who can cure illnesses. Let's take him!"* (Cao Gong possessed medical skills). Having said these words, the two visitors moved through the wall at the north side of the bedroom, and Cao Gong's body became light and sprang up from the bed like a rubber ball, following the pair through the wall. Cao Gong said that as he crossed through the wall, he had the same feeling as pushing through the cotton curtain doors used in the countryside. Because he did not have

272

time to put more clothes on, he felt extremely cold and muttered to himself, *"It's a little cold."* It was as if the woman could read Cao Gong's mind, as there was the reply, *"You will warm up very soon."* Sure enough, as soon as she had spoken those words, Cao Gong did not feel cold, but his head still had the sensation of wind blowing past.

According to what he remembered later, when they came out of the bedroom, they flew in a southeasterly direction, with him being drawn along in flight. As they flew past several towns and cities, Cao Gong heard in his mind the two entities telling him specifically the places that were below him. Thus he knew that first of all, he moved over the town of Liangxiang southeast toward Gu'an County. He then flew to the city of Bazhou, and then turned to fly in an eastwardly direction. Having flown past the city of Tianjin he then flew north. Then the two told him that below was the city of Qinhuang Dao. Then he flew north, and when he had traveled 50 or 60 miles distance, he started to float down to an uninhabited hilly region. Cao Gong though that the entire journey took seven or eight minutes. After they had landed, Cao Gong saw a giant unidentified object shaped like a ping pong (table tennis) paddle. The section that corresponded to the handle of the paddle was the size of a basketball court, the section that corresponded to the face of the paddle was roughly the size of a football field.

The two entities then took Cao Gong directly into the handle section of the object, and he experienced once again the same feeling of passing through a wall. Along with his two escorts, he ended up in a small room similar to a laboratory. This small room seemed to be positioned in a medium-sized room, which in turn was connected to a large-sized room by means of a door. In the small room they had entered, there was no seating, and the lighting was soft. At this point, the male entity nodded in a friendly manner towards Cao Gong and calm him down, saying that the reason he had been invited onto the craft was that they wanted to carry out an experiment using cosmic energy to cure an Earthling of illness. Thereupon the woman asked her companion and Cao Gong to wait there while she walked towards the large room. When she entered the door of the large room, Cao Gong heard from inside the room the sounds of machine equipment. He also heard the cries of pigs, dogs, oxen, sheep, and various other animals. The cries of these animals were wretched, as if they were being dissected or injected. The female entity returned with a 16 or 17 year old Chinese girl by her side. The girl appeared to be seriously ill. The female entity made the girl stand where there was a symbol on the floor. Then the male entity strongly patted Cao Gong on the 'da zhui acupoint' (between the seventh cervical and first thoracic vertebra). At once Cao Gong felt a burst of warmth flowing and surging around in his body. It was extremely comfortable, and from his elbows down to the palms of his hands and fingers he felt pins and needles like an electric discharge. The male entity signaled to Cao Gong to use the same method that he had just demonstrated in order to treat the girl.

At this point the female entity took some sort of instrument, five or six small metal bottles, and an object that resembled a black flashlight from a case on the floor. She placed the instrument and the small metal bottles in front of the legs of the seriously ill girl. She placed the object that resembled a black flashlight on top of the girl's head and pushed downwards. From inside the contraption came an air-tight object that had the appearance of a transparent raincoat. It smoothly began to cover the girl and the small metal bottles, sticking tightly to the floor. The male entity signaled for Cao Gong to start the experiment. Using his hands and strength Cao Gong began patting the 'da zhui acupoints' of the sickly girl, feeling some kind of heat flow from his hands into the girl's back. When Cao Gong wanted to move his arms away from the girl, a kind of giant absorbing force prevented him from doing so. The entire process lasted approximately five minutes, during which his arms became numb, and the sensation of an electric charge came out from his palms and fingers, flowing into the girl's back. The girl's body resembled something like a leather bag, all shaking and twisted.

Cao Gong was shocked by the fact that the transparent cover which shrouded the girl was now full of what appeared to be filthy gas. The girl now seemed to be full of vim and vigor, hardly resembling the person she was before. When the two entities saw that the experiment had been successful, they let out peals of laughter. They then invited Cao Gong to observe their large laboratory, but he was extremely frightened because he continued to hear the wretched cries of animals. The two entities seemed able to sense his feelings, so they decided to return Cao Gong to his home. They arranged their clothes and then leaned their bodies slightly forward.

Cao Gong was drawn up, flying into the sky. The two entities flew in front of him, drawing Cao Gong towards Beijing. They flew to the south side of Cao Gong's home, and returned him by moving through the wall as before.

For a long time after returning home, Cao Gong was unable to calm down. He thought deeply about his bizarre journey and at about 4am he hurriedly told his experience to a local Ufologist, miss Ma Linghuan.

HC addendum.
Source: Bill Chalker http://theozfiles.blogspot.com/2005   Type: G

Location: Santiago, Chile.
Date: Late December, 1999.
Time: 11:00 p.m.

The main witness, M.J. was visiting the house of some friends located in El Bosque street near the Pocuro section, on a fourth floor apartment and after having dinner he stepped out onto the terrace (balcony) and began taking in the view of the nearby Cordillera. Totally relaxed he perceived at a distance of about 1000 to 1500 m and at about 100 to 300 m in altitude a large red object that appeared to be approaching, which at first he thought it was a small plane, or more exactly an old two-seater vintage model, which were used a lot during the 50's. He was curious as to why such an aircraft would be flying so low. Concerned he thought that the pilot was lost as it was flying dangerously close to buildings.

Moments as the object came closer the witness was stunned to see that the "wings" appeared to be flapping up and down (the wings were long approximately 4 m in length). Stunned he could now see that the object was really some type of red colored winged creature which moved in a sort of zigzagging motion, always following the same track. Suddenly the strange creature was now in front of the witness at a distance of about 50 m, but maintaining the same height, parallel to Bilbao Street.

At this point the witness noticed that the creature's body appeared to be divided into two sections; the top section was less maneuverable and more rigid, while the bottom section was in constant motion. Terrified the witness thought he could make out huge claw like protrusions on the creature's feet which appeared to be indeed carrying "something" which the witness thought could have been a human body. (!) As the creature flew by moving swiftly away from the witness, he remembered that there was a large window on the other side of the apartment from which he could still be able to see the bizarre flying creature. So he yelled out to his friends *"UFO!" UFO!"* and ran towards the window. He managed to catch a glimpse of the creature again but in an instant it vanished behind some buildings. His observation lasted about 30-40 seconds. Later the witness commented what he had seen with close friends and contacted the source, convinced that he had seen some type of gargoyle type creature carrying a helpless victim, which the witness admitted it could had also been a large animal (let's hope).

HC addendum.
Source: Liliana Nuñez, Chile in: http://www.aforteanosla.com.ar
Type: E

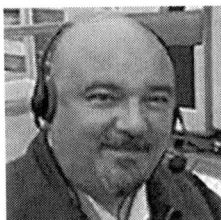

About the author

Albert S. Rosales, was born in Cuba on January 3, 1958. After living for some time in Spain, in 1967, his family moved to New York City before ultimately settling down in Miami where Albert became a US citizen and attended school. Albert had many strange incidents as a child and developed an interest in UFOs and unusual events from the time he was in high school.

He joined the United States Navy after high school and traveled the world. Later on, after being honorably discharged from the Navy, Albert went into the jewelry business with his father. After his father passed on, Albert joined a local law enforcement agency in Miami and has now been there for over 30 years. Albert is happily married, with five grown children, one girl and four boys.

For over 40 years, Albert has been studying UFOs, and since 1993, has been regularly updating his Humanoid Encounter catalogue. Albert's efforts are a continuation of the work of pioneers like Ted Bloecher, David Webb and others, who compiled the original HUMCAT.

You can forward your own humanoid encounters to Albert at:

garuda79@att.net

30921664R00158